Dedication

To our husbands and hiking companions, Bill and Ted.

NOTE:
See the back of this book for a **1995 UPDATE**

Satellite photo of the South Bay (looking roughly east)

SOUTH BAY TRAILS

Outdoor adventures
around the Santa Clara Valley

Frances Spangle
and
Jean Rusmore

WILDERNESS PRESS • BERKELEY

FIRST EDITION November 1984
Second printing August 1985
SECOND EDITION August 1991
Second printing March 1993
Third printing May 1995

Design by Thomas Winnett
Maps by Larry Van Dyke and Rann Schultz
Cover design by Larry Van Dyke
Cover photo taken in Henry W. Coe State Park by Robert K. Mark

Library of Congress Card Catalog Number 90-21511
International Standard Book Number 0-89997-118-0

Manufactured in the United States
Published by Wilderness Press
                2440 Bancroft Way
                Berkeley, CA 94704
                (510)843-8080

                Write or call for free catalog

PHOTO CREDITS

L. E. Bullmore Collection, courtesy of Michael Cox   137, 140
Fish and Wildlife Service photo   239, 248
Fish and Wildlife Service photo by Charles J. Johnston   233
Kenneth W. Gardiner   225, 263
Ellie Huggins   106
Robert K. Mark   cover
Midpeninsula Regional Open Space District photo by Carolyn Caddes   268
Jean Rusmore   5, 10, 14, 20, 26, 41, 43, 49, 51, 53, 61, 64, 67, 81, 84, 89, 93, 97,
101, 112, 123, 129, 131, 143, 147, 151, 154, 163, 171, 175, 181, 185, 186, 193, 197,
203, 207, 215, 231, 237, 255
Frances Spangle   8, 17, 39, 54, 70, 75, 91, 110, 195, 213, 218, 245, 246, 266
United States Air Force, courtesy United States Geological Survey   ii
Sheldon Woodward   33, 160

 Printed on recycled paper with soy-based ink

Library of Congress Cataloging-in-Publication Data

Spangle, Frances.
      South Bay trails : outdoor adventures around the Santa Clara
   Valley / Frances Spangle and Jean Rusmore. -- 2nd ed.
         p.   cm.
      Includes bibliographical references (p.) and index.
      ISBN 0-89997-118-0
      1. Hiking--California--Santa Clara Valley--Guide-books. 2. Parks-
   -California--Santa Clara Valley--Guide-books. 3. Santa Clara Valley
   (Calif.)--Description and travel--Guide-books. I. Rusmore, Jean.
   II. Title.
   GV199.42.C22S319957 1991
   917.94'73--dc20   90-21511
                                                                   CIP

Acknowledgments

We enjoyed the company of our families and many friends who joined us in exploring these trails. To them and to all those who helped and encouraged us during the preparation of this second edition of *South Bay Trails*, we extend our gratitude.

We are especially grateful for the assistance of the staffs of the public agencies whose trails we describe: San Francisco Bay National Wildlife Refuge—John Steiner and Michael Bitsko; California Department of Parks and Recreation, Henry W. Coe State Park, Kay Schmidt-Robinson and Barry Breckling; Santa Clara County Parks and Recreation Department—Douglas Gaynor, Director, and Park Planners Felice Errico, Mark Frederick, Julie Bondurant and Ruth Shriber; Midpeninsula Regional Open Space District—Herbert Grench, General Manager, and Planners Del Woods, Mary Gundert, and Sheryl Cochran; East Bay Regional Park District—Bob Doyle, Assistant General Manager of Land Acquisition; San Jose Park Planner—John Giusto; Sunnyvale, Campbell, Mountain View and Palo Alto city staffs; Sunnyvale Department of Public Works—Eugene Willroth, Operations Engineer.

Special thanks go to all the rangers and naturalists of South Bay parks and preserves, who inspired us with their dedication to the lands under their stewardship. Their suggestions and advice added greatly to the pleasure of our trips on these South Bay trails. Many helped us by reviewing early drafts of the manuscript.

We would like to thank Michael Cox and Kitty Monahan for detailed historical information on Almaden Quicksilver Park. Of the many helpful librarians, we would like to mention Catharine Fouts, Morgan Hill Public Library.

In the course of assembling material for this book we became increasingly aware of the valuable work of the Trails and Pathways Committee of the Santa Clara County Intergovernmental Council in developing the countywide Trails and Pathways Plan, the perseverance of the Committee members and the key role played by their staff coordinators, Donald Weden and Julie Bondurant.

Our gratitude goes to photographers Ken Gardiner and Sheldon Woodward, whose fine black and white prints enliven these pages; to the San Francisco Bay National Wildlife Refuge and the Midpeninsula Regional Open Space District for making available photographs from their files; to Evelyn Newman, who assembled her Henry Coe State Park slides for us; and to Bob Mark, whose photo of Henry Coe State Park graces the book cover.

To Noëlle Liebrenz and Larry Van Dyke of the Wilderness Press staff, we extend our appreciation for their part in the intricate steps toward publication; and to our patient editor and publisher, Tom Winnett, sincere thanks for his expertise in producing *South Bay Trails*.

Frances Spangle and Jean Rusmore
Portola Valley, CA, January 8, 1991

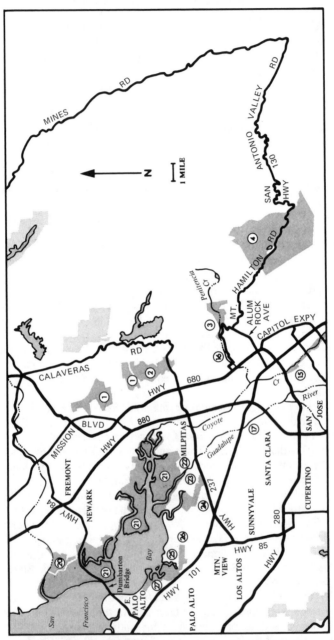

Location Map for South Bay Trails

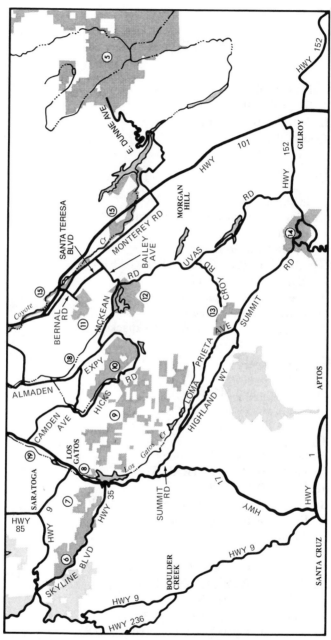

**Numbers in circles refer to Part 2 of Contents.
Shaded areas are parks and preserves.**

Contents

Foreword

South Bay Trails, the second trail guide written by Frances
Spangle and Jean Rusmore, is the result of their love of the area they
describe, their enthusiasm for the out-of-doors, and their ability to
bring its uniqueness and beauty into sharp focus.

Few places in our Golden State can compare with the mountains,
forests, and meadows to the east and west of the Santa Clara Valley.
South Bay Trails recalls, with delight, the early days when settlers
freely roamed the woodlands and grasslands of this now urban and
suburbanized region.

The authors then expertly describe the present trail system, which
forms a contemporary link from one natural area to another. In
South Bay Trails, Spangle and Rusmore detail the progress in
recreational open space preservation in the rapidly growing area,
while at the same time letting readers know how to get more enjoyment from its natural landscape.

From my experiences as a trail user in all parts of California, a
member of a state trails committee, and a hike leader in Japan and
Europe, I heartily recommend *South Bay Trails* not only for the true
trail enthusiast, but also for the armchair explorer.

Claude A. (Tony) Look
Member, California Recreational Trails Committee

Introduction

In the seven years since the first edition of *South Bay Trails* we saw public parklands grow to nearly 140,000 acres. Over these years public agencies carried out new park plans, adding new trails that today total close to 450 miles.

On revisiting our parks and preserves for this new edition of *South Bay Trails,* we met increased numbers of hikers, runners, equestrians and bicyclists along the way. In enlarged parks and preserves, on new woodland trails and on expanded paths by tree-lined creeks we found new and veteran trail users enjoying the wealth of open space in the South Bay.

We discovered improved park facilities, innovative displays at visitor centers and many trail events led by trained docents. We found that volunteers in record numbers are turning out to help with trail building, maintenance and trail activities.

Spurring local interest in trails are two recent regional programs. The first of these is the Association of Bay Area Governments' Bay Trail Plan to circle San Francisco and San Pablo bays with hiking and bicycle paths. South from Palo Alto many of the extensive Baylands paths described in *South Bay Trails* are now on the route of the Bay Trail. Along the east side of the Bay a new two-mile trail in Fremont is a significant step forward in completing the Bay Trail north from Alviso to the National Wildlife Refuge at Newark and on through Coyote Hills Regional Park.

In a second regional trail program the Bay Area Ridge Trail Council calls for a 400-mile route for hikers, equestrians and bicyclists on the ridgetops around San Francisco Bay. Over 120 miles of the Bay Area Ridge Trail have been officially dedicated, and within the area covered by *South Bay Trails,* are several dedicated segments of this trail.

The many hundreds of miles of trails in this guide cover terrain of remarkable diversity—from the western slopes of the Diablo Range to the ridges and eastern flanks of the Santa Cruz Mountains and from the Bayside marshes to the creekside park chains. To help the hiker, runner, equestrian and bicyclist explore these many trails, we arranged *South Bay Trails* by trips, often combining several trails to form loops. This distinctive feature suggests outings that vary from short easy strolls to long strenuous expeditions. Of special interest is an appendix listing "Trails for Different Seasons and Reasons", which groups trails so readers may choose those that fit their inclinations and abilities.

South Bay Trails includes the ring of parks and preserves around Santa Clara County on mountain slopes and in foothill woodlands together with the paths on the valley floor by creeks and by the Bay that enrich everyday living in this busy metropolitan area. Here is a wealth of recreation opportunities for everyone. A companionable walk or an invigorating bicycle ride is a few minutes from home. A creekside stroll along a newly restored river park during a noon lunch break is close to urban work places. Farther afield it is still possible to find cherished solitude on a long day's trip into the wilderness or a week's backpack trip to sight a golden eagle from a mountain peak.

Hiking in the backcountry entails unavoidable risk that every hiker assumes and must be aware of and respect. The fact that a trail is described in this book is not a representation that it will be safe for you. Trails vary greatly in difficulty and in the degree of conditioning and agility one needs to enjoy them safely. On some hikes routes may have changed or conditions may have deteriorated since the descriptions were written. Also trail conditions can change even from day to day, owing to weather and other factors. A trail that is safe on a dry day or for a highly conditioned, agile, properly equipped hiker may be completely unsafe for someone else or unsafe under adverse weather conditions.

You can minimize your risks on the trail by being knowledgeable, prepared and alert. There is not space in this book for a general treatise on safety in the mountains, but there are a number of good books and public courses on the subject and you should take advantage of them to increase your knowledge. Just as important, you should always be aware of your own limitations and of conditions existing when and where you are hiking. If conditions are dangerous, or if you're not prepared to deal with them safely, choose a different hike! It's better to have wasted a drive than to be the subject of a mountain rescue.

These warnings are not intended to scare you off the trails. Millions of people have safe and enjoyable hikes every year. However, one element of the beauty, freedom and excitement of the wilderness is the presence of risks that do not confront us at home. When you hike you assume those risks. They can be met safely, but only if you exercise your own independent judgement and common sense.

Part One
Background

The South Bay Setting

Geography

A 100-mile-long valley flanked by two arms of the Coast Range mountains lies at the southern end of San Francisco Bay. Through this valley flow tree-lined creeks that drain the steep, forested mountains and oak-dotted foothills of the Santa Cruz Mountains and the grassy and wooded heights of the Diablo Range. When the streams reach the Bay's edge, they widen into sloughs and meander through what were once broad marshes but are now diked salt ponds. This is the setting for *South Bay Trails*.

The eastern mountains, the Diablo Range, extend from Contra Costa County south to Pacheco Pass at the extreme southern end of Santa Clara County. The highest point in the range, 4372' Copernicus Peak, is near Mt. Hamilton, a few feet lower and known for its observatories. Other tall Diablo mountains are Mission Peak and Monument Peak in the north and Pacheco Peak and Mt. Sizer in the south.

These mountains, dry and grassy on their west- and south-facing slopes, are broken into parallel ridges with steep sides separated by narrow intervening valleys. The general trend of ridges and valleys is northwest-southeast, following the direction of major earthquake faults in the region. The Diablo Range separates the Santa Clara Valley from the San Joaquin Valley, coaxing moisture from the clouds that brush against its tall peaks.

Across the valley on the west side are the Santa Cruz Mountains and their foothills, slightly lower in elevation than the Diablo Range. This range extends south from Montara Mountain near San Francisco to Mt. Madonna, and then slopes to the valley of the Pajaro River, which flows west to Monterey Bay. A shallow notch in the Santa Cruz Mountains called Saratoga Gap has long been the route

3

from the valley to destinations along the Skyline ridge and to the west.

Farther south the Santa Cruz Mountains are interrupted by a low pass where Los Gatos Creek cuts through on its northeastward course to the Bay. The Spaniards called the northern mountainous area the Sierra Morena (dark mountains) and the southern area the Sierra Azul (the latter, perhaps, because of the blue haze that often hangs over its forested heights). The tallest mountain, Loma Prieta, is 3791'. Just north, other landmark peaks include Mt. Umunhum and Mt. Thayer, and Mt. Madonna is farther south.

The Santa Clara Valley lowlands enclosed by the two ranges consist of a number of alluvial fans and floodplains formed by deep deposits eroded from the surrounding mountains. The relatively smooth valley floor ranges in elevation from 150' to 400'. The valley rises from the Bay to a low, almost imperceptible divide at Morgan Hill, south of which the drainage flows to the Pajaro River.

Fifteen miles wide in the north, the valley tapers at the Santa Teresa Hills to a passage 2 miles wide, sometimes called the "Coyote Narrows," through which Coyote Creek flows.

Coyote Creek is the longest stream flowing out of the Diablo Range. Joined by tributary creeks, San Felipe and Silver, in the foothills, then by Penitencia, Calaveras, Berryessa and Scott on the valley floor, it empties into San Francisco Bay northeast of Alviso. The waters of Alameda Creek, now contained in a flood-control channel, flow into the Bay just north of Coyote Hills.

Major creeks that course down the east side of the Santa Cruz Mountains are Stevens, Calabasas, Saratoga, Los Gatos and Guadalupe, which flow into San Francisco Bay. Streams rising in the mountains southeast of Loma Prieta—Uvas, Llagas, freely across the valley. For purposes of flood control or ground-water recharge most are dammed at some point, diverted to percolation ponds, or channeled. Nevertheless, many stretches of these creeks flow toward the Bay, still bordered by the oaks, alders, sycamores and bay trees that have always lined their banks.

Plants and Animals

The great variety of South Bay terrain from mountains to plains accommodates a corresponding variety in plant communities—conifers on the mountains, chaparral on dry slopes, maples and ferns in damp stream canyons, grasses and occasional oaks in the meadows and distinctive salt-tolerant plants in bay marshes.

Grasslands cover the foothills on both sides of the valley as well as the south and west slopes of the Diablo Range. The familiar golden hills of summer and the sometimes brief green of winter and spring come from the predominant European oats and other annual grasses. In the grasslands are found the most spectacular wildflower displays. At times the low hills, even seen from a distance, are colored for miles with goldfields, tidytips and poppies.

Grasslands on the west-facing slopes of the Diablo Range are studded with magnificent open stands of deciduous valley oaks. In the bare hills of this range are canyons lined with live oak, California bay, maple, alder and sycamore. In both the Diablo and Santa Cruz ranges great areas of brushland or chaparral clothe dry hillsides with woody plants in various combinations—coyote bush, toyon, chamise and the ubiquitous poison oak. On much of the Santa Cruz Mountains are stands of live oak, madrone, canyon oak and black oak forming a dense canopy. In the damp canyons bay trees proliferate.

In the area of this book coniferous forests are found chiefly in the Santa Cruz Mountains. From the valley you can see the silhouettes of Douglas firs and redwoods. Associated with their forests is an undergrowth of blackberries, huckleberries and other shrubs and numerous fern species. Though some areas were logged in the past century, they now have maturing forests of good-sized trees. On the east slopes of the mountains are scattered knobcone pines— sometimes in thick young forests where they have sprung up after fires.

By a shady trail delicate blossoms of Alum Root grow from a rocky bank in Uvas Canyon Park

One can see the jagged outlines of another conifer on the hilltops of the Diablo Range in and near Coe Park, where the ponderosa pine has found a niche far from its usual Sierra habitat.

A special plant community borders the Bay where cordgrass, salt grass, pickleweed and other salt-tolerant plants grow in tidelands, wetlands and marshes.

Dark-green bands of trees still persist along the banks of creeks where they thread through the built-up cities on the valley floor. The alders, sycamores, oaks, maples and willows, shrubs and vines that make up the riparian vegetation provide a valuable habitat for wildlife.

In large parks and preserves where the land is relatively undisturbed, many animals that lived here before the coming of the Anglos can still be found. Gone are the antelope and the bear, but deer in numbers and coyotes and foxes, as well as many smaller mammals, still live here. You will see their tracks on and off the trails. Even a mountain lion is occasionally sighted in a remote part of a mountain park.

South Bay woods and fields contain myriad birds—over 300 species have been counted. Some more easily identifiable ones are mentioned in this guide because the authors saw them. The Baylands, reservoirs and percolation ponds are teeming with shorebirds and waterfowl. Resident birds that have long lived by the sloughs and marshes are finding new habitats by percolation ponds and salt ponds. Joining them in winter months are migrating birds by the thousands using the Pacific Flyway.

The South Bay's Past

In the years since the arrival of the Spanish in 1776 three distinct periods have together seen the changes that transformed the valley and the foothills at the south end of San Francisco Bay into today's densely urban scene.

For thousands of years before 1776 Ohlone Indians lived here, possessing a stable culture that had little impact on the land. After the founding of Mission Santa Clara in 1777 and Mission San José in 1797, the Indians were baptized and taken into these establishments. They left their villages, and their lands were divided into huge ranches that raised cattle for their hides and tallow.

The second transitional period began after nearly 100 years of Spanish and Mexican rule. The discovery of gold and the admission of California to the United States were followed by the break-up of the ranches into farms producing wheat, fruits and vegetables to supply the rapidly growing city of San Francisco.

Then, a century after the Gold Rush, the postwar boom ushered in the most profound alterations of the landscape as industry and housing swept away orchards, vineyards and truck farms. In less than two decades this agricultural valley became urban—home to more than a million people.

However, by the mid-1960s concern for the effects of unrestrained growth led to programs to create the parks, open-space preserves and trail systems we now enjoy. As we walk along these trails, we can still find much that evokes the earlier periods in South Bay history.

The Ohlone Indians

Of the earliest settlers, the Ohlone people, few remain, but we value the records we have of their lives and treasure the artifacts of their culture. They lived well on the abundance of this fertile, well-watered land, depending on the plentiful supplies of acorns, seeds, fruits, game, fish and shellfish. Their villages, circles of huts made of rushes over frameworks of bent willows, have disappeared, but traces remaining around their shellmounds have been studied by archeologists.

The Ohlone had no pottery, but their baskets of extraordinary fineness served every purpose. Of the very few that survived, one may be seen at the Los Altos Library.

The Ohlone were runners of great speed and endurance. We have no time records to compare them with the runners who follow our trails today, but an 1898 account testifies to their speed and endurance: ". . . one would run from my ranch at Edenvale to Santa Clara keeping up with the fastest horse, and laugh when he got there. . . ."

When Gaspar de Portolá came through the Santa Clara Valley, he described the people he found in large villages by the Guadalupe River as "generous affable heathen." Other early explorers commented on their curiosity and hospitality and noted that they were well-formed and comely. (Later reports on the Ohlone, when they were living in the missions, were not so complimentary. They were sometimes described as uncooperative—but perhaps their behavior was just a reaction to the frequently harsh discipline they faced.)

In a sad chapter in our history, the Ohlone population was greatly reduced and their culture destroyed as they were christened and taken from their villages to live in the missions. There they

Mural on old cannery shows Ohlone Indian life around the bay

succumbed to diseases against which they had no resistance. After secularization of the missions under Mexican rule, they were dispersed to work on ranches. By 1810 only a few Ohlone were living an aboriginal life. Under U.S. rule too, they were often badly treated.

Spanish and Mexican Rule

Soon after the founding of Mission Santa Clara and the establishment of the Pueblo de San José, Spanish and then Mexican governors of California granted ranches of thousands of acres as rewards for service or simply to settle the land. The economy was based on raising cattle and exporting hides and tallow. From this period Spanish place names abound. Streets, cities, creeks and hills carry the names of families and patron saints. Spanish words survive in our terms *chaparral, manzanita, arroyo, embarcadero* and *plaza,* among others.

The most visible heritage from these times covers our hills, which are colored golden in summer by the imported European oats that replaced the native bunchgrasses.

The supporting Pueblo de San José beside the Guadalupe River, at first just a double row of mud huts, has remained the focus of civic and cultural activity for the valley.

Neither Mission Santa Clara nor Mission San José has come down to us intact; floods, fires and earthquakes destroyed the early buildings. But fragments of old walls remain from an early Mission Santa Clara, and the museum of Mission San José occupies the surviving building of the old mission. A fine reconstruction of the 1807 mission is now completed. A few adobe buildings are still standing around the valley, some lived in today.

Many of the big parks in the hills are parts of former Spanish and Mexican ranches. Some have been used for grazing since those days, and grazing is still carried on. Mission Peak Preserve was a part of Mission San José lands; a part of the Higuera family's Rancho Tularcitos is now Ed R. Levin Park; in Santa Teresa Hills we can ride over José Bernal's lands.

The Coming of the Anglos and a Century of Agriculture

Even before the discovery of gold in California a steady trickle of immigrants from the east was arriving in the Bay Area. The first Anglos from an overland expedition reached San Jose in 1841. The war between United States and Mexico broke out in 1846. In the "Battle of Santa Clara," engaging only about 100 soldiers on each side, U.S. forces prevailed and the Bear Flag was raised over San Jose.

When California was admitted to statehood in 1850, San Jose became its first capital. The city soon changed from a sleepy Mexican village to a bustling center for the farms that supplied Gold Rush San Francisco. Stage lines and steamers made regular runs between San Francisco and Alviso, and by 1864 the San Francisco-San Jose Railroad was completed.

Bringing an exotic touch to valley life by the mid-1850s was the astoundingly productive New Almaden Quicksilver Mine. Seemingly inexhaustible supplies of cinnabar, mined from miles of tunnels through the hills, were processed in giant reduction works. The mines supplied needed mercury to California's gold fields and to international trade, chiefly with China.

But agriculture remained the basis of the South Bay economy. Fruit trees thrived in the valley, watered by creeks and irrigation ditches. Rich alluvial soil 30–40′ deep overlaid clay and water-bearing gravel substrata. For a while artesian wells gushed from the Bay plain.

Orchards and vineyards soon covered the valley floor and the foothills. Stock imported by French nurserymen produced the country's finest fruits, and Santa Clara Valley wines won awards in Paris. In the "wine boom" of 1880 grape vines were planted in thousands of acres across the valley and up to the summit of the Santa Cruz Mountains. But soon after came a glut of grapes, falling prices and a deadly root disease. As a result, vineyards were interplanted with prunes and apricots.

The valley continued to be one of the most productive agricultural areas in the U.S. Each spring, from the foothills, one looked down on a pink-and-white mosaic of fruit blossoms. This was indeed, the "Valley of Heart's Delight," as Santa Clara County people fondly called it. They made excursions out into the beautiful foothills surrounding the valley. Wagon trips to Lick Observatory were popular. As early as 1872 Alum Rock Park was set aside as a park by the State Legislature. Spas flourished around mineral springs and hot springs—at Congress Springs above Saratoga (which took its name from the New York resort), Gilroy Hot Springs and Warm Springs, near Mission San Jose.

In 1888 San Jose's Dashaway Stables advertised a large string of "useful, careful animals of fine appearance." It urged patrons to "revel in delights of spring through Santa Clara Valley, its foothills and adjacent mountains behind a Dashaway team."

The exuberance of these times took form in spacious farm houses, great mansions, luxurious estates, and even a few villas scattered through the foothills. Many of these handsome structures have

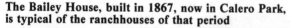

The Bailey House, built in 1867, now in Calero Park, is typical of the ranchhouses of that period

disappeared, but thanks to recent interest in historic preservation many notable buildings have survived. Among those in the parks are the Bailey House, the Gallegos Mansion, the Rengstorff House now in Mountain View's Shoreline, and La Casa Grande at New Almaden.

Expanding agriculture and a growing urban population increased demands on the valley's water supply. As water was pumped from wells to augment the once-ample supplies from creeks, the water table fell drastically. In consequence, the land around San Jose suffered massive subsidence. Periods of drought, with water shortages, and years of heavy rainfall, with disastrous floods, plagued the valley. In response, water-conservation districts were formed. They built dams to retain winter rains, control floods and replenish underground water supplies, and they constructed levees along creek banks to protect lands in floodplains.

These water-conservation measures have brought opportunities to create parks and trails beside reservoirs and ponds. The levees beside creeks and near the Bay have become routes for trails and bicycle paths. Streamside park chains along Coyote, Guadalupe, Los Gatos, and Penitencia creeks have expanding systems of trails.

From Orchards to Industry

With World War II came the beginnings of the transformation of the Santa Clara Valley and the East Bay south of Fremont. In a few decades it changed from a balanced agricultural community to a metropolitan area of more than a million people.

During the war, scientific expertise around Stanford University was developing electronic equipment for the military. A major naval air station was installed at Moffett Field. Then after the war came a spurt of urban growth as electronic plants offered employment in what we now call "Silicon Valley." Santa Clara County became one of the principal magnets for migration into California. Cities around the South Bay grew until many of their boundaries merged.

Progress Toward Parks, Preserves and Trails

By the mid-1960s valley residents began to realize that this phenomenal growth was eroding the quality of their environment, and they moved to restore some of the amenities lost in the fast pace of postwar building and to protect what was left.

Park Plans and Acquisitions

The East Bay Regional Park District, formed in 1934 in Alameda and Contra Costa counties, acquired Coyote Hills Regional Park in 1967, adding to its earlier holdings. The Alameda Creek Regional Trail was developed on each side of the flood control channel from the Bay to Niles. Mission Peak Regional Preserve was acquired in 1974.

In Santa Clara County a far-sighted plan for regional parks was spearheaded by Ed R. Levin, a planning commissioner. Adopted in 1972, it called for major parks throughout the valley and recreational corridors along the creeks. In the next year a policy plan for the Santa Clara County Baylands was adopted. Santa Clara County voters passed a tax allocation for parks in 1972. Today there are more than 37,000 acres of parklands in the county.

The citizen-initiated Midpeninsula Regional Park District (now the Midpeninsula Regional Open Space District) was established in 1972 for northern Santa Clara County. It now includes southern San Mateo County, and has over 32,000 acres of open-space preserves, nearly 10,000 in the area covered by this book. It is District policy ". . . to acquire land or rights to land for a regional trail system outside urbanized areas, and through cooperative programs to provide a trail system which ties together the urban area with major open space and recreation resources of the region."

An initiative measure on the November 1990 ballot proposed a Santa Clara County Open Space Authority to purchase and maintain open space land, to preserve agriculture and to protect viewsheds and watershed lands. This measure received 63% of the vote, narrowly missing the required two-thirds.

Meanwhile, alarm at the degradation of the Bay by pollution and by filling of marshlands and wetlands resulted in the establishment of the Bay Conservation and Development Commission. The San Francisco Bay National Wildlife Refuge in the South Bay now protects more than 23,000 acres of water, marsh and slough. Palo Alto's Baylands and flood-control basin encompass 720 acres of shoreline and marshland.

New Trails and Campgrounds

Of particular interest to trail users is Santa Clara County's Intergovernmental Council's Trails and Pathways Committee, formed in the 1970s. It has promoted trail issues and supported the County's adopted Trails and Pathways Master Plan, adopted by the county and cities in 1982. This plan serves as a guide to locating trails and to securing trail rights in areas where new development is taking place.

In the 1990s a new generation is joining veteran hikers and equestrians. A veritable army of runners and bicyclists is out on the trails. The Trail Center, organized in 1983, coordinates volunteer activities in trail building and maintenance, monitors trail issues and provides information to interested hikers, riders, bicyclists and runners.

Many parks and preserves now have active organizations of supporters and volunteers who train to become docents, to assist rangers, to staff visitor centers, to publish newsletters and in many ways to enrich the experiences of park visitors and trail users. A list of these groups is in Appendix II.

Five parks included in this guide provide overnight camping facilities. With an early start from a campsite the trail user can take long day trips through beautiful foothill and mountain parks. Then at day's end campers can watch for wildlife emerging at dusk and observe stars in the clear mountain air.

Grant Park's extensive trail system offers possibilities for a week of day trips exploring its 40 miles of trails. Mt. Madonna Park's forest camps and Uvas Canyon Park's oak-shaded camping areas are cool retreats from summer valley heat and bases for leisurely exploration of the trails.

Sanborn-Skyline Park's overnight campgrounds and the AYH Hostel are good starting points for hikes. Henry W. Coe State Park has thousands of acres of wilderness to explore from camps near headquarters and from backpack campsites.

Long Distance Trails Beckon Backpackers in the 90's

Of the parks included in this guide only Coe Park offers backpacking campsites which provide ample scope for a week's trip into remote canyons near springs and flowing streams. Several South Bay trails connect with other trail systems that provide opportunities for extended backpacking trips—west to trail camps on the forested slopes of the Santa Cruz Mountains and to the coast, north to Monte Bello Open Space Preserve, and east on the Ohlone Wilderness Trail in the eastern Diablo Range.

Early interest in trail connections between Castle Rock State Park on the Skyline ridge and Big Basin State Park near Santa Cruz led to the beginnings of the Skyline to the Sea Trail. With the support of the

Sempervirens Fund and the State Parks Department this famous trail has been continued to the Pacific Ocean. Today the 37-mile route descends through woodlands in Castle Rock Park on a trail easement beside Highway 9 into deep forests in the heart of Big Basin State Park, then continues over ridges and along creeks to the mouth of Waddell Creek.

Backpack camps are spaced at a distance of a day's walk or less. For information and reservations call the ranger at Big Basin State Park—408-338-6132. Excellent trail maps may be purchased from the state parks, the Sempervirens office and other map outlets.

Some day another crossing into the western Santa Cruz Mountains may lead to the Forest of Nisene Marks State Park near Aptos on Monterey Bay. Trail camps midway down the park's western ridge would provide stopovers for long distance trail users. However, until the status of intervening unimproved roads is clarified, this trip is not recommended.

The East Bay Regional Park District has opened its 29-mile Ohlone Wilderness Trail from Mission Peak Preserve across oak-dotted hills and forested canyons to Del Valle Regional Park south of Livermore. The route crosses San Francisco Watershed lands and the Sunol and Ohlone Regional Wilderness areas (see Mission Peak Preserve, Trip 4). Hikers, backpackers and equestrians can stop at backpack and equestrian camps along the way. For information, a

Backpacking in Henry Coe State Park

map and the permit required for the trail, call the East Bay Regional Park District: 415-531-9300.

Two New Long Distance Trails

Two regional trails are in the making—the Bay Area Ridge Trail and the San Francisco Bay Trail—one on the ridges and the other at water's edge.

The Ridge Trail for hikers, equestrians and bicyclists, well on the way to its 400-mile goal, had already dedicated nearly 100 miles of trail by the end of 1990. In a cooperative effort, public agencies and citizen organizatons in the South Bay are working to complete a route down the Santa Cruz Mountains and up the Diablo Range to join East and North Bay groups in completing the trail.

A plan to circle the shores of San Francisco and San Pablo bays with a paved trail for hikers and bicyclists, the San Francisco Bay Trail, is also being realized. Around the South Bay more than 50 miles of nearly continuous trail were in use in 1990 and more segments are in the planning stage.

Using This Guide

Each of the 26 parks and preserves in this guide is numbered on a locator map at the beginning of the book to correspond with its numerical listing in the Table of Contents. The Diablo Range parks and the Santa Cruz Mountain parks are listed from north to south; the Baylands parks are numbered around the Bay from east to west, as are the creekside parks.

The bulk of this guide contains descriptions of trips on trails in the public lands of the South Bay. Short hikes from park entrances are described, as well as longer and more extensive trips. Sometimes a car shuttle is suggested for long hikes. Where possible, trips are planned to end on a downhill stretch. Many trips are loop hikes which begin and end at the same place. Tips for planning hikes include times of day and seasons of the year when hiking is best—important on South Bay trails.

You will find a reference in Appendix I which lists trips for a variety of circumstances and difficulty. Trips on shady trails for hot summer days, hikes to high places, trails for wheelchair users, and long expeditions are some of the categories that may help you find the right trip for a special occasion or remind you of old favorites.

The time required for a trip is based on the authors' moderate walking pace—two miles an hour. This allows time for enjoying views, admiring flowers, examining animal tracks and taking short rests along the way. Bicyclists and equestrians, who may travel faster, can use these times to estimate their trip's duration.

Figures for elevation change tell the vertical footage gained or lost over the whole trip. To help estimate the time required for a trip where the cumulative gain is more than 1000 feet or there are steep climbs within a short distance, the authors used an old hiking rule, helpful to other users also: for every 1000 vertical feet gained, add ½ hour.

The authors aimed for accuracy in reporting, but enthusiasms for particular features are the authors' subjective responses. Sightings of birds and animals, the presence of individual flower species in bloom, the weather conditions on a certain day—all depend on the fortunate combination of being in the right place at the right time.

The authors attempted to include all public trails currently open in the South Bay, but new park trails will undoubtedly be added as enthusiasm for walking, hiking, jogging, running, bicycling and horseback riding continues.

How To Get There

Directions from the nearest major road to the parks are given. Although the car remains the quickest and easiest way to get to the trails, a few buses with adequate schedules can take you to several parks in the South Bay. The guide notes bus service where bus stops are within a few blocks of park entrances. AC Transit permits bikes on some buses on weekends. For up-to-date schedules call Santa Clara County Transit, 408-287-4210, or AC Transit, 415-797-6811, for East Bay parks.

Bike lanes and some separate bicycle paths lead to the creekside park chains, the Baylands and some of the foothill parks. Santa Clara County publishes a Bikeways Map that shows existing and planned bicycle routes chiefly on city streets. In Alameda County a long bicycle path leads from Niles Canyon to Coyote Hills Park, and there are bike lanes to the Wildlife Refuge.

Information and Maps

The maps in this guide show all the trails for trips described in South Bay parks, preserves, creek chains and Baylands. Although most jurisdictions offer park maps, they are not always available at the trailhead. You can call or write the public agencies listed in Appendix II for maps and further information.

Trails are indicated by dashed lines with no distinction made between foot trails, horse trails and bicycle trails. A number of trails

Well signed trails guide the hiker

are for hikers only and some are for hikers and equestrians only. The text treats this for each trip. Many of the trails are old, unsurfaced ranch roads, powerline service roads or fire roads. Unless the road is also used for public vehicular access, it is shown as a trail.

The Legend on page 22 depicts the symbols used on the maps. Trails are indicated by dashed lines, with no distinction made between those for hikers, equestrians or bicyclists. For each park or trip, such distinctions, where applicable, are made in the text.

Some parks and preserves offer hikes, nature walks, and guided field trips led by staff naturalists or trained volunteers and docents. The interpretive centers and science museums at park headquarters are well-worth a visit.

Excellent topographic maps for all the parks in this guide are available at the United States Geological Survey headquarters at 345 Middlefield Road in Menlo Park. Some outdoor equipment stores also carry them, as does The Map Center at Wilderness Press at 2440 Bancroft Way in Berkeley, and at 63 Washington Street in Santa Clara.

The specific topo map (s) for each park is listed at the beginning of its section. The quadrangles of the 7.5-minute series, on a $1'' = 2000'$ scale, are excellent for all trail users. Many local trails and old ranch roads are marked on these maps. There are symbols for natural features, such as vegetative cover, streams, lakes and mountaintops. Elevations and contour lines give information about the steepness of the terrain you will cover.

Rules for Parks and Preserves

The regulations for park and trail use are few, but important. Based on common sense, they are made for your safety and the preservation of the natural setting. All plants, animals and natural features are protected; leave them undisturbed for others to enjoy. Leaving your radio at home preserves the natural serenity and quiet. All archeological artifacts are protected and should be left undisturbed.

Smoking is prohibited on trails; no fires are allowed except in established fireplaces. Firearms and bows and arrows are prohibited except at organized ranges.

Stay on the designated trails. Do not shortcut switchbacks because this breaks down the trail, accelerates erosion and can dislodge rocks which could injure persons below you.

Where bicycles are allowed on South Bay trails, their riders are required to wear helmets.

Except where noted in the text, dogs are prohibited on all trails in Santa Clara County Parks, the Midpeninsula Regional Open Space Preserves, the San Francisco Bay National Wildlife Refuge and city parks. The presence of a dog, even a well-behaved one on a leash, disturbs wild creatures. Some parks allow dogs on a short leash in developed picnic grounds. Guide-dogs for the blind are always permitted.

These basic rules are common to all parks and not repeated in the individual park sections.

Park hours are generally 8 A.M. to ½ hour after sunset except in MROSD Preserves, which are open from dawn to dusk.

Some service roads, fire roads and wide paved paths have been opened to bicyclists in many parks, but narrow paths are restricted. Questions of speed, hazards to bicyclists themselves and to other users, liability of public agencies and impact of bicycles on the terrain are still under review. Some parks have limits on bicycle speed and many ordinances prohibit riding a bicycle in a reckless manner.

This guide attempts to note which trails are currently open to bicyclists and which are closed. However, since rules are still under study or subject to change by the agency in charge, trail users are urged to check with the agency in question and to observe trail signs.

Many South Bay trails are shared by hikers, runners, bicyclists and equestrians. Trail etiquette requires bicyclists to yield to hikers and equestrians. When hikers meet horses on the trail, the hikers should stand quietly uphill and wait for the horses to pass. Bicyclists, runners and joggers, traveling quietly but quickly on trails, may startle hikers and horses. Approaching from the rear, a bicyclist or runner should call to the hiker or horse's rider that he is passing.

To protect parks and their visitors, some parks or their outlying trails may be closed at times of extremely high fire danger. Some trails too, may be closed when muddy.

For safety's sake, always walk with a companion. Consult Appendix II for lists of groups that conduct hikes or start your own walking group with friends.

Cautions for Trail Users

Poison oak, that pesky plant of the California landscape, should be avoided. Touching its leaves or stems can produce an uncomfortable, itchy rash. Poison oak grows variously in the form of a low bush, a 20-foot vine or a man-sized shrub. Its shiny green three-lobed leaves turn brilliant shades of red in fall and are then easy to spot, but the bare branches in winter can still produce unpleasant effects. The best solution is to learn to recognize the plant and avoid it. Long-sleeved shirts and long pants give good protection. If you think you have touched the plant, wash the skin area in the nearest stream or use water from your canteen.

Rattlesnakes are native to this country. They have a triangular-shaped head, diamond markings or dark blotches on their backs and 1–10 rattles on their tails. Cold-blooded, these reptiles lie in the sun before the day gets hot, then retreat to cool crevices or holes in the grasslands. Though a rattlesnake will not attack you unless it feels threatened, give it a wide berth. Watch where you put your hands and feet, and stay on the trail.

A new hazard for trail users comes from the Western Black-Legged Tick. Bearing Lyme disease, it has recently spread to California and the Bay Area. This infectious disease is transmitted by a tiny black tick. The potentially serious symptoms of this disease begin with a blotchy rash and sometimes, flu-like fever and aches. Later, even more serious joint and neurological symptoms can occur.

It is important to avoid tick bites. Ticks brush off onto you from grasses and trailside bushes, primarily from December through June. The best protection is to wear long pants, tucked into boots or socks, and to check yourself and children frequently. An insect repellent containing DEET applied to clothing also helps.

Not-dangerous gopher snake digesting its meal on a sunny trail

Most parks display circulars about these ticks. You can obtain a free leaflet, "Facts about Lyme Disease and the Western Black Tick," from the Department of Health Services, 2151 Berkeley Way, Berkeley, CA 94704. Consult your physician if you believe you have been bitten by one of these ticks or if you develop early symptoms. Recognition of symptoms is important because early treatment can avoid complications.

Thirst and heat exhaustion can be problems on the trail. Although many days in summer are moderate, sometimes the temperature rises above 100°. On these days you should avoid long trips on steep, sunny hillsides. Always carry plenty of water—at least a quart per person per day. There are no drinking fountains on the trails, and stream and pond water is not potable. Wear a wide-brimmed hat to protect your face and head. With a little forethought you can plan your trip to avoid these hazards.

Climate and Weather

The South Bay's generally moderate climate makes good hiking possible throughout the year. Even the coldest months have unseasonably mild days to lure you out on the trails, and there are shady hillsides for those hot summer days.

In general, choose your trip to match the season and the day's weather. On hot summer days try the shady trails in the Santa Cruz Mountains or take trips along tree-bordered creeks. Start early in the morning or take an early-evening supper trip. Remember that ocean breezes blowing down the Bay keep summer temperatures cooler on the Baylands.

In spring and fall you have unlimited choices. For winter days try short hikes by the Bay or on sunny south-facing slopes. After a winter storm, when skies clear, try a peak climb for views of the distant Sierra.

What to Wear and Take Along

Hiking is not an expensive sport. The only special equipment you need is a pair of well-fitting shoes that give good support and have a raised tread. The authors have found running shoes to be very satisfactory except on the most rugged, rocky trails. For these trails lug-soled hiking boots are better.

Wearing several layers of outer garments topped by a windbreaker traps the heat when the day is cold and lets you peel off as you and the day warm up. On trips to higher elevations in winter, you will need a warm wool sweater and an insulated jacket. A cap or hat also helps reduce body heat loss.

Summer hiking calls for sun protection—the earlier-mentioned hat with a brim, a sunscreen and dark glasses. Even when the day is hot, a sweater or windbreaker is good insurance against freshening breezes or afternoon fog.

A small day-pack will hold your extra garments and the few necessities for your trip—lunch, water and this guide. If you have room, a bird book and binoculars are nice.

MAP LEGEND

═══════	Freeway	Ⓑ	Bus stop
───────	Road	Ⓟ	Parking
─ ─ ─ ─ ─	Trail	Ⓛⓟ	Limited parking
· · · · · · · · ·	Proposed trail	■	Restroom
── ·· ──	Park Boundary	▲	Picnic ground
── ··· ──	Stream	△	Campground
➤	Park entrance	✳	Park office / Visitor Center
▶	Trail entry point	Ⓗ	Horse staging area
⊢──⊣	Gate	□	Other structure

Part Two
The South Bay Trails
The Diablo Range

Mission Peak Regional Preserve

Mission Peak, that austere East Bay landmark, is more approachable than its steep west face reveals. In the Mission Peak Regional Preserve 15 miles of trails take you through wooded canyons, gently rolling hills, hidden valleys and sheltered glens. As well as the spectacular panorama from Mission Peak's summit, there are fresh vistas at each turn of its trails.

Mission Peak and the East Bay Regional Park District's 2546-acre preserve surrounding this landmark were part of the vast holdings of Mission San José, founded in 1797, whose lands once extended north almost to Oakland and east to the Livermore Valley. The mission's broad lands grew olives, fruits, grapes and wheat and grazed 12,000 head of cattle. Soon after its founding, this was one of the most prosperous of California's missions. From what is now Washington Boulevard a road led to the mission's embarcadero on Newark Slough. Later known as Jarvis Landing, this embarcadero remained a port for Bay traffic until early in this century.

When the mission was secularized in 1836, its lands were divided into ranches, and a settlement grew up around the mission and its supporting enterprises. During Gold Rush days the community became a bustling provision center, as it was on the route to the southern mines. Later, bypassed by the railroad, it again became a quiet village.

The 1806 adobe mission, handsomely reconstructed, and the adjoining museum in one of the original mission buildings are well worth a visit. In the community of Mission San Jose many buildings of the late 19th century remain, and they make a good walking tour. The valuable architectural heritage of this community, within the Fremont city limits, is protected by designation as a historic district.

23

Ohlone College, on Mission Boulevard, is on the hills once covered by the mission's vineyards. Palm and pepper trees are left from the site of an old park and estate. The double row of olive trees along Mission Boulevard marks the old road that ran from Mission Santa Clara to Mission San José.

In Mission Peak Regional Preserve, miles of trails lead to the summit of the peak through the rolling hills behind Ohlone College. Trails also reach the peak from Stanford Avenue, a few miles farther south. Another network of trails over college property behind the campus is open to the public. In 1985 the East Bay Regional Park District opened the first phase of its 29-mile Ohlone Wilderness Trail, which now reaches Del Valle Regional Park from Mission Peak Preserve.

The regional Bay Area Ridge Trail will some day link Monument Peak to Mission Peak and go north to Garin Regional Park.

Jurisdiction   East Bay Regional Park District.

Facilities   Trails, hiking, equestrian and, on designated service roads, bicycle. Equestrian staging area at Stanford Avenue with water, restroom.

Park Rules   Hours: Trails open daily. Curfew, Stanford Avenue staging area 10 P.M. to 5 A.M. Dogs under control allowed off leash only in undeveloped areas; leash required in parking areas.

Maps   EBRPD *Mission Peak Regional Preserve;* USGS quad *Niles Canyon.*

How To Get There

By Car   For Trips 1 and 5—From Freeway 680 in Fremont go north on Mission Boulevard 2.5 miles to Ohlone College. On weekdays, 50¢ parking fee in general parking lots; on weekends, free parking. For Trip 1 park on south side of campus above swimming pool—trailhead just beyond. For Trip 5 use parking lots at east end of Witherly Lane. For Trips 2, 3 and 4 up the west side of the peak—From Freeway 680 go north on Mission Boulevard 0.5 miles, then turn right (east) on Stanford Avenue and go ½ mile to trailhead staging area.

By Bus   AC Transit buses from Fremont Bart Station, R 24 and 28, Dixon Landing.

Trip 1.   **Peak Trail to the Summit from Ohlone College**

An exhilarating trip takes you to spectacular views, reaching the peak from its north side.

Distance   5.8 miles round trip.

Time   2½ hours up; 1½ hours down.

Elevation Gain   2100'

TRAIL NOTES

From the parking lot by the swimming pool on the south side of the campus, walk uphill to the eucalyptus grove, where you will see a sign for the Mission Peak Regional Preserve. The Peak Trail starts from a stile by a locked gate on the right, and the Spring Valley Trail starts uphill, veering to the left. Go over the stile to the Peak Trail, an old ranch road that goes steadily up the side of the mountain, rising about 600' to a saddle in less than ½ mile. The trail surface is well-compacted sandstone, making this a good trip in winter even shortly after rains.

More than halfway up the hill, note a trail junction to the left (north). Here a narrow footpath leaves the broad trail to cross over the hill to the Spring Valley Trail. This is the YSC Trail, built by the Youth Service Corps.

As you climb on the Peak Trail, the Bay plain comes into view, including Fremont and Milpitas, and beyond, the patterns of salt ponds and sloughs. In a half hour's walk the trail enters a wooded canyon. Just before you go into the woods, look back to catch the sweep of the Bay—from Mt. Tamalpais in the north down to Mt. Umunhum and Loma Prieta in the south.

For a short time you walk in one of the wooded canyons under oaks found in the folds of these otherwise bare East Bay hills. Then the trail comes out onto open grasslands in a saddle and turns toward the northeast boundary of the preserve. Before you come to the reservoir ahead, you see the Dry Creek Trail turning north, uphill, through a cattle gate to pastures beyond. Instead of going to the peak you could take this trail for a short trip back, turning down the Spring Valley Trail at the next junction.

To continue to the peak, go past the reservoir to the northeast boundary of the preserve. Here the service-road-trail comes to a locked gate providing access from Mill Creek Road for emergency vehicles. Your route, a signed path to the peak, turns southeast to the right of the gate, following the preserve-boundary fence. Mill Creek Road also follows the fence and then leads to a subdivision. There is no public access to the preserve from Mill Creek Road, and as you will see, there is no parking whatever along the road.

Your path leads into an oak grove, welcome shelter from the wind that funnels through the pass by the reservoir. The path along the fence rises gently through the trees and soon comes out into a small meadow. Beyond, you meet an intermittent stream lined with alders, where you turn away from the boundary to come out onto an open pasture. Here you pick up an old ranch road going uphill from another locked gate, providing access from Mill Creek Road. The road takes you through a handsome buckeye grove.

Here the climb to the peak begins in earnest, and you gain 520' in elevation in the next ½ mile. Your trail winds out of some oak woods, then veers south up a broad ridge in a steady pull to the peak. On a saddle below the peak you meet the Hidden Valley Trail coming up the west side from Stanford Avenue.

At a cattle gate and a trail marker for the Peak Trail, we enter another pasture and then circle east to approach the summit. Up a draw where the wind can be fierce, we come to a junction with the Eagle Trail, which loops around the high hilltops east of the summit

Milpitas and salt ponds seen from Mission Peak

and connects with the Laurel Canyon Loop, which descends to a canyon below and continues to the northeastern boundary of the park. From this junction it is a steady climb up the rocky footpath to the top of Mission Peak. We see below us the tops of the crags that face the west side of the summit. Stay on the trail. It is unsafe to explore the precipitous hillside below; a fence is there to deter the foolish.

A last clamber, and we are on the 2517' summit, marked by a low wooden post in a cluster of rocks. Stop for lunch here to enjoy the breathtaking view around the compass. Mt. Diablo stands out to the north. Southwest is Monument Peak, on the Alameda/Santa Clara county line, less than 2 miles away as the crow flies. Another part of Mission Peak Preserve adjoins Monument Peak, with a section of private property intervening. South of Monument Peak is Ed Levin Park, in Santa Clara County. It is expected that one day these two parks will be linked and provide a route for the Bay Area Ridge Trail south.

You may find yourself sharing the crags with a herd of goats that pose picturesquely on the pinnacles right below. This herd has gone wild, apparently finding the rocky summit to their liking. On clear days the peaks of the Sierra are visible across the San Joaquin Valley. Due east, you can see the lands where the new Ohlone Wilderness Trail goes over high, rolling hills studded with oaks.

The trip back from the summit is downhill all the way. You have alternate return routes of about the same length via the Hidden Valley or Horse Heaven/Peak Meadow trails west to Stanford Avenue, but they require a shuttle.

Trip 2.   Peak Climb from the West

A 2000' climb on the Hidden Valley Trail to the craggy summit offers views of landmarks from the Santa Cruz Mountains to the Sierra.

Distance   6½ miles round trip.

Time   3 hours up, 1½ hours down.

Elevation Gain   2100'

Connecting Trails   The Eagle and Laurel Canyon trails connect on the east side to the Ohlone Wilderness Trail to Del Valle Regional Park.

TRAIL NOTES

This is a strenuous climb to be taken in cool weather and with an early start up the exposed west slope. From the staging area at the end of Stanford Avenue go over a hiker/equestrian stile or through a gate, and then take the road to the left. This trail, a ranch and fire road, winds up a low ridge toward the peak. Its sign posts, marked with red dots, indicate the Ohlone Wilderness Trail route.

We walk with the sounds of Agua Caliente Creek rushing down the canyon below the trail and the song of meadowlarks in the grass. It is likely that Ohlone Indians occupied campsites in these pleasant foothills away from their permanent villages near the Bay. Archeological evidence from freeway excavations nearby suggests that Indians camped by streams in such sites to process bulbs and corms in the spring and acorns in the fall.

With the wooded depths of Hidden Valley indeed out of sight, our trail climbs out of the north side of the canyon, leaving the creek far below. As we gain elevation, the urban scene comes into view—suburbs, freeway arteries, the spreading General Motors plant, and to the north the blue waters of Fremont's Central Park Lake and its civic center. Bayward, the straight lines of salt-pond levees are intersected by curves of sloughs entering the Bay.

As the mountain steepens, our trail proceeds via switchbacks, three times approaching small streams shaded by bays and live oaks, then veering away over the bare hills. The shade and cool sounds of running water are welcome if the sun has risen high. At an elevation of about 1400' is a junction with the Peak Meadow Trail, which winds south across Hidden Valley. You can take this trail back to the staging area for a 3½-mile loop trip on the lower slopes of this beautiful mountain.

Continuing on the Hidden Valley Trail, in two more switchbacks we approach the rocky face of the peak, where uptilted layers of rock laid bare by landslides and erosion tower 700' above us, looking like the jagged spines of huge prehistoric animals. Eyeing these awesome cliffs, we walk up to a gate and through a stile and are suddenly in a gentle little valley at the foot of the crags.

Tucked behind a low ridge on the west are fields, a farmhouse and barns. This fertile valley, the McClure Ranch, homesteaded in the mid-1850s, was long an enclave of private property in the preserve, held in a life estate. The ranch came to the park district in 1982, when the last member of the McClure family died at age 93. There are plans to use the 130-year-old house as a group camp, by reservation, and as a backpack camp on the route of the Ohlone Wilderness Trail.

The trail turns north to leave the little valley, and a trail marker points to our route up around the north side of the peak. Soon we have climbed out on a grassy saddle to overlook the valleys and mountains on the east side of the peak—Mt. Diablo and the Livermore Valley. Right below are Mill Creek Road and the houses that edge the east side of the preserve. Here the wind blows with the force expected on such exposed heights, bending the grass in shining ripples with every gust. Across the saddle is a junction with the Peak Trail, which starts from Ohlone College; we can see the trail as it comes up the broad ridge from the north. From this junction continue on the Peak Trail. Then from the junction with the Eagle Trail take the footpath to the mountain top.

To complete the trip back to Stanford Avenue when you have come down from the peak, retrace your steps back to the little valley and continue down the switchbacks to the Stanford Avenue staging area.

Trip 3.   **Horse Heaven Trail to the Peak and down the Hidden Valley Trail**

A stiff climb from the Peak Meadow Trail on the steep Horse Heaven Trail crosses the headwaters of Agua Caliente Creek to ascend the peak from its south side, returning by the Hidden Valley Trail. This route is for hikers and equestrians.

Distance 5.5-mile loop.

Time 4½ hours.

Elevation Gain 2100′

TRAIL NOTES

From the Stanford Avenue staging area, start up the Peak Meadow Trail and turn right, downhill, almost immediately to cross Agua Caliente Creek. Your route is above the course of this sycamore-bordered stream as it winds up the canyon. The trail, on a ranch road, makes wide swings up grassy meadows where cattle graze. As the trail rounds a broad swale at an elevation of about 1200′, the Horse Heaven Trail turns right (south) up a draw to a little pass. From this point you can see into the ranchlands south of the preserve.

For the next mile the trail climbs an open ridge. Views are spectacular to the rocky face of Mission Peak, rising from the deep gorge cut by Agua Caliente Creek. Below the peak you will often see the herd of white goats that make this craggy outcrop their home.

Watch for a bedrock mortar with grinding holes made by the Ohlone Indians. This outcrop, with two holes worn by pestles, is on an open slope on your right beside the trail. There are no oak trees nearby, but it is believed that the Indians collected acorns elsewhere and ground them at sites with fine views such as this.

After an hour's climb on the Horse Heaven Trail you reach a small wooded canyon, sheltered by great outcrops, where Agua Caliente Creek cascades over rocks and crosses a small flat before descending into a ravine. The creek passes just south of the little valley of the McClure Ranch directly below the peak.

Another ¼ mile brings you to the 2200' shoulder of the peak, where your trail meets the Eagle Trail. From this point you look east over the Diablo Range. The Horse Heaven Trail turns north to the peak, a relatively easy climb from here. You can continue over the peak and down the other side to meet the Hidden Valley Trail that leads back to the start of your trip. If you have climbed the peak before, you can take the Eagle Trail, bearing right to circle a hilltop to the south, then turning north to traverse the hill below the peak on its east side. You can then swing left to take the Hidden Valley Trail downhill to the trailhead at Stanford Avenue, a round-trip loop of 5.5 miles.

Trip 4.   The Ohlone Wilderness Trail Route

This route is the beginning of the 29-mile Ohlone Wilderness Trail for hikers, backpackers and equestrians which extends to Del Valle Regional Park south of Livermore. The first segment, through Mission Peak Preserve, takes you over the north shoulder of the peak and down to the trailhead at the preserve's eastern boundary. From there the trail continues through San Francisco's Watershed lands, Sunol and Ohlone Wilderness and on to Del Valle Regional

Salt ponds glisten in the late-afternoon sun

Park. Red disks on the trail intersection signs mark the route all the way.

A permit/map is required. Send $1. and your name, address and telephone number to Ohlone Wilderness Trail, East Bay Regional Park District, 11500 Skyline Boulevard, Oakland, CA 94619. With the permit comes a fine map, trail regulations for the trip and a detailed description of this wilderness route through the Diablo Range.

Distance Within the Mission Peak Preserve, 5 miles. To Del Valle Regional Park, 29 miles; the backpack camp in Sunol Preserve, 12 miles.

Time 2½ hours, within the preserve.

Elevation Gain 1500'

TRAIL NOTES

The route starts on the Hidden Valley Trail from the Stanford Avenue staging area (see Trip 2). After you cross the north shoulder of the peak, turn east on the Peak Trail to the Eagle Trail. Follow the Eagle Trail ½ mile, passing the Ranch Trail, to the Laurel Canyon Loop, where you turn left, downhill. You very soon bear right when the Laurel Canyon Loop branches, keeping on the ranch road rather than the path down the creek canyon. After about ¾ mile the trail veers west as it reaches the preserve boundary fence. Continue to the gate, where you start on the trail along the route across San Francisco Watershed lands. You must have a permit, even for day use, and must sign the register at this trailhead.

Del Valle Regional Park is 24 miles east, on the red-disk-marked trail, over the oak-dotted hills of the Diablo Range. Camping at the backpack camps requires a permit and reservation from the East Bay Regional Park District.

Trip 5.   A Loop around the North Highlands

Try this easy walk over high grasslands behind the campus on a winter or spring day; for hikers only. Part of the route on the YSC Trail is not open to bicycles.

Distance 5-mile loop.

Time 3 hours.

Elevation Gain 400'

TRAIL NOTES

Park during weekends in one of the lots near the top of Witherly Lane. On weekdays park in one of the college parking lots, with a 50-¢ parking fee.

Starting from Witherly Lane north of Ohlone College, go through a cattle-guard gate above the campus. On the way up Witherly Lane you pass one of the town's handsomest old houses, the Gallegos mansion, still occupied and well kept. Continue on the road around the bend beyond Campus Building 29, an old house. There you will see the Dry Creek Trail going uphill. A short way up it, you turn left (north) on the Panorama Trail, which traverses the pasture lands and stays above a row of old eucalyptus trees. The trail for the most part is an old ranch road going in and out of small wooded ravines. Sandstone boulders dot the hillside and, above the trail, standing out against the sky, is a battlement of these huge boulders. Lichen as bright orange as the poppies that cluster nearby encrusts the rocks on this hillside.

Our trail rises on a gentle grade through pasture lands to meet the fenced northern boundary of the preserve, where we turn right and climb the trail by the fence, above a wooded canyon that drops steeply to Mission Creek, 400' below. The pattern of vegetation here is common in the East Bay hills—grassy slopes bare of trees on the warm south-and west-facing slopes, like those across the canyon, and a cover of oaks, bays and buckeyes on the shadier north slopes and canyons, like the wooded hill below our trail. At our eye level turkey vultures ride updrafts in the canyon, close enough for us to see their red heads and the spreading black feathers on their wingtips.

Soon our trail cuts across the north tip of the preserve, then zigzags up through the edge of some woods and chaparral to emerge on a grassy flat at the high point of this route. From here you have the panorama promised by the trail's name—views east to a succession of ridges of the Diablo Range and west across the Bay, with Mission San Jose below. Continue around and up the hill on the trail, which now roughly parallels the eastern boundary of the preserve. You soon drop to a small reservoir in a cleft in the hills. On a windy day (and wind is more usual than not on these hills), take shelter here for lunch if you're hungry by now.

Pick up the trail on the far side of the reservoir, where lupines and poppies bloom in a long spring season. From these high pasture lands you can fly kites, watch the soaring hawks and turkey vultures and perhaps catch sight of a glider overhead. The trail crosses under powerlines to a plateau. Then find your trail south of the powerlines, again on an old ranch road.

After going south and skirting the head of a canyon, the trail continues over a low hill. At the head of the next canyon, you leave the boundary fence and the Panorama Trail to go down the Spring Valley Trail in a streambed through the woods. The Dry Creek Trail continues southeast, climbing out of the canyon to join the Peak Trail over the hill.

A 10-minute walk under the oaks, coffeeberries and bays in this narrow ravine brings you to the spring, which gushes into a rocky basin by the trail. In a pleasant oak glade often filled with cattle coming to the watering trough fed by the spring is a crossing of the YSC Trail, for hikers only. One branch of it goes south through the woods and uphill to join the Peak Trail. You take the branch to the right (north), which climbs the bank between the spring and the watering trough. For the next ¾ mile your trail goes along grassy slopes, descending gradually to the Dry Creek Trail, where you turn left in a grove of eucalyptus above the road where you started, and ramble downhill to your car.

Leaves and unopened flowers on buckeye limb

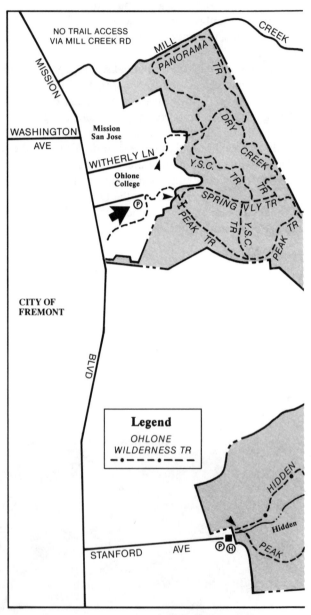

Mission Peak

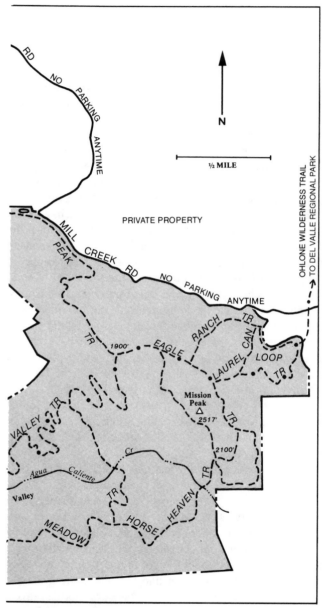

Regional Preserve

Ed R. Levin Park

Ed R. Levin Park, east of Milpitas, extends from low hills sheltering a 2-mile-long valley up to a high ridge rising to 2500' Monument Peak. The 1544-acre park's activities are focused in the valley, where lakes, ponds and spacious lawns draw crowds of weekend picnickers. An 18-hole golf course is busy every day. Rental stables and parking for horse trailers make the park popular with equestrians. Steady winds and good thermals make the park's hang-gliding launch sites some of the finest in the Bay Area.

Ed Levin Park is part of the 4000-acre Tularcitos Ranch, granted in 1821 to Juan Higuera, the mayor-domo of Mission San José, by the last of the Spanish governors in Alta California. This ranch extended from the confluence of Calera and Penitencia creeks to Calaveras Road and to the ridges at the headwaters of Calera Creek and Arroyo de los Coches. The large Higuera family built haciendas on its lands and were for years a dominant force on this side of the Bay. Of their seven adobe houses, one remains. It was rebuilt by the Curtner family, who later owned the Tularcitos Ranch. Recently restored, it stands surrounded by ancient fig, olive and pepper trees as the feature of charming little Higuera Adobe Park at Wessex Place and Park Victoria Drive, just east of Highway 680.

The little valley was considered as a reservoir site but was found to have poor geologic formations for holding water. The entire site is dotted with springs, which now fill the lakes and ponds and water the Spring Valley Golf Course.

Santa Clara County acquired the park in 1967, owing in good measure to the efforts of Ed R. Levin, the remarkable man for whom it was named—geologist, explorer, teacher, athlete and county planning commissioner. In 1979 the Minnis Ranch, on the north, was added to the park, taking in the hills rising above the valley up to Monument Peak. Under a lease agreement, cattle from the ranch continue to graze the hillsides. Aside from the communications installations on their heights and the hang gliders soaring above, these hills are much the same as when Juan Higuera's cattle ranged the slopes. European oats have taken the place of native bunch grasses, however, and the beef cattle from the Minnis Ranch that you meet on the trails are quite different from the Higuera cattle, which were raised for hides and tallow.

As you leave the flatland subdivisions and shopping centers on Calaveras Road, you slip through a cleft in the hills, following Arroyo de los Coches for a mile into a narrow canyon. The canyon opens up into the hidden valley that is the heart of Ed Levin Park. Directly ahead are the greens of the golf course. Turning right on Calaveras Road leads to park headquarters and a series of picnic grounds. From Downing Road to the left you reach pretty little Sandy Wool Lake, weeping willows trailing into its waters and ducks and geese bobbing on its surface.

Fine weekends draw crowds to the picnic tables by the lake. Fishermen line the shores to try for bluegill, crappie and bass. If the winds are right, you will find the meadow beyond the lake bright with hang gliders soaring above, alighting, testing their colorful wings. Graded launch sites range from 40' "bunny hills" for learners to the heights of the ridge for those who are Hang III. Hang gliders share the skies with red-tailed hawks, turkey vultures and an occasional golden eagle. The pilots watch the soaring birds to check the wind currents; some of them feel that the birds eye them in return.

The bare, grassy heights of the park are characteristic of East Bay hills. However, even on these slopes, so sere-looking in summer, are ravines lined with oaks, bays and sycamores watered by spring-fed streams. In contrast are the well-wooded east-facing slopes of the ridge above Arroyo de los Coches.

Although many of Ed Levin Park's trails have been laid out with equestrians in mind, a number of its trails offer fine trips for those on foot. A trail, also open to mountain bicyclists, was laid out in 1990. The long but exhilarating hike to Monument Peak over much tree-less hillside is a trip to take in the cool weather of spring or fall, but the trails on Los Coches Ridge are walks for all seasons, with shade on the east side and breezes on the hilltops.

Jurisdiction   Santa Clara County.

Facilities   Trails: hiking, equestrian and bicycle. Park head-quarters. Lake for fishing and boating. Picnic areas: family and group. Restrooms. 18-hole golf course. Horse-rental stables, horse-trailer parking.

Park Rules   Hours: 8 A.M. to ½ hour after sunset. Fees: $3/car. Dogs allowed only in Elm Group Picnic Area, on leash. Swimming and wading prohibited. Phone 408-358-3751.

Maps   Santa Clara County *Ed R. Levin Park;* USGS quads *Milpitas, Calaveras Reservoir.*

How to Get There

By Car   Turn east from Highway 680 on Calaveras Road exit.
Follow Calaveras Road 4 miles east to park entrance.

Trip 1.   Los Coches Ridge Trails

For fine walks in all seasons on shady hillsides and sunny hilltops, try the network of trails on this ridge.

Distance   4 miles round trip.

Time   2 hours.

Elevation Gain   200'

TRAIL NOTES

This trail system loops back and forth along the wooded east
slopes of the ridge and circles its 740' heights. Views from the hilltop stretch in all directions, and breezes from the west are cooling
even on bright, sunny days. You can walk the entire Los Coches
Ridge in a morning or an afternoon.

Start from the main parking lot by park headquarters on Calaveras
Road, following the Spring Valley Trail west to the Oak Knoll Group
Area. A trail to the right of the restrooms of this picnic area leads
east to the park boundary, then crosses the Arroyo de los Coches
("Creek of the pigs") and the private Vista Ridge Road to the trail on
the far side.

The Los Coches Ridge trails start on the west side of the road,
going uphill. Oaks and bays meet overhead, make this a refreshing,
pleasant climb. At the head of the little canyon, you turn right and
follow the trail west along the hill.

As you climb, the high hills on the east side of the park come into
sight. Take the first intersecting trail uphill, leading to the open
ridgetop. As this is a popular route for riding, you may be joined by
groups of equestrians from the park's rental stables. The trails are
not wide so it is important to observe trail etiquette: stand quietly
beside the trail until the horses have passed.

When you reach the hilltop, you will want to take in the sweeping
views. In the north Mt. Tamalpais rises above the frequent ocean
fogs and valley smogs. The Santa Cruz Mountains fill the western
horizon. To the east, the park's golden (sometimes green) hills rise to
Monument Peak. You may see bright-winged hang gliders drifting
gently down from the rocky point above the big green water tank on
the hillside above and north of Sandy Wool Lake.

After circling the knolls on the ridgetop, you have several choices
for your return. A good route is the trail around the boundary, going

The Los Coches Trail is a favorite of equestrians

north through the woods and making a loop above Calaveras Road where it enters the park. In early fall you will still find wildflowers on these slopes, such as clarkia and goldenrod. In the woods, the banks above the trail glow with colorful poison oak, which you can admire without touching; in April and May the whole hillside is flowery.

As the trail through the woods turns east, take the left fork for a lower and shadier trail back to Vista Ridge Road and cross it to the trail back to the Oak Knoll Group Area and to the parking lot.

Trip 2.   Climb toward the Heights of Monument Peak

An exhilarating hike across open hills and up wooded ravines beside spring-fed streams brings you to flower-covered high ridges of the mountain.

Distance   8 miles round trip.
Time   6 hours.
Elevation Gain   2000'

TRAIL NOTES

Start from the upper parking lot at Sandy Wool Lake and pick up the Tularcitos Trail to the right of a gate to Monument Peak Road. The trail goes along a fence to a cattle gate, which you pass through. Go straight up the hill to a left turn (north). From here you climb slowly on the Agua Caliente Trail that may be muddy in spring and dusty in summer. You cross a few wet ravines, veer left and contour around an open slope to a rise topped by a large water tank. You are now at 800′ elevation and 200′ above the lake.

Here you meet the Higuera Trail, which takes off uphill to a vista point and hang-gliding launch site 400′ above you that makes a good destination if you do not want to make the long climb to Monument Peak. The 0.8-mile round trip to the rocky promontory of this vista point offers a brisk climb up a zigzag trail. On a day with propitious winds you can watch the hang gliders taking off.

To continue toward Monument Peak, take the Agua Caliente Trail ahead, and climb by switchbacks to another cattle gate. This is a cattle range; leave gates as you find them. Your trail keeps climbing the side hill, with an elevation gain of 200′.

Immediately below, tucked into a small valley against a hill on its west, is the Minnis Ranch. As though looking through a window onto the past, we see the old ranchhouses with the palm trees that were a popular accent to gardens of the last century. A small orchard surrounds the barns. The ranch still manages the herds we have been meeting along the trail. In contrast to the condominiums, subdivisions and shopping centers on the other side of the hill, the ranch seems a century removed.

In ½ mile beyond the water tank you turn right on the Monument Peak Trail. The Agua Caliente Trail turns left here to zigzag down to cross Monument Peak Road below and continue west to Calera Creek and beyond.

The Monument Peak Trail soon crosses the road and starts the climb with a 1000′ elevation gain to go to the summit. Although the mountain is steep, a surprising number of flats break your climb.

Soon after crossing the road, the trail narrows for a stretch going through a shady ravine. As you head up meadows and cross ravines, with each turn new views open below, giving glimpses of the mountaintop above where pale yellow oat grass in summer is bright against a blue sky.

At an elevation of 1700′ our trail comes close to Calera Creek on a little flat where oaks and bays shade the trail. The road is nearby at this point. Although the trail crosses the creek just around a bend ahead, this is an inviting spot to pause under the trees for lunch.

As you move on, you hear a great chattering of mocking birds in the cottonwoods, then the softer sound of small waterfalls come from the creek as you reach the crossing. There are no comfortable perches for hikers here, but at least stop a while under the cotton-woods' white limbs before you continue.

You round the hill now on a gentler grade and enjoy wide views north over San Francisco Bay. After a rainy spring flowers blanket these hills, and the trail crosses flower-strewn fields of blue lupines, red maids, white forget-me-nots, yellow johnny jump-ups, lavender brodiaea and five-spot nemophila. Above the trail are sandstone out-crops encrusted with orange lichen as brilliant as the poppies in the grass.

The climb soon begins in earnest as you round another bend in the trail. Some steep stretches with loose rock underfoot make the going difficult. But around another bend is a gently sloping high plateau.

Right above is the peak, a gleaming moonscape, in summer covered with pale oatgrass, and surmounted with antennas and com-munications installations.

The climb continues still to another bend, where the trail crosses the head of Calera Creek at a small dammed pond. For the last ½ mile we bear right, (south), then turn to meet Monument Peak Road at the end of our trail—but not the end of our hike.

Monument Peak Road, a service road, turns north to the park's boundary, less than 100' below the summit. From this high ridge are encompassing views of the mountains of Contra Costa County and the Sierra on the eastern horizon and of the Bay Area to the west. Going straight ahead from the trail's end would take you on the short Sierra Trail, which passes the highest hang glider-launching site. Although the Monument Peak Road from the trail's end down to Sandy Wool Lake is for service vehicles and hang glider vehicles with permits, the roads along this ridgetop are open to hikers, too.

Hiker resting on Monument Peak Trail

Trip 3.   **The Calera Trail to the
Park's Northwest Boundary**

This trail, the only one designated for mountain bicycles in the
park, follows the western park boundary past open pasturelands,
then climbs beside Calera Creek to turn west on the Agua Caliente
Trail to the park's north boundary near Scott Creek.

Distance   5 miles round trip.

Time   (hikers) 2 hours.

Elevation Gain   1000′

TRAIL NOTES

Bicyclists are required to wear helmets and to observe, for their
safety and that of others, the trail rules granting right-of-way to
hikers and equestrians and to heed cautionary signs for steep sections of the trail.

From the parking lot at the northwest end of Sandy Wool Lake
find the mountain bicycle trail just left of a gate for hang gliders'
vehicles. The trail turns uphill, then goes right, through a cattle gate.

The trail then keeps near the park's boundary on the edge of a pasture and below low hills above which roofs of subdivision houses on
the far side are beginning to appear. As a small ravine opens up,
more of the subdivision is in view and the tees and greens of a golf
course. Our trail turns uphill to follow an intermittent creek edged
with cottonwoods, then crosses to the far side.

Toward the mountains an old, unmarked road, closed to bicyclists,
leads to the Minnis Ranch buildings. The ranch, extending up the
mountain, was added to the park, but their cattle still graze the hills.
The Calera Trail turns down by a pasture fence into a remote little
valley and soon passes under an immense live oak. Just beyond we
follow arrows pointing to a pasture gate and directing us down by the
far side of the fence.

Ahead groves of trees mark Calera Creek, which our trail follows
around a bend. Even in a dry year this spring-fed creek is running.
We follow it for a short distance, then cross to the far side, where
another gate ahead leads into an upper pasture.

The trail steepens and then climbs toward the Agua Caliente Trail
above. Veering away from the creek, our trail passes two even
steeper trails used by equestrians but closed to bicyclists. After a
final stiff grade, where there is a warning for bicyclists heading
down, you reach the Agua Caliente Trail.

The bicycle route turns left (west) on the Agua Caliente Trail.
From these heights are views of the urban valley, the San Francisco
Bay and the Santa Cruz Mountains. The trail contours around the

hill for about ½ mile to a vista point at 1000′ elevation near Scott Creek.

It is expected that a connection will some day be made to a trail, not yet completed, in the adjoining lands of the East Bay Regional Park District's Monument Peak Preserve.

Other Trails

West of Sandy Wool Lake and Downing Road, trails loop around the low Calaveras Ridge. Although these trails were laid out mainly for equestrians, they make good short walks within easy reach of picnic grounds around the lake.

White-barked sycamores on Levin Park hillside

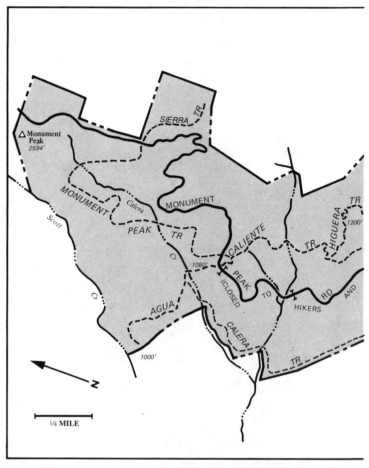

Ed R. Levin

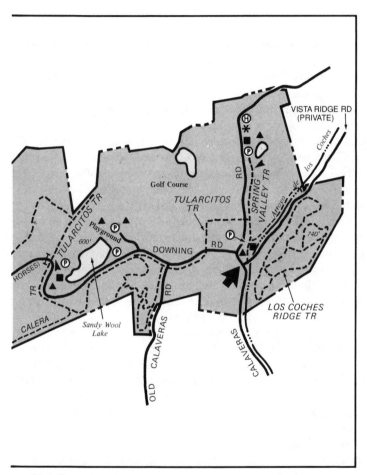

Park

Alum Rock Park

The lovely canyon of Penitencia Creek has been a popular excursion spot since 1872, when the park was acquired. This canyon was called simply "The Reservation" in its early days. The special charms of the cool, shady flats along its ever-flowing creek and the acclaimed medicinal qualities of its mineral springs soon brought it national recognition. Its present name, which came into being around the turn of the century, refers to a huge rock standing 625' above sea level on the north side of the canyon where the park's two entrance roads join. Both Alum Rock and the taller Eagle Rock nearby are of volcanic origin. The Calaveras Fault lies east of the park and a spur fault runs through Penitencia Creek Canyon.

After 1890 the park became widely known as a health spa. Its hot springs, containing seven minerals considered therapeutic, drew thousands. Stone grottos in the romantic European tradition gushed with a variety of supposedly healing waters. Mineral baths, an indoor swimming pool, a tea garden, a restaurant and a dance pavilion made this a fashionable retreat. A steam railroad brought visitors from San Jose on a 25¢ ride.

In the 1930s WPA workers added bridges built of gray stone from the canyon, and rock walls along the creek banks. With the advent of the automobile, the once-crowded train could not compete and it discontinued service in 1931. After World War II throngs of visitors overwhelmed the park facilities, and cars overcrowded parking lots. Eager explorers trampled the fragile plants and slid down the steep hillsides, eroding unstable soils.

To preserve this canyon required reorienting activities to ones emphasizing the natural setting. Now parking is limited, to control the number of visitors. However, parking restrictions do not apply to hikers, bicyclists and equestrians. Outdoor education programs at the Youth Science Institute are encouraging a better understanding of the park's ecology.

Gone are the baths, pavilions and restaurants, but Penitencia Creek still makes its way over the rocks in its shady canyon. You can still sample a mineral spring, stroll along the creek and relax on the lawns. Picnic tables and children's play areas invite you to enjoy family gatherings where San Jose society played in a former day.

Thirteen miles of good trails give you a chance to know the remarkable features of this 700-acre park. Some trails climb the steep hillsides for fine views; the wide Creek Trail, now designated a National Recreation Trail, follows Penitencia Creek through the length of the park. Joggers and hikers can use all the trails, horsemen are welcome on about half of them, and bicyclists may use the Creek Trail and paved roads. Following are four trips to help you discover the park's splendid features.

Jurisdiction   City of San Jose.

Facilities   Visitor Center, Youth Science Institute. Trails: hiking, equestrian and bicycle. Picnic areas with barbecues: family, group by reservation. Children's playgrounds. Day camps by arrangement. Wheelchair access to Visitor Center and to the paved Creek Trail from the Log Cabin to the Live Oak Area.

Park Rules   Hours: Park open every day in the year from 8 A.M. to ½ hour after sunset. Youth Science Institute open 9 A.M. to 4:30 P.M. Tuesday through Friday, noon to 4:30 Saturday; also open noon to 4:30 P.M. Sunday in summer. No dogs. No hard liquor. No smoking or motorized vehicles on trails. Park phone: 408-259-5477; for reservations. 408-277-5561. Fees: $2/car weekends, holidays. Youth Science Institute phone: 408-258-4322. Fees: child 10 cents, adult 50 cents, $1/family.

Maps   City of San Jose *Alum Rock Park, Joggers' Map;* USGS quad *Calaveras Reservoir.*

How To Get There

By Car   Main entrance: From Highway 101 or 680 take Alum Rock Avenue east to parking near picnic areas in lower and mid-canyon. West entrance at Penitencia Creek Road closed to motor vehicles. There is room for 8–10 cars at park boundary. *By Bicycle*   From Penitencia Creek Park at Mabury Road and Jackson Avenue take the paved bicycle path, sidewalks and trail along Penitencia Creek Road to the park's west entrance.

By Bus   County Transit 21 to Alum Rock Avenue and Miguelita Avenue.

Trip 1.   South Rim Loop

From the cool shade of the Penitencia Creek Trail you climb through oak woodlands to the chaparral-lined south rim of the canyon. In an easy descent you return to the lawns and picnic areas near the Visitor Center.

Distance   4 miles.
Time   2½ hours.
Elevation Gain   630'
TRAIL NOTES

From the easternmost parking lot go across one of the park's many bridges and head upstream on the Creek Trail. Penitencia Creek's waters tumble musically over sandstone boulders, with willows, big-leaf maples and sycamores lining its banks. You pass little grottos where springs seep out of the hillside, leaving minerals encrusted on the rocks. Only the mineral spring near the lawn area is tested for potability. If you would like to see other ornate grottos and still-active mineral springs, pick up the self-guiding, interpretive leaflet at the Visitor Center and follow the 0.3-mile Mineral Springs Loop Trail.

Having been close to the high south-rim wall, your trail now crosses a stone bridge over the creek. Under spreading live oaks is an array of picnic tables pleasantly removed from the busiest recreation areas of the midcanyon. At a sharp bend you see where the creek in its narrow gorge has cut through upended *chert* strata. Then your trail drops down into the creekbed and out to reach the other side, where an overlook invites a pause to enjoy the sight of Penitencia Creek cascading down over the rocks. Although the wooden bridge, a replacement for an old stone one, was washed out in a storm, you can still cross the creek at low water. In the near future a new one will be built.

Here Penitencia Creek is joined by Arroyo Aguague, whose waters originate in the mountains of Joseph D. Grant County Park, several miles south. The Indians called Penitencia Creek "Shistuc." The Spanish word *aguaje,* meaning "a rush of water," is still appropriate today.

From this cool retreat in summer you can look up to the hot, dry north canyon wall dotted with Digger pines. The rushing waters, quiet pools and dappled sunshine invite you to linger here. This place makes a good destination for an easy, short stroll and picnic, about a mile from the Visitor Center. Yellow blooms of monkey flower hang from a high stone embankment of the park's earlier days. Note the graceful circular stone steps, flanked by two trees, remaining from the original bridge.

To continue, take the South Rim Trail, for hikers only, up the precipitous canyon for a half hour's climb to the top. A trail sign warns of the dangers of shortcutting corners, not only to the hiker but to those walking below, who may be hit by dislodged rocks. You can see

Classic structure marks only potable spring in Alum Rock Park

the damage done along this trail by heedless hikers. Bicycles and horses are not allowed on this trail.

Ten switchbacks take you up the fern-clad and spring-flowered hillside. Bay and oak trees arch overhead, accented in late spring by light pink blooms of buckeye trees. At the last switchback of the South Rim Trail, a jumble of rocks seems to hang over the canyon. Easy footholds beckon the adventurous to find a perch from which to see the views. Or from the picnic table under the trees, you may hear the lively chorus of birds that inhabit this place. Hardly considered songbirds, the blue Steller jays call raucously from perches on limbs just above the trail. You can tell them from the scrub jays by their crest of deep-blue feathers. Chestnut-backed chickadees, with their sooty caps and white cheeks, may delight you with their acrobatics in the branches of a big Digger pine.

Leaving the woodlands, the trail, now open to horses, continues along a narrow ridge through high chaparral of coyote bush, sagebrush and scrub oak. Soon tall buckeyes, toyons and bays begin to give shade. About ½ mile from the summit, the trail forks. You can turn right, downhill, on a shorter route, the Switchback Trail, back to the canyon floor. That trail takes you to the Canyon Viewpoint, then zigzags many times until it comes out at the Creekside Picnic Area. From there it is less than ½ mile downstream to the Visitor Center.

If you stay on the South Rim Trail along the canyon heights, however, another ½ mile brings you to a sharp bend, from where you head north on a zigzag descent to the canyon floor. At the Woodland Trail intersection, turn right for a few yards and then go left down the stone steps and walkways of former park days. You emerge just a few paces east of the Visitor Center. A stop here to see the nature displays, the relief model of the park and the photos of yesteryear is instructive and entertaining.

Or go on a bit farther east and visit the Youth Science Institute to see its collection of live birds, snakes and small animals. The creatures here have injuries or defects that preclude survival in the wild. Most impressive are the huge hawks and owls chained to perches above you. This is also your chance to see a live rattlesnake—safely behind the glass walls of a cage.

Trip 2.   Circle Hike to Eagle Rock
on the North Rim

Hike up the north side of the canyon to Eagle Rock for an overlook of the park and the Santa Clara Valley. Return along the Creek Trail on the route of the old Alum Rock Steam Railroad.

Distance   2.2 miles.

Time   1¼ hours.

Elevation Gain   336′

TRAIL NOTES

It is best to take this trip from the east end of the park, for the trail goes up more gradually and the views out of the canyon expand as you walk. Start from the far end of the upstream parking lot where the North Rim Trail goes uphill. At the first intersection take the trail to the left; the other, a private road, is closed to all but service vehicles. A gentle climb brings you out above the steepest part of the canyon. Sounds of the creek and the cheerful cries of children from the playgrounds reach you from below.

In about ½ mile you reach a buckeye-shaded flat where the Loop Trail turns off uphill. An extra 10-minute push reaches a high ledge studded with a few deciduous oaks at the park's upper limits.

Where the Loop Trail rejoins the North Rim Trail along the upper boundary of the park, you'll find a few picnic tables set beneath clumps of evergreen oaks. On the hillside above are old palm trees on a former ranch site. Although subdivisions creep up to the park boundary on both sides, the rustic charms of the wooded creek canyon remain for the public to enjoy.

In a last short climb you arrive at the overlook on the uphill side of Eagle Rock. This is a good place to picnic on a clear winter day, when you can see for miles across the valley to the Santa Cruz Mountains.

Now, retrace your steps to the first intersection, turn right, and take the trail below Eagle Rock. From the steep downhill side this upthrust of volcanic rock is impressively tall and rugged. Signs ask hikers to stay off this slope. The authors saw two deer grazing there, oblivious of signs and people.

To reach the valley floor, take the next left bend to meet the Creek Trail going east. This trail, open to bicyclists, passes right below Alum Rock and crosses over the main park-entrance road on the old bridge that once carried the Alum Rock Steam Railroad. On the south side of the bridge, a railroad tunnel went through rock, now crumbled away. A metal plaque on the rock walls tells the story of the old railroad.

The Creek Trail continues upstream on the railroad right-of-way. As you walk here, you can imagine the pleasant and exciting trip in the days when the railroad passed under the trees beside the creek. The sycamore trees, with gray-and-white mottled trunks, now tower more than 100' above the creek. On the grassy banks magenta farewell-to-spring blooms in June and July. Farther on, thickets of wild rose, snowberry and blackberry bushes cover the banks under the alder, cottonwood and bay trees.

The wide, slightly uphill Creek Trail is a popular stroll. On the way back to your starting point, you will find yourself in the company of many families enjoying this easy excursion from their tables at one of the pleasant picnic areas nearby.

Hills on north side of Penitencia Creek canyon

Trip 3.   Circle Hike from the Park's West End

Starting along the Penitencia Creek Trail, a National Recreation Trail, this trip climbs through an oak forest on the Woodland Trail and circles back on the open hillsides of the north canyon wall.

Distance   3 miles.

Time   1½ hours.

Elevation Gain   360'

TRAIL NOTES

Although the west entrance is closed to vehicles, there is room for 8 to 10 cars beside Penitencia Creek Road at the park's west entrance. However, bicyclists may use this entrance, ride through the park on the paved road and return on either the Creek Trail or a service road on the south hillside.

You will see signs for the Creek Trail that goes east through the edge of a former quarry, created in the 1960s when the San Jose Airport runways were lengthened. Once past the barren quarry site, you come to year-round Penitencia Creek, its banks clothed with several species of fern and snowberry, wild rose and blackberry bushes. The bright red rose hips and waxy white snowberries are important food sources for birds and animals. On a quiet morning walk you may see a black-tailed deer coming down from the woods to drink. The ample waters of this creek sustain the park's plants and abundant wildlife and then flow west to percolation ponds to improve Santa Clara Valley's groundwater supply.

After about ½ mile you will note some steps on your right leading up the bank to a marker honoring Richard H. Quincy, an early San Jose wood and coal dealer who promoted the Alum Rock Steam Railroad. At first a narrow-gauge steam line, the train was electrified in 1901. It crossed the creek here on a trestle, which was completely destroyed by floods in 1911. Remnants of pillars supporting the trestle can be found along the creek at low water. This old trestle is commemorated here at an interpretive overlook and rest area.

Relaxing on this high, sunny platform above the alders and cottonwoods, you can look far up the wooded canyon to the hills on its north side. You may hear woodpeckers in the forest or see a brown red-shafted flicker showing its white rump patch and red wing and tail linings as it flies.

Return to the Creek Trail, going upstream, and arc right on the Stable Trail, which is closed to bicyclists. Now zigzag up the south side of the canyon through oak woodlands interspersed with occasional buckeyes and red-berried toyons. When you come to the park's main entrance road, cross over and go left for a short distance on an old paved road, now a bicycle trail. Watch for a footpath on the left, the Woodland Trail, and take this winding path under the trees along the canyon side.

You could continue on the Woodland Trail all the way to the Visitor Center, but for this circle hike from the park's west entrance, turn off to the left after about 0.6 mile. A sign points the way downhill to the Creek Trail. Just beyond this junction is the 4H Alum Rock Ropes Course. Securely fastened to huge oaks, rope ladders and swings are used by groups of young people under strict supervision of qualified instructors. Call 408-299-2630 for information.

Here and there on the gentle descent to the Creek Trail, you pass 3–6' conglomerate rocks, masses of rounded pebbles and clays cemented together by geologic forces. Probably once in the creek bed but now high above it, they are clothed with gray-green mosses and lichens.

This is a well-designed trail with easy switchbacks, but shortcutting has badly eroded the turns. Park rules caution hikers to stay on the trail for their own safety and for protection of the hillside from scouring erosion.

At the Creek Trail go left again for about 200 feet. Before the creek crossing, you find another remnant of the railroad. Once a tunnel went through the rock walls of the canyon, but, by 1909 the rock was crumbling and so the walls were removed. Now at this Alum Rock Rest Area explanatory plaques tell about the railroad and the early days of Alum Rock Park.

Schoolchildren hear about mineral springs from a park docent

Back on the Creek Trail, bear west to cross over the park road and the creek, passing right under Alum Rock, towering 200' above you. On the far side you can see the Rustic Lands Picnic Area, reached by a small footbridge that is removed in winter. At the first trail junction veer right, taking the Eagle Rock Trail, which shares the alignment of the North Rim Trail here. In 500 feet the trail to Eagle Rock turns right but you continue straight ahead (west) on the wide North Rim Trail, traversing the open hillside. At a slight rise the sawed-off top of Loma Prieta, standing tall in the distant Santa Cruz Mountains, appears framed in a notch in the hills.

In less than 0.2 mile a junction sign points right, to Lariat Lane, but you continue on a trail bearing left about 45 degrees. Follow this trail on a steep hillside past scattered large evergreen oaks, until you meet the other segment of the North Rim Trail, which more or less parallels the road below. Turn right (west) on this trail, contouring around the hill. The trail soon crosses Penitencia Creek Road and leads to the creek, which you can ford in the dry season to reach the Creek Trail. During the wet season, stay above the road; an informal trail comes out farther down the road by the maple-lined creek. The creek and the road continue west, bending around a hill.

A narrow bridge built in 1909 is flanked by round pillars ornately set with fossil-bearing rocks, probably from this creek bed. Cross the creek on this bridge and move to the other side of the road, where you find a gated, wide entry to the service area. The barrier is for

A graceful stone bridge built by the Works Progress Administration

motor vehicles only; hikers go right on through. Tall big-leaf maples and willows line the creek side of this large flat. You head south, intersecting the Creek Trail in the quarry area where your trip began. Arc to the right, and over a little hillock you'll find the park's west entrance.

If you go west from here on Penitencia Creek Road, you will be following the creek for several miles. The City of San Jose and Santa Clara County are completing land purchases to form a chain of creekside parks. At this writing a tree-shaded, paved trail borders Penitencia Creek for several miles downstream. (See page 201, Penitencia Creek Trail.)

Trip 4.   Loop Trip to Inspiration Point

An easy, shady hike for the dry season on the Woodland and Creek trails features the interpretive overlook that explains the park's geologic origins.

Distance   2½-mile loop.
Time   1¾ hours.
Elevation Gain   400'
TRAIL NOTES

This little trip, for hikers only, can be taken from any of the picnic areas in the park starting in either direction, but is not possible in winter because the portable bridge is removed. Since most of the trail segments are described in Trips 1 and 3, only brief directions are given here. Inspiration Point, the highlight of the trip, makes a pleasant destination for a picnic lunch.

Starting at the Visitor Center, go upstream to a spur of the South Rim Trail. Turn right on this horse and hiker trail, which goes abruptly uphill on the steep south canyon wall. After about 500 feet and several zigzags, the trail turns west and levels off. At the junction of the main South Rim Trail you bear right, continuing west. In less than ½ mile and just after your trail crosses the surfaced bicycle path, take a trail to your right a few hundred yards to find the log-fenced overlook at Inspiration Point.

Wooden benches shaded by young oaks invite you to pause here to read the information panels and enjoy the views. A plaque on the overlook tells of the canyon's volcanic and seismic origins. It informs you that a Calaveras Fault branch cuts through the park and Penitencia Creek follows its alignment. From this vantage point you can see the tree-lined path of the stream through the canyon.

While enjoying the views from here, look out across the canyon to the opposite hillside, where Eagle Rock rises to 795', some 300' above the level of the creek bed. East of this rocky promontory you can see shelves, or ledges, probably formed by landslides following earthquakes in past centuries. Part of the North Rim Trail traverses one of these shelves (see Trip 2).

Refreshed and more knowledgeable after your stop here, retrace your steps to the Woodland Trail and resume your hike west. Where the trail intersects the main park-entrance road, cross over it and descend for the next ½ mile on the tree-canopied Stable Trail, for horses and hikers only. A path takes off left to boarding stables uphill, but you continue zigzagging downhill. In the fall acorns cover the trail underfoot. In winter and early spring you will also find large, shiny, orange-brown balls on the ground here—the seed of buckeye trees. If you come in late spring, the fragrance of pink-and-white buckeye blossoms fills the air.

At the creek, turn upstream (east) on the Creek Trail and go past

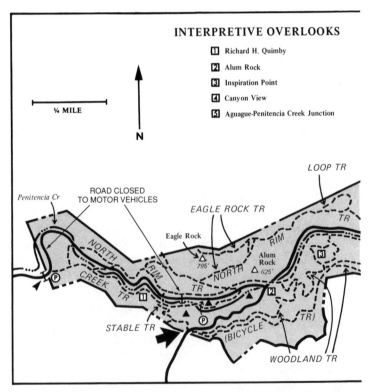

INTERPRETIVE OVERLOOKS

1 Richard H. Quimby
2 Alum Rock
3 Inspiration Point
4 Canyon View
5 Aguague-Penitencia Creek Junction

¼ MILE

N

Alum Rock

the Quail Hollow Picnic Area. You can ford the stream here at low water, but the Creek Trail stays on the south side and in the dry season crosses farther upstream on a portable bridge, removed in winter, to the Eagle Rock Picnic Area. The trail then weaves informally past parking areas and picnic places and eventually crosses the park road opposite the Rustic Lands Picnic Area.

Two switchbacks take you to the trail coming down from Eagle Rock, the North Rim Trail. You go right here, heading due east to the old railroad-bridge stream crossing. Now the wide Creek Trail, shaded by alders and sycamores, makes its way on the south bank past the Log Cabin and Tot Lot picnic areas back to the Visitor Center. More than 100 years from its founding, Alum Rock Park, in the lovely, narrow valley of Penitencia Creek, continues to provide relaxation and pleasure in a rustic setting.

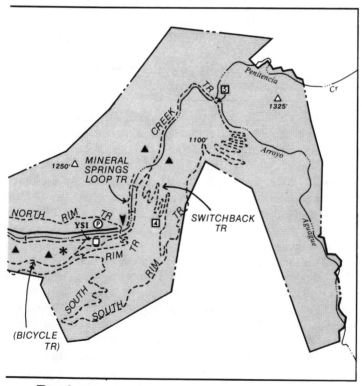

Park

Joseph D. Grant Park

The 9000-acre Joseph D. Grant Park, in the Diablo Range, includes secluded Hall's Valley, sheltered on the west by a high, wooded ridge and on the east by worn, rounded hills dotted with great oaks. The Grant ranch was a part of Rancho Cañada de Pala, awarded to José Jesus Bernal in 1839. The ranch was owned by the Bernal family until 1870, when the family's holdings were broken up. Owners of these lands during the next decade included Barbara Bernal and Frederick Hall, an attorney and local historian who lived on the ranch and for whom Hall's Valley was named. In 1880 a major owner sold the property, now the present park, to Adam Grant.

Adam, who had moved to San Francisco in Gold Rush days, started a successful dry-goods store and then became a banker and director of a number of corporations. His son, Joseph Donohoe Grant, born in 1858, was raised in San Francisco but was interested in the ranch and tried to raise polo ponies there. He was a patron of the arts, a trustee of Stanford University, and a founder of the Save the Redwoods League.

Josephine, one of Joseph's three children, eventually became the sole owner of the property, operating it as a cattle ranch and living there much of the time. After the break-up of her marriage to Captain Sheldon McCreery, she lived at the ranch year-round. At her death in 1972 the ranch, willed to the Save the Redwoods League and the Menninger Foundation, was offered for sale. Santa Clara County bought the ranch in 1975. Now Joseph D. Grant Park, the county's largest, is enjoyed by increasing numbers of visitors each year as its facilities expand.

The handsome old ranchhouse at the head of Hall's Valley, now park headquarters, contains a museum with early ranch artifacts and an interpretive center with fine displays of wildlife. The 40-acre Grant Lake and two small lakes are stocked and are popular with fishermen. Beside Grant Lake an environmental protection area in marshy land is set aside for research. Twenty three campsites are scattered under the trees on a wooded hill near the park entrance. Two of these are for the handicapped. A trail for the physically limited is planned. Hikers welcome the chance to camp at the park and to be out early on the trails.

Spring nature-study programs and conducted hikes are scheduled on some weekends. A group called Friends of the Grant Ranch Park, formed to stimulate interest in the park, trains docents who assist at the Visitor Center. Membership in this association brings you a subscription to the *Hall's Valley Journal,* which will keep you up to date on activities in the park.

Trips on the park's 40 miles of trails range from short walks close to headquarters for picnicking or fishing to hikes around Hall's Valley and into the hills. The adventurous will want to take the challenging climbs out of the valley to the park's high ridges.

Hall's Valley slopes gently south for 2 miles from the old ranchhouse. San Felipe Creek meanders through its broad hayfields and pastures to the hills at its lower end, where it cuts through a narrow canyon on its way to San Felipe Valley, 5 miles downstream.

Two very easy trips skirt the valley and cross the valley floor on short excursions. A third, longer trip circles the valley, fording San Felipe Creek in the narrows, then climbs partway up the eastern hills before returning to the valley floor.

For comfortable trips adjust your hikes to the weather and seasons. The open, west-facing hills are hot in summer and early fall,

Grant ranchhouse serves as Park headquarters

but trails on these hills make for good flower gazing in spring and fine walking on crisp fall days. Trails on the wooded western hills offer shady summer trips.

Trails in Grant Park are for the most part ranch and service roads, broad and well signed. With some exceptions they follow reasonably comfortable grades. Because so many of the trails are old ranch roads, they are clearly shown on the USGS map of the area—*Lick Observatory*—which gives detailed topographic information that cannot be shown on either the park map or the one in this guide.

Some trails up the eastern slopes of the park are open to bicycles—the Hotel Trail and other trails up to the southern boundary and as far north as the Los Huecos Trail, and the trails in the upper northeast park—the Cañada de Pala and Pala Seca trails. The Hall's Valley Trail is open to bicycles going uphill only.

Bicyclists are required to wear helmets. On trails on the western hills, used extensively by horses, bicycles are not permitted from the San Felipe Trail up to the western boundary. The Washburn Trail is for hikers only.

Jurisdiction   Santa Clara County.

Facilities   Headquarters with interpretive center and museum. Trails: hiking, equestrian and bicycle trails. Picnic areas: family, group by reservation. Camping: 23 drive-in sites for families; group sites by reservation. Horse-trailer parking; horse rental at private stables nearby. Handicapped facilities: ramps, restrooms, 2 campsites.

Park Rules   Hours: 8 A.M. to ½ hour after sunset. Dogs on 6' leash, but no dogs in primitive areas or on trails. No fires except in designated areas and in provided stoves. No smoking on trails. Hikers must stay on trails. No swimming or wading. Fees: Day use, $3/car on Saturdays, Sundays and holidays, May 21 to September 10, fee collected daily. Camping, $8/night/car, limit of 8 people/site and 2 vehicles/site, $4 for second vehicle. Pets $1/night; limit 2 pets/site. Senior citizen camping rates: $4 Monday through Thursday and $8 Friday, Saturday, Sunday. Camp open daily April 15 to October 30; Friday, Saturday during November and March. Closed December, January, February. For information call 408-274-6121.

Maps   Santa Clara County *Joseph D. Grant Park;* USGS quad *Lick Observatory.*

How To Get There   From Highway 680 go east on McKee Road or Alum Rock Avenue about 2 miles to Mt. Hamilton Road. Turn right, uphill, and go 8 miles to park entrance on south side of road. Park by Visitor Center.

Trip 1.   Hall's Valley to Snell Barn

An easy walk down into tranquil Hall's Valley goes over low hills and crosses the valley past old Snell Barn.

Distance   1¾-mile loop.

Time   1 hour.

Elevation Gain   120′

TRAIL NOTES

Leave the headquarters parking lot going west under the giant valley oaks toward the old ranch buildings and corrals ahead on your left. Turn south at the corrals and pick up the San Felipe Trail for hikers and equestrians only, which follows the road to the family camping area. Continue past the campsites tucked among the trees on the low ridge to your left. Beyond, your trail enters a small, grassy swale dotted with oaks.

In spring when the flower-strewn grass is green, when new leaves are coming out on the oaks, when the air is filled with songs of birds, and when watercourses are running, this trip is a delight. You pass patches of shooting stars, a whole field of buttercups, much blue-eyed grass, and johnny jump-ups accented by pink mallow and a scattering of lavender brodiaea.

The old Snell barn is still used to store hay

Watch for the Barn Trail in ¾ mile from the corrals and turn left on it toward Hall's Valley. Your trail passes the big white Snell Barn at the edge of the valley. This sturdy old barn, built in the 1800s, still stores hay cut at the park. You start down to the valley floor here, heading for the Hotel Trail on the far side. Through this gently sloping valley San Felipe Creek flows south, joined by intermittent streams from the hills on both sides.

In wet weather, crossing San Felipe Creek on the far side of the valley can be muddy. Just beyond the creek, we turn back up the valley, picking up the Lower Hotel Trail. It skirts the edge of the valley and soon joins the Upper Hotel Trail. For the next mile, the trail winds north around the base of a hill past hayfields. Ahead we see the old ranchhouse and its tank house on a little rise at the upper end of the valley—the end of our trip.

Trip 2.   Hall's Valley to the Circle Corral

This is another excursion for hikers and equestrians on the San Felipe Trail, going halfway down Hall's Valley, as far as the Circle Corral, to enjoy open fields and views up to the surrounding hills.

Distance   3¾-mile loop.

Time   2 hours.

Elevation Gain   210′

TRAIL NOTES

Start this trip on the San Felipe Trail, as in Trip 1, but continue past the Barn Trail turnoff. Your trail runs along the side of the valley, at the edge of the woodlands that clothe the western ridge of the park. As you walk through open meadows, the valley opens up below you, and the high eastern ridge of the park comes into sight. From some points you can even see the white gleam of the Lick Observatories on Mt. Hamilton.

The fields in spring are busy with scampering ground squirrels, sitting on their hindquarters to nibble at grass seeds or parting the grass to scurry to their holes to avoid hawks sailing overhead. Later, as the grass dries and summer comes, ground squirrels disappear into their holes, seldom to venture out again until the grass turns green. A store of seeds "squirreled away" will last them until the next crop.

The trail takes you close to the edge of the woods, where you can expect to catch sight of the many deer that find a protected home in the park. About ¾ mile beyond the Barn Trail turnoff, look for the Corral Trail, the next trail across the valley. Turn here, drop down to the valley floor, and head for the round corral you see on the far side.

You can lean on the corral fence, imagine round-ups of not too long ago, and reflect on the good fortune of Bay Area residents to have this tranquil valley for relaxation and exploration. And remember the generosity of Josephine Grant McCreery and the wisdom of the Santa Clara County Supervisors who acquired this vast ranch for a park. Look up and you may see one of the golden eagles that nest in this park and need open places like this to survive. Return by the Hotel Trail up the valley.

Trip 3.   Around Hall's Valley to Rattlesnake Pond

The longest of the Hall's Valley trips, for hikers and equestrians, makes a circle around the valley to reach the ford at its end, with a way-stop by a pond.

Distance   4¾-mile loop.

Time   2½ hours.

Elevation Gain   300'

TRAIL NOTES

Although you can make this trip in a few hours, you will want to take your time to admire the flowers, catch a soaring eagle in your binoculars, watch deer at the edge of the woods and enjoy a long lunch under a spreading valley oak.

Start this trip as in Trip 2 but continue past the Corral Trail to a junction with the Brush Trail. Veer east and climb to a meadow cut off from Hall's Valley by low hills. This is a flowery garden in spring; in summer tawny grasses contrast with valley oaks. You gain a few hundred feet in altitude through oak woods and then, near a small pond that fills with winter rains, turn left (east) and downhill onto the Cañada de Pala Trail.

After a steep descent you are soon at San Felipe Creek. Swollen by the waters of many small tributaries, the creek is here a year-round watercourse, so in rainy months you may have to wade the ford. This is the lowest point in the trip; ahead is an elevation gain of 200' to the Hotel Trail. Switchbacks on the east side of the creek take you into shady little ravines where the banks blossom with Chinese houses and shooting stars. After the last bend of the trail, you come to Rattlesnake Pond, edged with reeds and, as its name suggests, a place where rattlesnakes are often found. This is a spot to heed the warning to STAY ON THE TRAIL and to watch where you put your feet. Past the pond, the trail levels out, crossing a damp meadow. The sod is often torn up here, a sign that feral pigs have been rooting for

**One of many small streams flowing through Hall's Valley
to join San Felipe Creek**

bulbs. Up a rise ahead, the Cañada de Pala Trail intersects the Hotel
Trail, your route back. The way is downhill from here.

For ¼ mile the broad trail continues through sloping grasslands.
Then it goes over a little rise, through one of those stony meadows
where wildflowers flourish with particular intensity. It is worth a special trip in spring to see this garden of close-growing pink mallow,
orange poppies, blue lupines, goldfields, blue-eyed grass, and johnny
jump-ups. Serpentine soil in this meadow inhibits tall grasses but
provides the conditions for such flowers to thrive.

In contrast to this brightness, the next stretch of trail leads down
to a little stream in the shade of cottonwoods. This is a welcome,
cool place to stop on a warm day. The stream turns here toward the
valley and runs a gravelly, tree-bordered course to meet San Felipe
Creek. Our trail too turns toward the valley, and soon comes to the
Circle Corral. From here at the edge of Hall's Valley either Hotel
Trail—Upper and Lower—will take us back to headquarters.

Trip 4.   The Lake Loop

On this loop footpaths take you to Bass and McCreery lakes for
fishing and picnicking.

Distance   3-mile loop.
Time   1½ hours.
Elevation Gain   340'

TRAIL NOTES

About ¼ mile from park headquarters a footpath takes off uphill from the Hotel Trail. The path climbs grassy slopes and then follows a small stream up a rocky, wooded ravine. You will find Bass Lake— a small reservoir stocked with fish—in a bench on a hillside at the head of the stream. A picnic table under a tree invites you to make this your destination for lunch. The high meadows at the south end of the lake, where great valley oaks are silhouetted against grass and sky, make for pleasant strolling.

Taking the path that leaves the west corner of Bass Lake, you continue to McCreery Lake. A quick, steep climb brings you to the side of the Mt. Hamilton Road, where your trail turns left to parallel the road. Watch for a stile in the fence, where you cross the road to the stile on the opposite side. Here a footpath takes off downhill into a ravine leading to McCreery Lake. At this point, however, if you have time, walk up at least a few bends on the Yerba Buena Trail, a broad fire road ahead of you as you go through the stile. From April to June the grass is filled with flowers, and valley oaks make dramatic patterns against the rolling pasture lands that extend to the ridgetop.

Returning to the footpath with McCreery Lake as your destination, go down the ravine beside a stream. You are soon under the cool shade of oaks and buckeyes, and in spring the little stream ripples musically down its rocky course. The damp banks of the ravine are strewn with nearly every species of flower to be found in the park. Lavender Chinese houses cover the ground in sheets, and apricot-colored monkey flowers bloom luxuriantly in this well-watered location. Lavender brodiaea of several species and deep blue larkspur's spikes blossom here against the intense magenta of clarkias. The uncommon wind poppies, with their pale orange, papery flowers, grow in the moist shade (in contrast to their not-too-close relatives, the California poppies, which thrive in the sun).

This pleasant, woodsy trail continues beside the stream to where it meets a larger stream; here the ravine opens up into a small meadow. Sheltered from wind and shaded by overhanging trees, this trail is a good one for either a warm or a blustery day. We soon come to McCreery Lake, popular with fishermen, who catch bass here, and with picnickers, who enjoy a place by the water in the sun or in the shade of sycamore trees.

To return, take the path at the northwest end of the lake out to Mt. Hamilton Road. A stile across the road leads to the Hotel Trail, which you take down to park headquarters, ½ mile away.

Trip 5.   Hike to the Park's East Ridge

The Hall's Valley Trail, for hikers only, is fine at any time of the
year, but don't miss it in spring, when leaf buds on the oaks are
bursting in pale green and hillsides glow with sheets of wildflowers.
Distance   4-mile loop.
Time   2½ hours.
Elevation Gain   1100'

TRAIL NOTES

The Hall's Valley Trail starts from the parking lot at Grant Lake
on the north side of Mt. Hamilton Road, ¼ mile east of the main park
entrance. The lake is popular with fishermen, who try for black bass
and bluegill, and with birders, who find a wide range of birds, from
orioles and magpies to great blue herons that nest by the lake.

The Hall's Valley Trail leaves the lake on its east side, dipping
below the earth dam and crossing a ditch carrying water from springs
uphill. The trail turns north around a clump of tall eucalypti that
once surrounded an early ranch building. Golden eagles sometimes
alight in these trees.

In May you will have a flowery walk to some of the Bay Area's
finest displays. On the slope ahead great clumps of blue-eyed grass
take over a meadow. Around the bend is the Los Huecos Trail, on
which you will return. Continue on the Hall's Valley Trail, which
winds up a wooded canyon. On an easy grade up an old ranch road,
it makes a pleasant climb. Your route enters the woods on the can-
yonside above a creek. Flowers line the shady banks in April and
May—iris, shooting stars and pagodalike collinsias. Splashes of
buttercup gild the slope under the oaks.

As you gain altitude, leaving the canyon depths, you come out on
an open, grassy hillside dotted with valley oaks. You look down on
Grant Lake and across to the hills on the west side of the park and to
the Santa Cruz Mountains beyond. The air is loud with cries of
woodpeckers and jays in the canyon. You may see torn-up patches of
turf in damp places on the hillside, the work of the wild pigs you find
here and there in the park. Look for their splay-toed footprints in
muddy places on the trail.

On up the hill in springtime are deciduous oaks whose dark
branches are tipped with new leaves, young grass shimmers in the
breeze and flowers are everywhere. As you approach the ridgetop,
where soils are thinner, flower displays are even more lavish—
yellow johnny jump-ups, orange poppies, more buttercups, pink
mallow mixed with blue brodiaea, big gray- leaved clumps of yellow-

Trails up the east ridge wind through oak woodlands

blossomed false lupine. Here the Hall's Valley Trail meets the Cañada de Pala Trail at a 2400' saddle—a blaze of flowers in spring and a golden glow of oats against blue sky in summer.

From the saddle you look down into Smith Canyon and its east-facing slope, edged with scrub oak, Digger pine and buckeye. Turn right (south) onto the Cañada de Pala Trail (open to bicycles) and go uphill for 0.3 mile to the Los Huecos Trail intersection. Looking east from here, you see the white observatory buildings atop Mt. Hamilton. Established in 1886 through the gift of James Lick, the original observatory here was the first permanently occupied mountain observatory in the world. The work begun in those early days is carried on by astronomers from the University of California at Santa Cruz.

Pause here for the fine views all around before you make the steep descent on the Los Huecos Trail. The Los Huecos Trail is open to bicycles so you may wish to return by the Hall's Valley Trail to avoid sharing this downhill run. Go with care; the loose rock surface of the trail makes the footing treacherous. Down the trail ¼ mile is a large-scale rock garden—a stunningly composed stone outcropping, weathered and lichen-covered, surrounded by a swath of orange poppies, with accents of blue larkspur, goldfields and yellow johnny jump-ups in spring.

The trail continues steeply down to a lower ridge, where it levels off on a grassy hogback edged with oak woods on its north side. Here buttercups blossom in golden profusion. After a few more steep drops, the trail joins the Hall's Valley Trail a short distance from your parking place near Grant Lake.

Trip 6.   Dutch Flat Trail to the
West Ridge

On this trip for hikers and equestrians views over the Santa Clara Valley alternate with panoramas of the Grant Ranch, its pasture lands and Mt. Hamilton to the east.

Distance   6-mile loop.

Time   3 hours.

Elevation Gain   1000'

TRAIL NOTES

On this trail you sample the environments of the west side of the park—chaparral, oak woods, gentle meadows, wooded pasture lands and streamsides. The views from Dutch Flat alone are worth the climb.

Start west from the headquarters parking lot on the road to the corrals and to the San Felipe Trail. After rounding the corrals, turn off uphill, west, on the Dairy Trail. This trail ascends with pleasant changes in grade through familiar-looking oak woods and chaparral, crossing small meadows and climbing up wooded slopes. We soon can look out over the valley to the eastern hills and pick out Mt. Hamilton Road where it cuts through the park on its way to Smith Creek and the observatories.

After about ½ hour's climb the Dairy Trail turns south, and we leave it to climb to the ridgetop on the Dutch Flat Trail. On long switchbacks we go north through tall chaparral of greasewood, wild lilac and elderberry and then climb through deep woods where we are grateful for the shade of bays and oaks.

As the trail turns south again, we come out onto Dutch Flat, a broad lofty plateau that extends along the west boundary of the park. We can see across the Santa Clara Valley to the Santa Cruz Mountains with landmark Mt. Umunhum, a blocky building atop it. Far south is the Gavilan Range. We are nearly at the level of the park's eastern ridge and can make out the wide fire road that is the Yerba Buena Trail.

From this point the undulating Dutch Flat Trail rises to over 2400'. Gently rounded hills are dotted with fine oaks, making this a lovely walk. For the next 2 miles we are near the fenceline of the park's western boundary. The old wooden fence, still in good shape, was put up in the days when the Grant family operated the ranch.

This is a trail to linger on, to find landmarks in the urban valley on the west or in the ranch on the east, and to watch hawks as they soar on the updrafts. The 2-mile walk along the ridge makes the 1000' foot climb worthwhile. After a jog in the trail, it continues near the park boundary, bending east with it for ½ mile, then turning north. You pass the start of the Cañada de Pala Trail, then pick up the Brush Trail and follow it north. Continuing through more delightful meadows and woodlands, we finally come to a reservoir edged with reeds.

Near the reservoir quail make their dignified way along the trail ahead until startled into whirring flight. Rabbits rest in the shade by the trail, leaping to safety only when we approach too closely.

At the reservoir we meet the Dairy Trail and turn to the right, downhill. In the swampy seepage from the reservoirs, yellow mimulus and cattails grow. Shortly, the trail turns north and we are headed back. The valley and Snell Barn come into view just below us as we approach the San Felipe Trail, which takes us back to park headquarters.

Trip 7. The Cañada de Pala Trail on the East Ridge

Here is a dramatic trip for hikers, equestrians and bicyclists that traverses the park's eastern heights to hidden Deer Valley.

Distance 8 miles round trip.

Time 4 hours.

Elevation Gain 450'

TRAIL NOTES

Although the ridge is beautiful in spring, when the grass is green and wildflowers bloom, it is most striking in early summer, when the oats are pale gold against a blue sky. Try for a day when the weather is not too hot, and make an early start. If you leave a car at the Grant Lake parking area, hikers and equestrians can shorten the trip by returning on the Hall's Valley Trail, which is closed to bicyclists going downhill. Bicyclists can return on the Los Huecos Trail.

This trip on the Cañada de Pala Trail runs north along the park's east ridge from Mt. Hamilton Road as far as Deer Valley, at the north edge of the park. The trail, on a ranch road, takes a sinuous route over high grasslands, winding around the smooth hilltops.

Park at the crest of Mt. Hamilton Road before it descends east to Smith Creek, about a 10-minute drive from the main park entrance.

Hikers above the ridgetop on the Cañada de Pala Trail

Enter the trail through a gate on the north side of the road and go through a dense grove of oaks to climb to the hilltop, a rise of 200'. From this viewpoint you see down into Smith Creek Canyon, a steep 500' below, and up to the white domes of Lick Observatories. In the other direction you see Grant Lake at the head of Hall's Valley and the wooded hills of the park's west boundary.

About ½ mile north is a junction with the Yerba Buena Trail, a wide fire road coming up from Mt. Hamilton Road. The ridge ahead is open grazing land, with a scattering of deciduous oaks. Grasses, now mainly European annual oats and some rye, grow fast to take advantage of the short "spring" after the winter rains. By April the hilltop blooms brilliantly with poppies, mallows, lupine, brodiaea and gold fields, followed in June by farewell-to-spring and mariposa lilies.

The oaks, fine specimens of the valley oak, *Quercus lobata,* depend not on rain falling around them but on deep water found by their long roots. In such dry areas they are spaced widely and are often found lining ravines, where there is more underground water. On this ridge the oaks are broad-trunked old trees. Here and there broken stumps and fallen dead branches remain where age has finally overtaken them. You see few young trees. More than a century of grazing has replaced native perennial bunchgrasses with imported annuals and prevented the sprouted acorns' growth into young trees. The maximum life span of these giants is 500 years, so without a positive program to protect young trees, these hills will someday be bare.

Soon you cross the high point of this part of the ridge and descend past a junction with the Los Huecos Trail, open to bicycles. Then, 0.3 mile farther, you reach a broad saddle where you meet the Hall's Valley Trail, another route up from Grant Lake. Continuing on the Cañada de Pala Trail, you climb north along the ridge, passing still-used corrals and cattle chutes. After ¼ mile you come to a junction with the Pala Seca Trail, which leads east and then follows the ridge north to the far end of the park. Staying on the Cañada de Pala Trail, you descend the hillside past watercourses in each small ravine, where reeds and marshy spots mark springs, and enter the head of Deer Valley, which drains to the north.

Ringed with parklike oak groves, this mile-long valley is one of the wildest and most remote parts of the park. From the stately blue oaks, acorn woodpeckers swoop with flashing black-and-white wings, endlessly exchanging their sharp cries. Less visible, dark-blue Steller jays call to each other from treetops. The stillness is sometimes further broken by the cries of golden eagles, whose voice the Audubon Society's field guide describes as "soft mewing or yelping notes." These magnificent raptors with wingspreads of 6–8' can sometimes be seen soaring above the treetops and swooping down into the grasslands.

In this highland valley you will often catch sight of small bands of deer bounding out of the brush, and on rare occasions might even glimpse a mountain lion. These shy and rare animals pose little threat to deer populations; most of the deer they kill are weak or crippled. They pose no threat at all to hikers, from whom they will flee.

Hikers who have left a car at Grant Lake can retrace their steps to the Hall's Valley Trail and take it for 2½ miles downhill to the car. Bicyclists can return on the Los Huecos Trail.

Trip 8. Eagle Lake Loop

This trip takes you along open pasture lands to Eagle Lake, down a creek canyon and then up through a Digger pine forest.
Distance 5.5-mile loop.
Time 3½ hours.
Elevation Gain 840'

TRAIL NOTES

Park beside Mt. Hamilton Road at its highest point before descending to Smith Creek. This trip is described starting on the Cañada de Pala Trail and returning on the Bonnhoff Trail. By parking another car at the Smith Creek entrance to the Digger Pine Trail, however, you can avoid the steep, exposed Bonnhoff Trail and shorten the trip by ½ mile.

The Cañada de Pala Trail goes southwest from Mt. Hamilton Road on an easy grade on switchbacks into Hall's Valley. This route, a utility service road under tall powerlines, takes us over grassy slopes, here and there shaded with valley oaks, and into cool, wooded ravines where creeks run in winter and spring. In May the green grass is dotted with flowers—magenta clarkia, blue-eyed grass and purple brodiaea in the sun, and masses of yellow buttercups and lavender and white Chinese houses on shady, north-facing slopes.

Ahead Hall's Valley opens up to view—the ranchhouse at the head of the valley, Grant Lake beyond and Snell Barn to the right across the valley. Over the wooded hills to the west we see the Santa Cruz Mountains and far south the mountains east of Monterey. The melodious songs of meadowlarks and the sharp calls of wood-peckers stand out in the general chorus of bird song.

After four switchbacks our trail rises out of a small ravine to meet the Hotel Trail. Early in this century a road on the route of the Hotel Trail up Hall's Valley eventually reached a popular inn (no longer extant) on Smith Creek near the fire station. Enterprising excursionists spent a night at the hotel before taking a wagon up Mt. Hamilton to Lick Observatory.

The Hotel Trail rises gradually through gentle meadows and past small reservoirs for watering cattle. After about 1½ miles we go through a small draw and come upon tranquil Eagle Lake, brimful in May. Frogs splash into the water at our coming, and fish sometimes jump from its surface.

On a May visit the authors looked up to see large, dark gray animals moving through tall grass on a nearby hilltop. As they approached, they proved to be a small herd of the wild pigs that have become numerous in the park. A boar nearly 3 feet high, with long, menacing tusks, accompanied by two sows and a piglet, trotted down the hill and out of our sight. These feral pigs, descendants of wild boars imported to the East Coast from Europe in the past century, were brought to California as game animals. They will avoid you if they can, but leave them alone; they might be dangerous if cornered.

Before you leave Eagle Lake go just beyond the south rim of the lake for a view down the San Felipe Valley. Mt. Misery is the tall peak you see at the south end of the valley, and beyond is a succession of hills and mountains all the way to the Santa Lucia Mountains near Monterey. To continue your trip, take the well-signed Digger Pine Trail, once a footpath, now graded for service vehicles, from the northeast end of the lake. It descends abruptly into a narrow-walled canyon, then turns down beside an intermittent stream, which you cross and recross before turning uphill. In warm weather this stretch is a pleasant, cool interlude. Sycamores edge the stream, and masses of Chinese houses blossom along its shady banks. Here, also, are wind poppies, with their delicate orange-red flowers.

After several stream crossings your trail takes off straight uphill and climbs out of the canyon in a series of short, steep pitches mixed with easy grades shaded by bays and oaks. In season the hillsides are clothed with more white and lavender Chinese houses. Some purple larkspur and a small-flowered blue flax grow in scattered clumps beside the trail After a 10-minute climb up the canyon, you begin to see the blue-green, long-needled Digger pines found on dry heights such as these. Their unusually large seeds were an important food for the Indians, sometimes traded to tribelets farther west.

Another ¾ hour's walk brings you to a flowery, damp meadow where a pond catches runoff from surrounding hills. A trail junction sign here points to the east entrance to the Digger Pine Trail, 0.3 mile down a gentle slope at Smith Creek. There a short lane from Mt. Hamilton Road leads to a stile and a gated entrance to the Digger Pine Trail. This is the trail to take if you wish to avoid the uncomfortably steep parts of the Bonnhoff Trail.

But to complete the trip on the Bonnhoff Trail, turn left (north) up a steep ranch road. The trail is named for a man who was for many years Josephine Grant McCreery's ranch manager. The climb from the meadow is one of several difficult, steep stretches without switchbacks on this trail. However, the route along the hilltops has magnificent wide views of Hall's Valley. The trail is slow going on the upgrades, but in less than a mile you come around the last bend and are in sight of Mt. Hamilton Road and the end of the trip.

Trip 9. The Washburn Trail to Deer Valley

A stiff climb for hikers only to the high, remote northeast corner of the park takes you to lush Deer Valley, to hilltops of flowers, to forests of great oaks and to breathtaking vistas.

Distance 9.7 miles to Grant Lake; 11.2 miles to Washburn
trailhead.

Time 8 hours.

Elevation Gain 1800'

TRAIL NOTES

This is a challenging, spectacular trip with long uphill climbs, one
for cool weather and an early start. (The early start is easier now
with camping allowed in the park.) The Washburn Trail starts from
the east side of Mt. Hamilton Road about 1 mile below the park
entrance, and the trip ends on the Hall's Valley Trail at Grant Lake,
½ mile above the park entrance. The distance between the two will
seem long at the end of the day, so try to arrange a car shuttle.

A stile by a gate on the east side of the road leads to a trail passing
north of the White Barn. Head down the ranch road straight toward
the hills. You can look up from here at the 2900' heights you will
cross on the Washburn Trail. A 20-minute walk through a pasture
brings you to oak woods, then a quick descent to a branch of the
Arroyo Aguague. Sycamores and alders meet overhead where two
streams join in a small flat to flow west to Alum Rock Park. This
makes a pleasant destination for a picnic in late spring before the
creeks dry up. Children would be happily occupied here.

For those who continue, the trail crosses the creek and climbs
steadily up a ravine beside a branch of the creek. Leaving the ravine,
we climb around bend after bend for another mile. The trail is now
out in open pasture lands dotted with the valley oaks that are a constant delight in this park. The ranch road we have been following
approaches the northern boundary of the park and then crosses it
through a locked gate into a ranch beyond. We stay in the park,
turning right on a jeep track going uphill, which the Washburn Trail
now follows.

Here in a draw by the trail one of Grant Park's windmills pumps
water to fill a cattle trough. We are at an elevation of 1700', with
more than 1000' to go before reaching the high point of the trail. It is
a steady, steep climb now, up hillsides bright with yellow mariposa
lilies, lavender brodiaea and magenta godetias, to reach a narrow
ridge shaded by a grove of blue oaks. This is a good place to rest
before the last push to the hilltop. Then the trail continues in a series
of steep pitches mixed with level stretches. Repeatedly, the feeling
that surely the brow of the hill ahead is the summit gives way to
dismay that another climb is beyond, and then still another.
However, you can stop along the way to look off to the Bay far below
and to admire the grassy slopes, where silvery-headed blow-wives

Remote Deer Valley is an exhilarating destination for a day-long hike

glisten and more mariposa lilies and brodiaeas blossom. At last you reach the high point of the Washburn Trail at an elevation of 2956'. On the Pala Seca Trail beyond, you reach nearly 3000'.

From the south side of the trail a series of hogbacks, or shoulders, extends from the ridge down to Grant Lake. Along these heights the mile-long Tamyen Trail takes off to a windmill on a hilltop.

Continuing on the Washburn Trail, you follow along a fence to a gate, where you turn sharply downhill. The trail goes through a grove of magnificent oaks—some of the finest in the park. A long arc of the trail brings you to the south end of Deer Valley and the Cañada de Pala Trail. A leisurely lunch here will give you time to enjoy this beautiful setting.

Remote Deer Valley is a place of eagles and deer herds. Mountain lions have been seen here too, but that is little cause for alarm; their shyness keeps them out of our way. At times the valley is filled with grazing cattle. A herd may include a bull—an animal to treat with cautious respect. Give him time to move out of your way.

This mile-long valley is enclosed on the west by a ridge forested with blue and black oaks; on the east by rounded, grassy hills rising above 2900', dotted with valley oaks and furrowed by wooded ravines. Here and there are great outcrops of lichen-covered rocks.

At the head of the valley where the Washburn Trail joins the Cañada de Pala Trail, you have alternate routes for your return trip. The shortest way is by the Cañada de Pala Trail south for 1.0 mile to the Hall's Valley Trail for an easy trip down to Grant Lake. A longer, more circuitous and more spectacular route for those still feeling energetic after lunch is to follow the Cañada de Pala Trail north down the valley, then take the Pala Seca Trail over the east ridge to join the Cañada de Pala Trail going south to the Hall's Valley Trail.

If you choose the long way, take the Cañada de Pala Trail down the marshy valley, which drains northward. Its waters gather into a meandering stream through some sycamores before it descends to join a branch of Arroyo Aguague. As Deer Valley narrows at its lower end, we pass a sycamore-filled canyon cutting into the hills on the east side of the valley. Our trail begins to climb the rocky, enclosing north hills near the park's north boundary.

A trail marker points to the Pala Seca Trail, where you turn south to continue climbing out of the valley. A highlight of this part of the trail is a profusion of yellow mariposa lilies, which makes the trip very much worthwhile in spring. These exquisite blossoms grow in such surprising numbers that the ridgetop sparkles with glints of pale gold. Along the trail in the thin soil are patches of lavender, flaxlike linanthus, and popcorn flowers add white accents. In April dwarf lupines echo the blue of the sky. Listen for the song of meadowlarks. They sometimes fly close, trying to distract you from their nests in the grass or from their fledglings.

Looking out from the colorful grasslands, you have one of the park's most commanding views. To the east stretch ridge on ridge of the rugged Diablo Range, at this point about 35 miles wide—an expanse of remote ranches where cattle graze much as they did a century ago. More than two centuries ago Juan Bautista de Anza led an expedition through this formidable country from the east side of Mt. Diablo down the San Antonio Valley east of Mt. Hamilton, through what is now Coe Park and out to Gilroy.

After walking for about a mile along the broad, nearly level summit of the Pala Seca Trail, you turn down to meet the Cañada de Pala Trail under the generous shade of an immense, lone white oak. From this intersection it is a short 0.4 mile down to the saddle and the Hall's Valley Trail. From there it is downhill all the way to the parking lot at Grant Lake.

The Pala Seca Trail is one of the park's most dramatic stretches, though a long, strenuous walk to reach by way of the Washburn Trail. An easier way to the Pala Seca Trail is by the wooded Hall's Valley Trail.

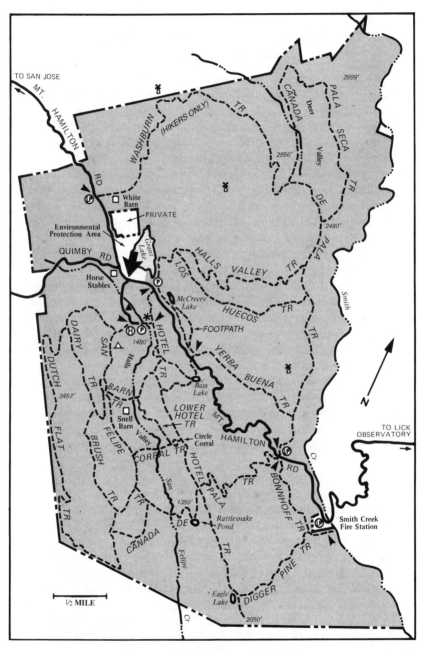

Joseph D. Grant Park

Henry W. Coe State Park
SEE MAP ON PAGES 102-3

Rising to over 3500' on the southeastern flank of the Santa Clara Valley, this wild, undeveloped region is the largest mountain park in the South Bay. Thousands of acres of ridges, deep canyons, upland meadows and flowing streams beckon the ambitious visitor to days of long hikes and rides or a week's extended backpacking trip through nearly untrammeled wilderness.

The original park of 13,000 acres was a gift of Sada Coe Robinson to Santa Clara County in 1953. Subsequent additions of several cattle ranches brought the size of the park to over 67,000 acres. Following the acquisition of these ranches, the California State Parks Department reclassified a large area of Henry W. Coe State Park as wilderness. Now only a few man-made structures remain in the park, and the land retains a wilderness character.

The park is open all year, although spring and fall are the most popular visiting periods. Temperatures can drop below freezing in winter, and summer maxima reach well above 90°. However, the variety of terrain provides opportunity to enjoy the park in any season. Sunny, south-facing slopes offer warm pockets in winter, and shady stream canyons are cool in the heat of summer.

Thousands of people visit this vast and challenging park every year. Whether they hike to Sada's Spring in the northwest section of the park or climb to the monument honoring Sada's father, they can enjoy the beautiful setting of her ranch. Later acquisitions multiplied and extended her gift to the people many times.

History

The Ohlone Indians were the first inhabitants of the lands that now make up the western part of Henry W. Coe State Park. They made their homes on several sites near year-round streams where fish were plentiful. Acorns, the staple of their diet, were supplemented by berries, nuts, deer and an abundant supply of small animals. Recent research indicates that the Northern Valley Yokuts, a tall, light-complexioned, peaceful tribe, came to the eastern areas of the park (now the wilderness area) from their villages in the San Joaquin Valley. (Please note that all archeological artifacts are protected and should be left undisturbed. Visitors should report any such finds to a ranger.)

During the westward movement of the mid-1800s, among the many pioneers settling in the South Bay was Henry W. Coe, Sr., who bought a 500-acre ranch in the San Felipe Valley, north of today's park.

Henry Coe's sons, Henry Jr. and Charles, homesteaded lands in this vicinity in the 1880s. By the early 1900s Henry Jr. had purchased the Pine Ridge Ranch and built a house there. He married Rhoda Sutcliffe in 1905, and they lived at the ranch with their two children, Henry S. and Sada Sutcliffe Coe, until 1913.

Henry Jr.'s daughter Sada lived during several years of her childhood at the Pine Ridge Ranch. Many years later she and her husband, Oscar Robinson, managed the ranch. At the death of Sada's father in 1943, it was sold to a cattle company. But Sada bought it back in 1947 and ran cattle there herself until she gave the ranch to Santa Clara County in 1953.

Sada Coe wanted to preserve the ranch from development and to give others the opportunity to experience the peace and tranquility of its remote location. She dedicated it ". . . as a living memorial to those great and sturdy pioneers" of early California, as she wrote in *My Log from the Hearth*. Santa Clara County held the ranch until 1958, when the State of California took it over.

Sada Coe Robinson lived until 1979, 26 years after her generous gift of Pine Ridge Ranch to the people. During these years she followed the development of the park as the campgrounds and some trails were built. In 1971 Sada gave money to construct the museum, donating many of her family's furnishings as well. A collection of antique carriages is housed in one of her barns.

Natural Resources

This outstanding park provides a remarkable diversity of plant and animal life. With almost every ecological zone of the Coast Range represented, one can find all the usual plants of the oak woodlands, grasslands, coniferous forests and riparian communities. Fields of wildflowers are spectacular in spring throughout the park, but there are exceptional displays on Pine Ridge near the monument, in Miller Field and in many remote wilderness areas. In addition, some unusual plant species of the western United States are found here, including the giant manzanita on the park's western ridges. Most unusual are the stands of ponderosa pine.

The Pine Ridge Association volunteers and park rangers lead wildflower walks in the spring to the best displays of the season.

Saturday evening programs in spring and early summer highlight
biological and natural features of the park. A stop at the charming
farmhouse Visitor Center at park headquarters offers a glimpse of
the region's cultural and natural history. Call the park office or write
for the schedule of activities.

Seldom seen, but known to be inhabitants of the park, are mountain lions and bobcats. Golden eagles and red-tailed hawks patrol the
skies. There is an abundant animal population of deer, fox, rabbit,
squirrel and many small rodents. Wild pigs (hybrids of European
boars and domestic pigs) are also seen.

Geology

Coe Park presents an excellent cross section of the Diablo Range,
stretching from the eastern foothills of the Santa Clara Valley to the
low-lying hills and valleys west of the San Joaquin Valley. The
mountains consist largely of Franciscan Formation rocks, a jumble
of rocks that accumulated as the Pacific Plate slid under the North
American Plate some 90 million years ago.

The southeast part of the park contains some of the largest blue
schist blocks found in California. Compared with the surrounding
sediments, crystalline blue schist is resistant to erosion. Consequently, isolated blocks of this schist stand out prominently on
hillsides. They are known throughout the area of the Franciscan
Formation as "knockers." In Coe Park some are as large as ½ mile
across.

The park visitor can see some examples of well-preserved marine
sediments in the chert layers on road-cuts near the park headquarters and on top of the Rooster Comb in the wilderness area.
With a hand lens one can see the tiny marine fossils whose shells
make up this rock.

Most creeks in Coe Park run northwest-southeast, following the
general trend of earthquake faults in California. Soda Springs Creek,
following this alignment, runs through the canyon that contains the
Madrone Springs Fault.

Trails in Coe Park

Within the original Coe Park area are some 40 miles of hiking and
riding trails. These trails climb ridges to mountaintop views and
descend to wooded canyons and secluded campsites beside streams.
In the entire park there are 175 miles of trail, including many miles
to explore in the remote, 23,000-acre wilderness.

Stone dairy house
kept milk cool
at the Coe Ranch

Maps for Coe Park are available at the Visitor Center at park headquarters. A large-format map, covering the entire park, designates the major trail routes to the park's three main areas: (1) the Coe Ranch section from park headquarters, (2) the lands in the park's southwest corner—the Lakes Area—and (3) the Orestimba Wilderness. Available too, are maps showing trails open for bicyclists and equestrians. In addition, there are a number of books and brochures about the park, including The Pine Ridge Association's, *Trails of Henry W. Coe State Park,* by Winslow R. Briggs.

Most of the park trails are old ranch roads, today used only by patrol vehicles and the few people with private inholdings in the park. These ranch roads are open to hikers, equestrians and bicyclists, but some trails are designated exclusively for hikers. Only hikers and equestrians are allowed in the Orestimba Wilderness. Trails that follow or cross creeks may be impassable just after heavy rains. Consult the ranger and park maps for an alternative route at these times.

Spring and fall are the best times for trips in this park, when the weather is usually cool and the skies clear. California's mild winters can also offer periods of excellent hiking or riding weather. The authors have even hiked in Henry Coe Park on summer days that were pleasantly cool, but it is well to remember that on hot-weather backpack trips you should plan to do the long uphill stretches in the early morning and reach your campsite by midday. For day trips a long rest in midday is wise; summer's long afternoons allow many hours of light for a cooler return.

Although running streams and springs are found throughout the park, the water supply is undependable and may not meet state drinking water standards—so following the trails in Coe Park requires that you carry plenty of water or the means to purify the park's spring and stream water. Even though each campsite is located by a spring or flowing creek, most of the streams dry up in summer and many springs stop flowing. Therefore, you should carry water—at least a quart of water per person per day is recommended, more in hot weather.

Trips from the Coe Ranch Headquarters

This guide details six trips from the park headquarters—short walks of about a mile up to the Henry Coe memorial monument and out over the gentle meadows to flowing springs. Beyond are trips of a few miles and one as long as 17 miles.

Backpack trips to outlying camps from park headquarters enable the hiker to explore the far reaches of the park's original area. All overnight park users must have a permit from the ranger and must get current information on routes and their seasonal limitations.

The climbs up rugged ridges and descents into steep canyons present physical challenges that the user must recognize. The extra time required for such elevation gains is reflected in the time suggested for hikers on each trip.

The Southwest Corner—The Lakes Area

South and east of the headquarters area are three lakes, Coit, Mississippi, and Kelly, fine destinations for long and demanding backpacking, equestrian and bicycle trips. The North Fork of Pacheco Creek drains most of this section of the park, fed by Mississippi, Coon and other minor creeks. Along Pacheco Creek are some steep canyons and a spectacular, but remote waterfall in rugged terrain. Between Coyote and Kelly Cabin Canyon creeks is the long slope of Mahoney Meadows with its high grasslands and oak savanna. Higher ridges covered with blue oak and live oak separate creeks to the north. Along streams are denser stands of bay, live oak and sycamore trees. Digger pines and blue oaks are found on the dry, steeper slopes and chaparral thrives on the dry, hot south- and west-facing ridges.

The Orestimba Wilderness

In 1985 23,000 acres were set aside from development in Coe Park as a State Wilderness (under the California Wilderness Act of 1974). This area of relatively undeveloped land, often called the Orestimba Wilderness, has retained its primeval character without permanent improvements or human habitation, other than a few structures that pre-dated acquisition. The Orestimba Wilderness, affected primarily by the forces of nature, has outstanding opportunities for solitude and unconfined types of recreation. It contains natural features of scientific, educational, scenic and historical value.

Steep ridges, high peaks and some broad flats and wide gravel washes characterize much of this wilderness. Digger pines and blue oaks cover the hills, while grassland on the long Paradise Flat is dotted with magnficent oaks. The South Fork of Orestimba Creek drains north, fed by Red and Robinson creeks. Sycamore, live oak, willow and bay trees flourish by these streams with occasional clumps of holly-leaf cherry and toyon.

From ridgetops one has immense vistas south to the Pacheco Pass peaks and southwest to Monterey Bay and its nearby mountains. From the northern part of the wilderness you look down into the wide San Antonio Valley and up to Mt. Hamilton.

Not included in the wilderness area is a vehicle access to Coe Park from Bell Station on the Pacheco Pass Highway (152), which will some day be an entrance to the vast backcountry and the Orestimba Wilderness. Bell Station was an important center of cattle operations for the great ranches of this part of the Diablo Range. The road from Bell Station follows a 6-mile, State-owned corridor through private property to the Dowdy Ranch. This former cattle ranch site will some day provide a trailhead and staging area into areas north and west. Beyond this ranch is a 6-mile dirt road to Orestimba Corral, where trailhead parking will provide access for day and overnight use by hikers, bicyclists and equestrians.

From the Dowdy Ranch and the Orestimba Corral extends a network of unimproved roads that serve as trails along creek valleys and over ridges. The wilderness area just north of the corral will be open to hikers, backpackers and equestrians, who will have better access to unimproved campsites. No bicycles are allowed in the wilderness area.

Camping in the Park

Coe Park offers many opportunities for camping. For car campers, 20 primitive family campsites are near the park headquarters on Pine Ridge. Each has a barbecue and picnic table; some have sun shelters. Water and latrines are nearby. Popular with youth and church groups are the 10 reservable group sites at Manzanita Point. Campers must walk the 2½–3 miles into the site, but one vehicle for each group may drive in with supplies and water and stand by for emergencies.

Backpack Camps

Scattered throughout the park are backpack camps, with one to five campsites each, near water and some level bedsites. There are no prepared fire rings; in fact, fires are not allowed at backpacking sites, although you can carry a backpack stove, if you have a permit from the park office. The camps, set in scenic places, are less than a day's hike apart and visiting a combination of these can make an extended trip of several days.

Horsemen can camp behind the ranch headquarters, and there are eight horse camps, including those at Schafer Corral, at Mississippi Creek and at Coit Lake in the eastern section of the park. One of the

Old ranch buildings house park headquarters and history museum at Coe

Manzanita Point camping areas, Blue Oak Horse Camp, near Manzanita Point, can be used by horsemen's groups. Horsemen may also camp in the Orestimba Wilderness.

Whether you plan an extensive backpack trip or just an overnight in one of the backpack camps, you must check in with the ranger to get a permit, pay fees and obtain a campsite assignment. Day hikers and equestrians must also pay fees and check in with the ranger. For your safety the park staff should know visitors' destinations and estimated return times.

Jurisdiction State of California.

Facilities Headquarters and Visitor Center. Trails: More than 175 miles; hiking, equestrian, bicycling, 40 miles in area covered by this guide. Horse-trailer parking. Family picnic area. Camping: 19 backpack plus backpacking in zones for up to 33 more groups; 20 family drive-in; group camps—12 hike-in, by reservation; 8 horsemen's camps. Fishing under regulations of State Fish and Game. Handicapped access to one campsite.

Park Rules Hours: Open daily throughout the year. No open fires, except at camps near headquarters and those designated in Manzanita Point Group Camps. Bicycles allowed on dirt roads and some trails, but not in the Orestimba Wilderness. Dogs not allowed on trails or roads; on leash in headquarters area only; dog fee, $1/day, $1/night. Fees: $5/car, day use; $7/car campsite/night; $3/person/backpack site/night; $14/horse campsite/night; $4/night/additional vehicle. Phone: 408-779-2728.

Maps State of California *Henry W. Coe State Park;* USGS quads *Gilroy Hot Springs, Mississippi Creek, Mt. Sizer, Mt. Stakes, Mustang Peak, Pacheco Peak* and *Wilcox Ridge.*

How To Get There From Highway 101 near Morgan Hill take East Dunne Avenue for 13 miles to park entrance.

Trips from the Coe Ranch Headquarters

Trip 1.   Lion Spring Jaunt
A short walk from the park office on the south side of Pine Ridge visits a cool retreat.

Distance   1½ miles round trip.

Time   1 hour; Springs Trail for hikers only.

Elevation Gain   340'

TRAIL NOTES
When you leave the Visitor Center, cross the road near the stop sign and enter the trail next to the cattle-loading chute. Take the trail going left, downhill, into a little ravine below the barn. Signs point the way to Frog Lake and Manzanita Point. But you go toward Manzanita Point for ½ mile on the Corral Trail, which roughly parallels the Pacheco Route (a wide service road).

The large black oaks growing on the north-facing slopes have shiny, deeply lobed 6″ leaves with sharp points. The new leaves, fuzzy and reddish in spring, become deep green in summer. By fall, especially in colder locations, they become yellow tinged with red.

In and out of oak-wooded ravines, the trail gently contours along the hillside where chaparral grows on the drier, south-facing slopes. In less than ½ mile you come out into a tree-studded grassland, or savanna. Tall oats, green and lush in spring and golden brown in summer, provide food and shelter for small animals, which in turn, are food for hawks, coyotes and owls.

At the Fish Trail junction the Corral Trail becomes the Springs Trail and goes right. Shading your way are scattered Digger pines, oaks and ponderosa pines. Very soon you come to a clearing. Stay on the trail another 50 feet to find an obscure trail on the right which traverses on a good grade back to the Lion Spring campsite. If you can't find the trail, you can spot the campsite location by the chemical toilet. If no one is occupying the site, you might have your lunch at the table under the trees.

But first circle around the outcrop of big gray boulders to find Lion Spring, originally developed to water the Coe Ranch cattle. Many years ago its cool shade lured the ranch children here to spend hot summer afternoons. Legend has it that sometimes they saw a lion crouching on the shadowy ledge above the spring. Today, only a lucky and very observant visitor would ever see a mountain lion in the park, although it is a known inhabitant. This beautiful, shy creature is much too wary of humans, so enjoy the children's retreat without trepidation.

Returning to the Springs Trail, you can continue east on this level trail to visit Blackberry, Arnold and Plum springs, some of the 100 or so springs in the park. Or you can retrace your steps to the Fish Trail junction. From here you can look up on the hillside to see Sada Coe's old corral. The huge ponderosa nearby is named "Sada's Pine," in memory of the park's donor. Bear left at the junction and take the Corral Trail back to your starting point.

Trip 2.   Loop Trip to Middle Ridge
via Frog Lake

Two good climbs on the outbound trip take you to ridges capped with pines and tall manzanitas. The return is on the Fish Trail.

Distance   5.7-mile loop.

Time   4 hours.

Elevation Gain   1400'

TRAIL NOTES

When you leave the Visitor Center, go 300' back up the entrance road and take a gated road on the right. At the first bend take the foot path, the Monument Trail, that goes left up the grassy hillside. Equestrians and bicyclists take the dirt road, the Pacheco Route, then go north on the Northern Heights Route. Although the way is steep, a glade of oaks soon gives some shade. Deep blue lupines stand out in the grass, and drifts of shiny, yellow-petaled buttercups grace the shady places in spring. Even in fall the fields of golden oats are brightened with lavender asters and the purple spikes of blue curls.

The Monument Trail veers to the right and in a few minutes reaches a junction where you can detour 600' east and across the ranch road to reach the monument to Sada Coe's father, Henry W. Coe, Jr. This monument is surmounted by some of the tallest ponderosa pines in the park, landmarks that are identifiable from other high points in the park and even from some places in the Santa Clara Valley.

Your trip to Middle Ridge continues on the foot trail to the 3000' crest of Pine Ridge among the towering ponderosa pines that give the ridge its name. These trees have grown to stately proportions—a little biological island found in only a few places outside their usual habitat, the Sierra Nevada and the Rocky Mountains. The sounds of the wind in the pines and the birds singing give one the feeling of calm and peace that Sada Coe described in stories based on her life on this ranch. "Slowly the peace of the hills crept into her heart," she wrote in *My Log from the Hearth.*

Now the foot trail joins the ranch road, known as the Northern Heights Route, and you make a long descent down the north side of the ridge through forests of black oaks, madrones and tall manzanitas. Since the discontinuance of cattle grazing, biologists note, the oaks and pines too are regenerating faster.

At the Little Fork of Coyote Creek, 0.7 miles from Pine Ridge, the road veers left and crosses the creek past the trail on your right that goes to the marshy shores of Frog Lake. This little green reservoir, ringed with reeds, is a peaceful destination offering good picnic places under the trees.

In the fall you might watch for holes in the ground the size of a quarter, where the hairy-bodied, long-legged tarantula makes his home. The largest of spiders, the tarantula lines its little underground well with a silky web that catches the insects it eats. Also within the park lives the tarantula hawk, an insect that stings the tarantula and lays its eggs in the victim's body.

From Frog Lake you head up the road for a longer, less steep route to Middle Ridge. Or take the steep, but shorter foot trail to your right just after crossing Little Fork. In either case, at the ridgetop you meet the Middle Ridge Trail, leaving the Northern Heights Route, and turn to the right through a grassy meadow. From your vantage point on Middle Ridge you see northeast to 3000' Blue Ridge, which cuts diagonally northwest-southeast through the park for about 5 miles.

The Middle Ridge Trail, for hikers and, except after rain, for bicyclists, descends gently to a saddle before climbing again, to 2700'. On this rise you enter an amazing stand of large spreading manzanitas. Their shining mahogany-red trunks support a broad canopy of leaves that casts a deep shadow. On a still day you can hear the faint rustle of the little papery curls of bark peeling from the trunks and falling to carpet the ground. Here and there straight trunks of pine trees grow up through the manzanita.

Your trail makes a gradual descent along the ridge to the Fish Trail. Here you turn right and then go down the south slope through chaparral and mixed woodland to cross the Little Fork of Coyote Creek once again. Fifteen minutes takes you down to the boulder-strewn creek bed, usually dry in summer (after heavy rains, however, you may have to take off your shoes and wade across).

Manzanitas grow very large in Coe Park

On the Fish Trail you make a few switchbacks through the woods and soon arrive at a small, open, grassy valley. In summer and fall, the magnificent specimens of valley oak here stand out darkly against the pale gold grass. In spring the new leaves unfolding on gnarled, bare branches shine light-green in the sun, and deep-blue heads of tall brodiaea wave above the emerging oats.

Your trail then bends around the hillside to enter a tight, shady little canyon. On a hot day this is a welcome, cool climb under dark bay trees beside a watercourse which is dry by summer. Emerging on the open savanna of Pine Ridge, the trail levels off. Before it crosses the main ranch road to Manzanita Point, you can see east to the fences of a corral that Sada Coe built when she managed Pine Ridge Ranch. She expected to drive the cattle here for loading, but the road proved too narrow for trucks. Today a backpack site, Old Corral Camp, stands under the oak and pine trees just north of the corral.

Across the ranch road you pick up the Springs Trail for a few yards, then take the Corral Trail going west, back to park head-quarters. Scattered through the grass on a ¼-mile stretch of hillside trail are bright yellow tarweed blossoms on tall delicate stems, purple spikes of blue curls and pink heads of buckwheat. Then the trail winds through the woods back to your starting point.

Trip 3.   **Poverty Flat Circle Hike**
                  via Middle Ridge

This trip follows the route of Trip 2 as far as the Fish Trail, then
continues southeast down Middle Ridge through its shady north-
slope woods to the confluence of the two forks of Coyote Creek near
Poverty Flat.

Distance   9.3-mile loop.

Time   6 or 7 hours. Middle Ridge Trail for hikers and bicyclists
only.

Elevation Gain   2280'

TRAIL NOTES

From headquarters this is a full day's hike or an easy 2-day backpack trip. Follow the directions for Trip 2 and when you reach
Middle Ridge, turn southeast and follow the trail down the ridge
through the meadows and forests to the Fish Trail junction. Instead
of branching off to the right here, as in Trip 2, continue down Middle
Ridge for 2½ miles to Poverty Flat.

For the first mile your way lies on the sloping plateau of Middle
Ridge, at first through the shade of a dense growth of huge
manzanitas. Then the footpath emerges onto grasslands under blue
oaks and ponderosa pines. Shortly the grassy area widens, and you
walk through a magnificent, broad, undulating savanna, with
immense, widely-spaced valley and blue oaks. The trail slopes down
on the south side of the broad ridge past a few old oaks riddled with
woodpecker holes. As you descend, your view south over the canyon
of the Little Fork is of Pine Ridge. You can pick out the main ranch
road winding up through the rugged woodlands of the ridge's north-
facing slope, where this trip will eventually take you.

About a mile from the Fish Trail junction, the trail turns northeast, crosses the ridge, dips into a few ravines and then drops down
the north side. Here the forest deepens, and trees of many species
crowd the steep slopes—madrones, tall ponderosa pines and gray-
green Digger pines, blue and black oaks interspersed with a few
canyon oaks. Toyon, manzanita and poison oak fill the understory.
Since the discontinuance of cattle grazing, the native bunchgrass is
flourishing on this hillside.

The authors felt truly remote from civilization here. The only
noises were the calls of many birds and the splashing of the creek in
the canyon below. When a 2'-long animal (perhaps a fox) silently
crossed the trail ahead of us, we sensed we were privileged humans
in this wilderness.

On many switchbacks you continue east and down the steep slope for more than a mile. You arrive at the confluence of the two forks of Coyote Creek at the foot of a narrow peninsula between them. Sunlight filters through the trees, and patterns of light dance on the waters of grass-edged pools.

If you are going to the Poverty Flat backpack camp, you will find the first site under the oaks on the broad flat just across the stream. Hop across on the rocks—no bridge here. At high water you may have to wade through the chilly water. If you are going back to head-quarters, walk about ¼ mile past the first campsite, then cross the creek at the ford (or wherever you can make it over the rocks) and pick up the ranch road, now known as the Pacheco Route, going west, uphill. After two very steep climbs on a zigzag route of slightly less than 2 miles and an elevation gain of 1200', you reach the open meadows on Pine Ridge. The spring flowers of the woodlands— white milkmaids, shooting stars, blue iris and pink-blossomed currant—bloom beside the trail. Scarlet flowers of the California fuchsia stand out on open road cuts late in the year.

The authors found a striped racer snake sunning its 18 inches on the warm, dusty road. And if you wonder what birds you saw perched in the trees beside the trail, stop in at the Visitor Center when you get back to headquarters and look over the many helpful pamphlets and books. The knowledgeable ranger or one of the trained volunteers will answer your questions or tell you where to look for the information.

The year-round waters of Coyote Creek at Poverty Flat

Trip 4.   The Big Loop

From the heights of Blue Ridge to the cool waters of East Fork
Coyote Creek, this hike samples most of the unique terrain of Sada
Coe's original park gift. It is a very strenuous, long day's hike or a
good weekend backpack trip.

Distance   14.2-mile loop over Jackass Trail cut-off; 17.1-mile
   loop.

Time   10–12 hours.

Elevation Gain   3940′

TRAIL NOTES

Leave the park office as in Trip 2, and take the Monument Trail, a
footpath, toward Frog Lake, which climbs quickly to the 3000′
summit of Pine Ridge. After crossing the top in the shade of the
majestic ponderosa pines, your trail descends the north side of Pine
Ridge.

Many very large manzanitas grow treelike here, their mahogany-
red branches ending in gray-green, leathery foliage. If you come here
in the fall, you may see their red fruit, *manzanitas,* the Spanish
name for little apples. These fruits were one of the many that the
Ohlone Indians used to make cider.

Before long the foot trail joins the road, the Northern Heights
Route, and plunges downhill to Little Fork Coyote Creek. There
hikers take a turnoff north for the ascent to Middle Ridge. A
generous scattering of black oaks gives you shade on the way up the
steep trail. At the broad, grassy ridgetop dotted with huge oaks and a
few pines, turn left and rejoin the road. An alternate and less abrupt
uphill route for equestrians and bicyclists, though longer, follows the
ranch road west past Frog Lake to Middle Ridge.

Now, continuing on the Northern Heights Route, you go through
oak woodlands where a recent controlled burn eliminated heavy
undergrowth that had accumulated for over 50 years. Soon the road
heads downhill, losing about 1300′ in less than 2 miles, and rounds a
bend. On the right is Deer Horn spring, one of the park's many
springs. Its waters are piped into a large trough, beside which a sign
warns that they should be purified before drinking. During the heat
of a summer's day, the flow often stops, perhaps because of the high
rate of transpiration from the trees, and then resumes in the evening.

A short distance down on the opposite side of the road is the site of
the Widow Hobbs' cabin. The only remaining signs are the chimney
stones and an apricot tree struggling to survive. In good years it
bears fruit, enjoyed mostly by birds. Here you will find three campsites for today's adventurers. Whether you stop for the night or just

**Clear waters of the Middle Fork of Coyote Creek
flow past Skeel's Meadow**

for a moment in the shade of the big black oaks, you can enjoy the view across to the south face of Blue Ridge. Its grassy flats and chaparral-covered slopes do not look blue. From Henry Coe's first homesite north of the ridge, however, the heavier woods, blue oaks and manzanita on the north slope do, in fact, look blue—hence its name.

Continuing downhill toward the Middle Fork of Coyote Creek, you soon come to a right turnoff that leads to the Skeels' Meadow Camps. In a grassy opening above the creek are three campsites, some of the choicest in the park. The year-round waters of the lovely Middle Fork form small pools. Bright green sedge grass edges pools between the rocks, giving a Japanese garden effect. If you made an early start from the park headquarters, this creekside would be a delightful place for lunch. Ringed by maples, oaks and buckeyes, this appealing site drew Indians long before campers. Here and there on large boulders by the creek are grinding holes where they made acorns into meal.

Retrace your steps to the main trail and in a few hundred feet come to the left turnoff for Upper Camp. Big sycamores twine their roots around the boulders in the creek, and several little waterfalls splash into big pools, one large enough for swimming. Both Skeels' and Upper Camp by the Middle Fork of Coyote Creek are inviting enough for a few days' stopover for relaxing and exploring. The waters of the Middle Fork originate north of the park boundary. The stream swings around the northwest corner of the park and flows between Middle Ridge and Blue Ridge. At Poverty Flat the Middle Fork joins the Little Fork, and they continue down to the confluence with the East Fork at China Hole.

Along the creek banks or in the water, you might see a common amphibious snake, the California aquatic garter snake. You have to look carefully for it, as the single yellow stripe running the length of its dark back gives the snake the appearance of a twig lying on the rocks or floating in the water.

The next part of the trip on the Northern Heights route takes you up a very steep mountainside on The Short-Cut—something of a misnomer, as it is the only way to reach the crest of Blue Ridge, where you turn right. You will certainly want to make this 1.3-mile, steady 1500' climb while the day is young and you are fresh.

Your reward for this strenuous stretch lies at the top of Blue Ridge, crowned with a magnificent forest and open for sweeping views. On very clear days you can see the Sierra Nevada peaks, sometimes even identifying Half Dome. Pause awhile under the shade of a black oak or one of the fine specimens of ponderosa pines scattered along the ridge. This is a good vantage point from which to watch for golden eagles. Their tremendous wingspread of nearly 8' and their smooth flight distinguish them from the smaller turkey vultures, with their wobblier flight. You may see an eagle soaring high above the ridge make a stunning dive of thousands of feet into the canyon. Or look for eagles perched in the top branches of a dead tree.

The Northern Heights Route continues southeast, rising slightly for about a mile toward 3216' Mt. Sizer, near the north park boundary. Looking back northwest, you can see Mt. Hamilton. At the east boundary of the park is Mustang Peak, and beyond in the southeast lie the peaks near Pacheco Pass. More than 67,000 acres of remarkable country, relatively untouched by man's activities, are yours to explore. Notes from De Anza's diarist Pedro Font, exploring here two centuries ago, tell us that "on the ridges and at intervals there are seen strips and stretches of very white gravel." You too can see them shining to the north.

A scattered canopy of large trees gives the impression of walking down a shady sky-lane with ridge after ridge of mountains falling away on every side. In less than a mile you pass the trail to Black Oak Spring on the left. This trail takes you to the Black Oak Spring backpack camp, just ½ mile down the mountainside. As a second-night stop on the Big Loop, it makes a good base for exploring Hat

Rock and Rock House Ridge farther east. You will find spectacular wildflowers here in the spring.

If you take this alternate route, then from Hat Rock take the Rock House Ridge Trail and descend gradually southeast for 2½ miles, staying on the exposed ridgecrest most of the way. After you drop down into the canyon of the East Fork of Coyote Creek, you turn south and follow the fork downstream to Los Cruzeros.

Eschewing the Black Oak Spring alternate and staying on the Northern Heights Route for 1 mile more, you meet the Jackass Trail, a foot path on the right, which offers a 3-mile shorter version of this trip, bringing you to the main trail, the Pacheco Route, near Jackass Peak. There you turn west to Poverty Flat and back to the park headquarters. This cut-off eliminates the Narrows-to-China Hole section, described later, which is impassable after storms.

To continue on the longer trip, stay on the Northern Heights Route, descending gradually in light shade for 3 miles to Miller Field. Named for a former cattle baron whose herds once grazed here, these grasslands are now noted for a spectacular display of spring wildflowers.

The canyon of East Fork Coyote Creek lies below, and the Northern Heights Route drops quickly to meet it. Here you leave the Northern Heights Route, which arcs north to Bear Mountain and the Orestimba Wilderness. However, you follow the creek downstream (south) in a wide, gravelly wash, wherever you can find a good path. Passing Schafer Corral, a horsemen's campsite, and the ranch road to Jackass Peak on your right, you continue down the arroyo to Los Cruzeros. In April of 1776, when Juan Bautista De Anza and his men came from the San Antonio Valley along this creek, they named it "Arroyo del Coyote."

The easiest way for hikers to return to park headquarters is to follow the creek route through The Narrows to China Hole, as described in Trip 5. (This route, however, is impassable after storms.) Then climb to Manzanita Point and follow the trail back to headquarters.

Bicyclists turn uphill on the north side of the creek just before Los Cruzeros, where the road crosses the creek. This wide road, the Pacheco Route, goes over open grasslands, gaining about 400' in elevation before entering the forest near Jackass Peak. Here the foot trail from Blue Ridge joins the Pacheco Route, which then drops to the Middle Fork Coyote Creek at Poverty Flat. From here back to headquarters the Pacheco Route gains 1480' in 3.4 miles. (See Trip 3.)

Two Trips from Manzanita Point Group Area

Trip 5.   Loop Trip from Manzanita Point
to Poverty Flat

This trip, for hikers only, features over 2 miles of shady streamside trails, with a stop for lunch and swimming at China Hole, and a steep climb back from Poverty Flat through a forest of oaks, bays and manzanitas.

Distance   5-mile loop.

Time   3½ hours.

Elevation Gain   1160′

TRAIL NOTES

This trip is described starting down the Madrone Springs Trail, because crisscrossing up this south-facing slope can be hot in late afternoon. On a cold spring day, however, you might enjoy climbing back to Manzanita Point with the warmth of the sun on your back. In winter or early spring, high water makes this trail impassable; be sure to check with the ranger.

The trail takes off to the right from the main road through the Manzanita Point Group Area, just opposite Camp 7. At first it goes through rolling grasslands marked by brilliant displays of wild-flowers in the spring, including purple Ithuriel's spear and orange poppies. Here and there are clumps of valley and live oaks that offer shade for hikers. About 15 switchbacks traverse the nose of this ridge.

In half an hour you can be at Soda Springs Creek, the site of one of the park's backpack camps—Madrone Soda Springs. Cross the creek and explore the wide flat where Indians once lived. In 1879 Dr. Clinton Munson and Marshall Hunter bought Madrone Soda Springs and built a hotel offering the inducement of the springs' special healing properties. In 1881, at the height of the resort's popularity, a stage made four runs a week here from Madrone (Morgan Hill). A wagon road led from the hotel up Soda Springs Canyon and then climbed the 1000′ ridge on the southwest side of the creek. Madrone Soda Springs was later operated as a hunting resort. It was used into the 1940s.

Few vestiges of the old resort remain. Surrounding the flat, stands of native madrone trees still flourish, and hikers can now spend the night at two backpack campsites here.

After exploring the area, cross the creek again and head down-stream toward the junction of Soda Springs and Coyote creeks, a dis-

Deep pools near China Hole tempt swimmers

tance of about 1.3 miles. The trail goes through a narrow canyon, crossing the creek many times. It usually stays close to the water's edge, among shade-loving plants—snowberry, mint and ocean spray—sheltered by evergreen bay trees and deciduous big-leaf maples and black oaks.

About one-third of the way down the trail you come to an abandoned, tumbledown cabin built out over the creek. You can imagine how pleasant it was to live here with the sounds of water flowing over the rocks and the deep shade of trees in summer. Continuing downstream, the trail, now the MileTrail, follows the creek, crossing it several more times. In spring, new shoots of ferns uncurl their light-green fronds, and columbine, star flower, trillium and woodland star thrive in this damp canyon. In fall the golden maple and red poison-oak leaves stand out against the dark green of bays and oaks, and the California fuchsia adds its scarlet touch to the rocky banks.

Emerging from this narrow, woodsy canyon, Soda Springs Creek flows into the wide streambed of Coyote Creek. Turn left, upstream, staying on this side of the creek for 0.3 mile. At China Hole deep pools and rocky beaches invite you to stop for a swim. On the far side of the creek you will find the China Hole backpack camp in the shelter of big boulders, a popular goal of weekend pack trips.

Continue upstream a few yards to the confluence of the Middle and East forks of Coyote Creek. Here you look right into the steep-sided canyon of the East Fork, aptly named "The Narrows." But your route, except when impassable after storms, lies north along the Middle Fork, following the stream to Poverty Flat. You may have to do some rockhopping or wading in the creek.

In less than ½ hour you clamber over big boulders to the main ranch road, the Pacheco Route, which comes in from the east side of the park. Follow this road west to reach a broad flat with backpack campsites under oaks and sycamores. This is Poverty Flat, an inviting base from which to explore this part of the park. You can understand why one of the park's largest Indian settlements was in this pleasant flat, which had water, abundant fish and game and plentiful fruits and berries nearby. And you can sympathize with the reluctance of the homesteader who resisted Henry Coe's efforts to buy him out.

To return to your campground at Manzanita Point, cross the creek and head up the steep zigzags of the Cougar Trail under cover of handsome oak and bay trees. This is a shady trail, appropriate for the afternoon of a hot day. Cattle fences were cut to let the trail go through, but no cattle have grazed here since the state took over these 13,000 acres for a park in 1958.

In 0.6 mile, at a junction, you take the right-hand trail, the Coit Route, along the spine of Manzanita Point through the chaparral and manzanita forest. Deep mahogany branches of the large manzanitas fan out to leafy, rounded crowns of gray-green. Their dark red, glistening trunks contrast sharply with the gray of dead limbs and the nearly white lichen frosting the branches. When you come to openings in the forest, pause to enjoy the views south across the green, wooded canyon of Coyote Creek and southeast to the grassy flats of Mahoney Meadows.

Soon your trail levels out and enters the clearing at Camp 9. Continue along it to your campsite at Manzanita Point or onward for 2½ miles to park headquarters.

Trip 6.   Loop Hike to Mahoney Meadows

A vigorous trip takes you to China Hole, out to the high, oak-dotted grasslands of Mahoney Meadows and through The Narrows of East Fork Coyote Creek. On foot trails and jeep or fire roads, it goes to the eastern sections of the old Coe Ranch.

Distance   6.2-mile loop.
Time   4½ hours.
Elevation Gain   1560'
TRAIL NOTES

Starting from the end of Manzanita Point Road near Camp 9, take the trail, the Coit Route, out along the narrow east end of the ridge through a forest of giant manzanitas that grow as high as trees. On the forest floor is a carpet of the manzanita's small, spent leaves. Occasional taller madrone trees, also of the heath family, are interspersed among the dense stand of manzanitas. Your trail stays along the ridgetop, which is no more than 40 feet wide in some places.

As you come out of the manzanita forest, you find a fork in the trail. The left one, the Cougar Trail, goes to Poverty Flat, but you take the right one, the Coit Route, to China Hole, and begin your descent through thick chaparral. In spring your path is brightened by the light pink, bell-shaped flowers of spiny gooseberry plants. The terrain soon becomes more open, with occasional clumps of oaks and an understory of poison oak, holly-leaved cherry and honeysuckle. After a couple of zigzags the trail heads downhill, almost due south, skirting an open, grass-covered hillside. A few more switchbacks and you are at the creek's edge. Right after heavy rains, this crossing may require wading, but in summer and early fall it is easy to rock-hop across the stream. Along the creek banks grow green clumps of wild roses, bearing clusters of pink flowers and, later, red rose hips. Indians who once lived along Coyote Creek dried the hips for tea.

Across the creek, the Coit Route to Mahoney Meadows goes steeply up the hillside under a cover of bay trees, with an occasional black oak towering overhead. The trail makes a few switchbacks as it climbs beside an intermittent streambed. Large boulders on the hillside offer protection to clumps of bright-magenta-and-white shooting stars in spring. Moving out into rolling grasslands, the trail contours around the hill. On a clear day you see ridge after ridge of mountains to the south and southwest, as far south as San Benito County. On a fall day the authors found the diggings of wild pigs beside this trail. These creatures, descended from boars imported as game animals from Europe, have adapted well to the coastal mountains of California. Though seldom seen or heard by man, they reveal where they have been by the marks of their rootings in soft soil.

Here and there you see the feathery-looking, gray-green Digger pine, sparsely branched and bearing 8″ cones. It grows in hot, dry locations, usually below 4000′. Soon you emerge on the open grasslands that mark the beginning of Mahoney Meadows. Here you meet the wide road from Los Cruzeros.

From this point you can look east across a steep canyon to Willow Ridge, chaparral-covered except for thick stands of bay trees filling its canyons. On its northernmost reach a clump of straggly-looking Digger pines, known as the Eagle Pines, appear indeed to be perfect lookout perches for eagles. The canyon between you and Willow Ridge is Kelly Cabin Canyon, named for an early settler.

If you are on a backpack trip, continue on this road, the Coit Route, to campsites at Kelly Lake, or go a mile farther to those at Coit Lake.

When you are ready to start back, head north on the Coit Route to the junction with the Lost Spring Trail. Take this shady, gentle, downhill trail, which bypasses the steep gravelled road to Los Cruzeros. Along the way you may see rusty-breasted western bluebirds flying among the great oaks where they nest. The grasslands blaze with wildflowers in spring, the blue of lupines contrasting with the yellow of johnny jump-ups. Fall has its share of color, too, with the brilliant scarlet California fuchsia and yellow and white species of tarweed. Ubiquitous poison oak, climbing high in the trees, shows its scarlet, red, bronze and yellow foliage then.

In about ½ hour you reach Los Cruzeros, marked by magnificent specimens of California sycamore with gnarled white trunks. Its large leaves, golden brown in fall, make a bright contrast to the dark-green foliage of the oaks and bays on the canyon walls. This is the point where East Fork Coyote Creek enters the canyon called The Narrows, steep-sided in some places and impassable after heavy rains. At Los Cruzeros, under the sprawling sycamores, is another of the park's backpack camps.

Turn left, downstream, at Los Cruzeros, and walk on the dry, gravelly streambed or step from rock to rock over the water, depending on the season. At some points, even in summer, you have to climb up the banks and around large boulders because the water is too high to cross on the rocks.

Shortly beyond the tightest place in The Narrows, you emerge at the confluence of the Middle and East forks of Coyote Creek. Look for the beautiful and uncommon scarlet larkspur here. Just downstream are several fine swimming holes. But in late spring and early summer you can find many good and less crowded swimming holes back in The Narrows.

From here you retrace your steps uphill on the northwest bank toward Manzanita Point on the Coit Route. Take the left fork at the junction with the Cougar Trail from Poverty Flat, and go up through the manzanita forest. This 1.2-mile climb back to the trailhead at Camp 9 in the Manzanita Point Group Area gains 840', so allow a good hour to negotiate it, especially if you are carrying a backpack. From Camp 9 it is 0.2 mile to Camp 7, your starting point. If you continue to park headquarters, about 2½ miles farther on an easy grade, it takes another hour.

A giant oak on the slopes of Pine Ridge in Coe Park

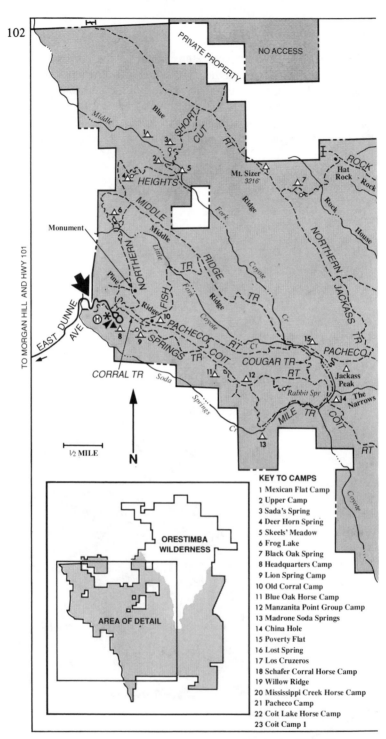

PRIVATE PROPERTY

NO ACCESS

TO MORGAN HILL AND HWY 101

Monument

EAST DUNNE AVE

CORRAL TR

½ MILE

N

ORESTIMBA WILDERNESS

AREA OF DETAIL

KEY TO CAMPS

1 Mexican Flat Camp
2 Upper Camp
3 Sada's Spring
4 Deer Horn Spring
5 Skeels' Meadow
6 Frog Lake
7 Black Oak Spring
8 Headquarters Camp
9 Lion Spring Camp
10 Old Corral Camp
11 Blue Oak Horse Camp
12 Manzanita Point Group Camp
13 Madrone Soda Springs
14 China Hole
15 Poverty Flat
16 Lost Spring
17 Los Cruzeros
18 Schafer Corral Horse Camp
19 Willow Ridge
20 Mississippi Creek Horse Camp
21 Pacheco Camp
22 Coit Lake Horse Camp
23 Coit Camp 1

Henry W. Coe

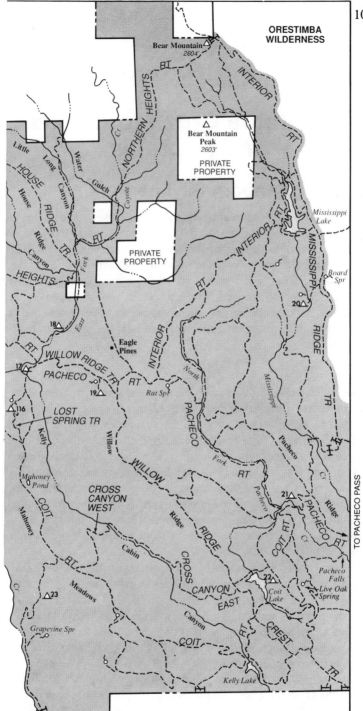

ORESTIMBA
WILDERNESS

Bear Mountain
2604'

Bear Mountain
Peak
2603'
PRIVATE
PROPERTY

Mississippi
Lake

Board
Spr

20△

PRIVATE
PROPERTY

NORTHERN HEIGHTS

INTERIOR RT

Little

Long Canyon

Water

Gulch

Coyote

House

HOUSE

RIDGE

TR

Ridge

Canyon

HEIGHTS

Eau

Fork

18△

17△

116△

19△

Eagle
Pines

WILLOW RIDGE TR

PACHECO

RT

RT

INTERIOR

North

Rat Spr

Mississippi

MISSISSIPPI

RIDGE

TR

PACHECO

Fork

LOST
SPRING TR

Kelly

Mahoney
Pond

COIT

Mahoney

RT

WILLOW

RT

WILLOW

RIDGE

CROSS
CANYON
WEST

Ridge

Cabin

CROSS

Meadows

23△

Cr

Grapevine Spr

CANYON

EAST

Pacheco

Pacheco Cr

21△

COIT RT

PACHECO

Ridge

RT

TO PACHECO PASS

Pacheco
Falls

Live Oak
Spring

22△

Coit
Lake

Canyon

Canyon

COIT

RT

CREST

TR

Kelly Lake

State Park

The Santa Cruz Mountains and Foothills

Sanborn-Skyline Park

The park's 3000+ acres extend up the heavily wooded canyons of the Santa Cruz Mountains west from Sanborn Road to the Skyline ridge, its steep hillsides cut by a number of year-round creeks. The park stretches for nearly seven miles along the east side of the ridge, from Castle Rock Park southeast through Lyndon Canyon. A southern corner of the park touches the El Sereno Open Space Preserve. Park headquarters, picnic areas, campgrounds and a hostel are concentrated off Sanborn Road near the park entrance.

History

For thousands of years this mountainside was frequented by Ohlone Indians, who came from their villages in the valley below to hunt deer and rabbits and gather wild blackberries, strawberries and seeds. The arrival of the Spaniards in the 18th century brought little change. The steep canyons and hills were not suited to cattle grazing and the land was not included in any Spanish land grant. After U.S. acquisition of California, land-hungry settlers came to the Bay Area, and this land was opened to homesteaders. Soon Swiss, Italian and German settlers from Alpine regions of Europe, who felt at home in these hills, were farming the slopes of what is now Sanborn-Skyline Park.

The work was hard—clearing, ploughing and planting orchards. There were vineyards and small wineries in every family's holdings. These farms were largely self-sufficient. The early farmers' names survive on creeks and roads— Bonjetti, Taudt (now Todd), McElroy. Kendall Clark Sandborn, an early settler, petitioned for improving a road to Lake Ranch. Although he left these parts soon after, his name remains on Sanborn Road (without the "d").

The demand for lumber to build rapidly growing San Francisco during the Gold Rush brought loggers to the groves of redwoods and

Douglas firs. Then came wood cutters, who marketed oak for firewood and tanbark for tanning leather. Large-scale lumbering, however, was over early in this century.

As the Santa Clara Valley was settled, these lands attracted families for excursions to the forests, orchards and mountain streams. Over the dirt roads, which crisscrossed the hills, they came on horseback and in wagons to fish, hunt and enjoy the flower-covered hills that we take such pleasure in to this day.

The great earthquake of 1906 struck the Sanborn-Skyline Park area, which is crossed by the San Andreas Fault, with great intensity. Cracks opened up in the ground 5 or 6 feet deep and as long as 100 feet. Though there were few houses here, the quake took its toll on the forests as trees were toppled and split. Spring flows were changed and landslides left cliffs as high as 40 feet. Chaparral and forest now conceal this destruction except from the trained eye of a geologist. The quake also shook down water tanks, all too vulnerable on their wooden foundations, and damaged wineries.

By the early 1900s many landholdings were consolidated. Judge James Welch, a Superior Court Judge of Santa Clara County, purchased the Lotti and McElroy lands. On this 800-acre estate he put up a lodge of redwood logs, which today serves as Welch-hurst, an attractive American Youth Hostel, included in the National Register of Historic Places. It was largely due to Judge Welch's efforts that Skyline Boulevard rights-of-way were acquired.

About this time the holdings of Taudt and Baille, and later Pourroy, were purchased by H.P. Dyer. He engaged a stone cutter to cut building blocks of local sandstone for his house. To safeguard his water supply from Sanborn Creek, Dyer bought Pourroy's holdings upstream. On his estate he cleared land around his house, planting orchards and vineyards. Santa Clara County bought Dyer's land in 1974. We now enjoy this handsome building as Sanborn-Skyline Park's headquarters and his orchard as the picnic grounds.

Meanwhile Judge Welch's family sold their place in 1950, and it changed hands again when Vernon J. Pick, who had made a fortune mining uranium, bought it. During Pick's tenure he tunneled into the hill to make an elaborate bomb shelter. However, he soon sold the land. In 1976 Santa Clara County purchased the piece.

A master plan for the park, under preparation at this writing, is evaluating trail design and use, which may result in new trails or different alignments. However, 8.4 miles of trail take hikers through forest and meadow, by streams and ponds.

Included in the park trails is the Skyline Trail, now a dedicated segment of the Bay Area Ridge Trail. This trail, for hikers and equestrians, follows the Skyline Scenic Corridor, providing important trail connections to parks and preserves to the north and on the west side of the Santa Cruz Mountains. This opens up backpacking possibilities for trips from the Welch-hurst hostel to the Skyline ridge and on to the chain of backpack camps extending to the coast. Northward, trails lead to the backpack camp on Monte Bello Ridge and to a trail down Black Mountain to the AYH hostel at Hidden Villa.

Jurisdiction   Santa Clara County.

Facilities   Headquarters and Youth Science Institute exhibits. Trails: hiking, self-guiding nature trail; equestrian, Skyline Trail only. Picnicking: family and group by reservation. Camping: 40 walk-in family sites, RV sites and youth-group site by reservation. Phone: 408-867-3654 or 408-358-3751. Youth hostel reservations: 408-741-0166. Fishing at Lake Ranch Reservoir, under State Fish and Game regulations.

Park Rules   Dogs on leash in picnic grounds and RV campgrounds. No dogs on trails or in walk-in campgrounds. Bicycles on paved trails only. Hours: 8 A.M. to ½ hour after sunset. Off-season hours as posted. Fees: $3/car, Saturdays, Sundays, holidays. Camping $3/night/car, walk-in sites; $3/night/second car; $6/RV site/night, $3/night/second car.

Welch-hurst, the judge's old lodge, is now a hostel in Sanborn-Skyline park

Maps Santa Clara County *Sanborn-Skyline Park;* USGS quads *Castle Rock Ridge, Cupertino.*

How To Get There From the town of Saratoga at the intersection of Saratoga-Sunnyvale and Saratoga-Los Gatos roads take Highway 9 for 2 miles west to Sanborn Road. Turn left and go 1 mile to park entrance. For the hostel, turn right at the AYH sign before the park entrance and follow the road 0.4 mile to the hostel.

Trip 1. Circle Hike to the Todd Creek Redwoods

A climb up the mountainside on the Sanborn and San Andreas trails takes you to a tall redwood grove on a creekside flat where ancient redwoods were cut.

Distance 4-mile loop.

Time 2 hours.

Elevation Gain 1200'

TRAIL NOTES

The Sanborn Trail leaves the west side of the picnic grounds, going uphill under redwoods on the service road through the walk-in campgrounds. You pass inviting camps scattered under the trees within the sound of Sanborn Creek.

After you leave the campgrounds the route crosses the creek, which cascades into the canyon below. Rounding an open slope of an old clearing, you pass a deer trail, where you often come across deer going down to the creek.

Soon you turn back into fir, madrone and maple woodlands. You will see grape vines left from an old family vineyard growing through the chaparral that edges the road. The road you have followed reaches a small flat and circles the site of an old house that once perched on this hillside.

From this point the broad road dwindles to a narrow, steep, rocky way where greasewood crowds the trail. After a few minutes' climb, though, a left turn (south) takes you back into a cool canyon where firs and tanoaks rise above a ground cover of wood ferns. From here a good trail winds up a ridge on an easy grade. You realize how far up the mountain you have come when you see the summer fog drifting over the heights of the Skyline ridge above and feel its cooling breezes.

A long switchback into a canyon and out takes you higher into the forest. Now on a delightful section of the trail, you find the woods are open and the path underfoot softened with the leaves of tanoak and madrone. The duff on the trail reflects the tree cover—pink and gold under madrones and buff under tanoaks. As you go north, the trail appears to fork. Keep left (south); the other trail is a shortcut over a steep, uncomfortable route.

Continuing up and around the ridge, you come to the San Andreas Trail, which has climbed south on the east side of Todd Creek. To reach the Todd Creek Redwoods, continue south on the Sanborn Trail, up a steep slope broken by many sandstone outcrops. The mountain falls away precipitously below the trail.

Just beyond the San Andreas Trail you will see the first of the redwoods that herald the Todd grove. The straight red-brown trunks become more numerous as you near Todd Creek. These second-growth trees are now 2–3' in diameter. Large stumps with young trees circling around them are signs of old logging.

In ¼ mile from the San Andreas Trail junction in a little flat crossed by the creek, we reach the largest of the Todd Creek Redwoods. We see 8–10' stumps of giant old trees that grew where water from the creek was most plentiful. This flat was once dominated by a dozen or so huge trees that had grown for thousands of years along the creek. The flat is now thickly grown with new redwoods and some of the Douglas firs that spring up after a forest is cleared. The creek banks are lined with giant chain fern. The creek, disrupted over a century ago by logging and still clogged with debris of broken limbs and fallen trees, is regaining its fern gardens and its mossy-rocked appearance. A few redwoods of considerable size lend dignity to the grove.

As you stop here, you can imagine the scene when loggers were felling trees in the 1800s. Redwoods were felled uphill to avoid splitting, then cut in 10–20' lengths. Chained together, teams of bulls dragged them down chutes along the creek to a mill, perhaps at Saratoga. You can see notches on the stumps, cut by lumberjacks to hold springboards on which they stood while sawing the trees. Lumbermen lived in a camp at the foot of McElroy Creek, but sometimes camped near this grove. Mules carried their supplies over trails you traveled on to get to this grove.

The Sanborn Trail continues uphill through the Todd grove to join the Skyline Trail, the route of the Bay Area Ridge Trail, in 0.3 mile. But to return to park headquarters you can make a loop back on the 1.8-mile San Andreas Trail. This trail may be re-routed upon completion of the park's master plan to avoid some eroded sections.

For now, retrace your steps to the trail junction. The San Andreas Trail goes on switchbacks down a ridge above Todd Creek. Your trail first leads under an airy forest canopy of young madrones where in summer the ground is golden from their leaf fall, then under dark-foliaged firs. Finally the trail descends a hill above the redwood-covered east bank of Todd Canyon. As your trail turns east, it enters the quiet of another redwood forest. Along the way you will see rings of redwood trees. Each ring, marking the site of an ancient tree, long crumbled to duff, is now circled by younger trees. Each young tree, cut in the last century, now in turn has an outer ring of third-generation trees around its stump.

Out of the redwoods the trail descends to a flat and turns east toward park headquarters. For 0.7 mile we go along old roads past the scene of early farming to reach a segment of the Nature Trail, which leads us back to headquarters, picnic grounds and parking lot.

Trip 2.   Level Walk to Lake Ranch Reservoir

On a short, level service road through the steep forested water-shed of Lake Ranch Reservoir you wind in and out of ravines to reach the reservoir that was once an important water source for the City of San Jose.

Distance   3 miles round trip.

Time   1½ hours.

Elevation Gain   Nearly level.

How To Get There   On Black Road go 4 miles west from Highway 17 or 1 mile east from Skyline Boulevard. At this writing there is room for a few cars by the gated park entrance, which must be kept clear, and room for a few cars in turnouts nearby. At present this road is the only public route to Lake Ranch. The extension of Sanborn Road from the main park entrance south to the reservoir is a private road.

TRAIL NOTES

This trail starts from Black Road near the park's south boundary on a service road used by the San Jose Water Company. Trees meet overhead on this level road, making it a cool walk in summer. Along the steep, forested slope, young firs predominate, but with a scattering of very large old firs. On small flats and ridges are oaks and madrones. Thimbleberry, creambush, ferns and wild blackberry form a pale-green understory. In steep ravines where streams tumble down rocky watercourses, small groves of redwoods thrive in the ample moisture, and shoulder-high giant chain ferns grow where they find underground water.

Lake Ranch Reservoir is an easy walk from Black Road

From a bend in the road you can see the dry, chaparral-covered hills on the far side of Lyndon Canyon. The road comes out at the reservoir's south end. New construction for bank protection and outflow pipes shows that this reservoir is still part of the Valley's water supply.

The reservoir, dammed at both ends, lies in a saddle between the drainage of Saratoga Creek to the north and that of Lyndon Canyon, flowing southeast into Lexington Reservoir. One should not be misled by the USGS topographic map showing the Lake Ranch Reservoir brimful of blue water. The present draw-down of water in summer leaves bare banks and murky green waters.

The San Andreas Rift Zone runs through the reservoir at the head of two narrow canyons. Earth movement here during the 1906 quake was violent. Present concern for the seismic safety of earth dams requires lower-than-designed-for water levels.

The road circles the east side of the reservoir toward the wider, higher dam at the far end, ⅓ mile away. There is no trail on the west side of the reservoir, where tree cover is heavy and banks steep. The southeast hillside above the lake, part of which is included in the park, is chaparral-covered—predominately chamise which turns bronze in summer. As you reach the far end of the reservoir, two dirt roads turn uphill. On a cool day you can walk up one in the sun for a view of the lake and its forest backdrop.

Shady flats at the north end of the reservoir are appealing on warm, sunny days. From the top of the earthen dam, where several spreading maples give you shade, there is a nice view out over the water. In a grove of tall live oaks west of the dam you will find some remnants of the ranch that was here years ago—fine stone foundations of an old winery, a stone-lined creek channel and fragments of farm machinery. After lingering in the pleasant shade by the reservoir, retrace your steps back to Black Road.

Trip 3. Loop Trip to Summit Rock and Bonjetti Creek

Climb Summit Rock, descend to homesteader Bonjetti's creek and an orchard in the canyon, and then take a side trip to a nearby knoll.

Distance 1.6-mile loop; additional 1.2-mile side trip to knoll.

Time 1 hour; add ½ hour for round trip to knoll.

Elevation Gain 400'

How To Get There From the Highway 35/9 intersection at Saratoga Gap, go 1½ miles southeast on Highway 35 to a turnout on the east side of the road. There is ample parking.

TRAIL NOTES

A loop trip down to Bonjetti Creek and back is good in any season, for the compacted road surface is not muddy in winter and the way is sheltered from winds. In spring, meadows are flowery and irises bloom in the woods. Apple trees blossom in May in the little orchard by the creek.

You start your trip following the old Summit Road route southeast on the well-marked Skyline Trail, also the route of the Bay Area Ridge Trail. You pass through a fir, oak and madrone forest typical of the mountains east of the Skyline ridge. Sunlight filters through the young fir trees to an understory of pale green, soft-leaved thimbleberry and prickly-stemmed roses. Here and there an old giant of a fir towers above the rest of the forest, its thick gray trunk 5' or so in diameter.

After ½ mile, at a trail junction, a well-worn path turns left off the Skyline Trail, leading to Summit Rock, a large outcrop of sandstone rising 20' or more above a little plateau. The dropoff on the valley side is alarmingly long. Eroded pits in the rocks make good handholds and footholds for the nimble climber to reach the top. From this vantage point you can look up and down the Santa Clara Valley.

After enjoying the views, retrace your steps to the junction where the Skyline Trail turns south along the ridgetop. Take the first trail left (the Summit Rock Loop Trail) down into the canyon of Bonjetti Creek, one of the wild canyons that furrow the east face of the Santa Cruz Mountains. Your trail, on an old wagon road, crosses a sloping meadow of bracken fern and—in spring a flowery grassland—to enter the shade of majestic firs. Trees 5–8' in diameter rise above a thick growth of younger firs. The cool depths of the canyon make this a good route on hot summer days. The old road rounds a ridge and comes out again on an open slope which slants down to Bonjetti Creek.

Our journey down this old wagon road takes us into the past when it reaches a small clearing on a flat, where an old apple orchard marks a long-abandoned homestead. A few large redwood stumps and some 100' tall redwoods are what is left of one of the groves of redwoods that punctuate the fir forest of the east slopes of the Santa Cruz Mountains along creeks where water is plentiful.

In May you could celebrate the blossoming apple trees with a lunch in the sun. When you are ready to move on, cross the stream at the lower end of the clearing to pick up the trail that leads 0.4 mile back to the Skyline Trail.

But a fine side trip from this little orchard is a 20-minute walk east to a knoll. Pick up a trail turning left from the sign TO SKYLINE TRAIL. A path goes through a corner of the overgrown apple orchard, then widens to an old ranch road on an easy grade that spirals up the knoll to reach its 2800' summit.

The road passes below a steep clearing on the left where a few old pecan trees cling to the slope, their nuts now harvested only by squirrels. To the right a young Douglas-fir forest clothes the hillside up to the Skyline ridge, and your route soon enters the edge of this forest. Finally the road turns through chaparral to the top of the knoll, probably the site of an old house, now overgrown with oaks.

Summit Rock has great views over Santa Clara Valley

To return to the Summit Rock Loop Trail retrace your steps to the last trail sign and go uphill, west. On this shady route through the forest, you climb a narrow ridge between cascading Bonjetti Creek on one side and a waterfall spilling over a 20'-high mossy rock on the other. In winter and spring, the sounds of cascade and waterfall are heard in counter point. Seeping springs keep banks fern-clad, and big-leaf maples flourish alongside the stream.

You soon meet the Skyline Trail, now also signed the Bay Area Ridge Trail, where it passes below the Skyline ridge. Turn right (north). In ¼ mile the trail rises to a flat ridgetop close to the highway, as you can hear from traffic sounds. Under black oaks and through small meadows, then through a fir forest, you walk for another ½ mile to rejoin the Summit Rock Loop Trail. The Skyline Trail bears left (northwest) and you continue on it back to the parking area.

Trip 4.   The Skyline Trail to Saratoga Gap

Follow the old wagon route along the ridge paralleling present-day Skyline Boulevard and today a dedicated segment of the Bay Area Ridge Trail, In the shade of madrone woods and fir forests you pass trails taking off to destinations in Sanborn-Skyline and Castle Rock parks.

Distance   6 miles one way.

Time   3 hours.

Elevation Gain   300'

Connecting Trails   Skyline to the Sea Trail west, Castle Rock trails west, Canyon Trail north.

Jurisdiction   (1) Sanborn-Skyline Park, Santa Clara County; (2) Castle Rock to Saratoga Gap, State of California.

Maps   Santa Clara County *Sanborn-Skyline Park;* USGS quads *Castle Rock Ridge* and *Cupertino;* Sempervirens Fund *Castle Rock to Big Basin* and *Trails to the West.*

Facilities   Hiking and equestrian trail. No water or restrooms.

Park Rules   Hours: 8 A.M. to ½ hour after sunset. No dogs on trails.

How To Get There

By Car   To reach the south end of the trail, drive about 5 miles southeast of Saratoga Gap on Highway 35 to Sanborn-Skyline Park's day use trailhead parking area, known as The Peak, on the east side of the road. There is also off-road parking space at the following access points to the trail: at Indian Rock Trail, Castle Rock, northern entrance to the Summit Rock Loop Trail and Saratoga Gap.

By Bicycle   There are bike lanes on Skyline Boulevard and a narrow, climbing lane on Highway 9 for experienced riders.

TRAIL NOTES

Although the scenic and recreation values of the Santa Cruz Mountains Skyline have long been recognized, the ambitious concept of a 100-mile recreation corridor from the Golden Gate Bridge to the Pajaro River has been carried out only in part. Santa Clara County plans for the Skyline have been realized to a large extent in the Skyline Trail, completed in the 1980s and now a dedicated segment of the Bay Area Ridge Trail.

Part of the trail is in Santa Clara County's Sanborn-Skyline Park, where the trail is open to hikers and equestrians. North of the park the trail goes through Castle Rock State Park. This section of the trail to Saratoga Gap is not a suitable route for horses. Bicyclists use Skyline Boulevard, which parallels the trail.

This trip is described from the trail's higher south end at Sanborn-Skyline Park's upper parking area. The trail climbs gradually for 2 miles to its highest point near Mt. Bielawski, gaining more than 300' in elevation, then slopes down to Saratoga Gap, 600' lower.

From the marked trail entrances where there is parking, you can do the Skyline Trail in short segments, or you can take the whole trip from one end to the other utilizing a car shuttle. With a longer car shuttle, you can leave the Skyline Trail and take the Sanborn Trail down into Sanborn-Skyline Park.

Begin your trip at The Peak, the day use trailhead parking area at the Skyline Trail's southern end, on the east side of Skyline Boulevard. A wooden county sign and the blue, red and white logo of the Bay Area Ridge Trail, point to the trail heading north on an old ranch road.

Your trail lies west of a grassy meadow under big black oaks. Rounding a bend, you walk through an abandoned pear orchard and come to the site of an old ranch residence. This originally belonged to a sea captain named Seagraves. The house is long gone, but among the domestic plantings to the right of the trail is a mighty oak, at least 6' in diameter. Its giant limbs, once trussed by cables, have now split, yet the tree lives on.

The trail now veers west and from several viewpoints you can look 25 miles south across the western flanks of the Santa Cruz Mountains to Monterey Bay. Farther along, the trail returns to Skyline Boulevard at a point where two picnic tables sit under the shade of a clump of redwoods behind a high stone wall, which suffered some damage in the earthquake of October 17, 1989. Through the old wall was the entrance, now blocked, to the Seagraves homesite.

When the trail forks just beyond here, keep to the upper one—the lower one deadends at a flat below the main trail. After the trail narrows, you pass through another abandoned orchard in an overgrown clearing. Back in the shelter of the woods, 10–25' sandstone boulders by the trail have been eroded to form niches roomy enough for small children to crawl into. The tree cover of multi-trunked madrones spreads a pink and yellow carpet of spent leaves on the trail in summer.

Around numerous bends and back into ravines, the trail continues through a quiet forest. After 1.8 miles from the starting point you make a wide swing away from Skyline Boulevard, round a bend and descend to the Sanborn Trail junction. From here it is only 0.3 mile down to the Todd Creek Redwoods. Second-growth trees now shade the little flat by the creek where giant redwoods were cut. (See Trip 1.)

At this trail junction the county park sign tells you that it is 1.9 miles to the Castle Rock Trail and another 2.0 miles to Saratoga Gap. The forest is deep here and the trail surface is covered with leaves and a light layer of duff—your feet fairly spring off the soft ground. In the tops of Douglas firs, some as much as 4' in diameter, Steller's jays call.

Continuing north on the Skyline Trail, you emerge into a clearing where you may find bright patches of goldenrod blooming beside the trail in the fall, and still a few magenta flowers of farewell-to-spring coming through the grass. Just west of Skyline Boulevard Mt. Bielawski rises to 3231', shielded from your view by the tall trees above your trail, which is only a few hundred feet below its summit. Eastward, the mountainside falls away steeply as your trail passes around the headwall of the canyon of McElroy Creek.

When the trail once again comes out near Skyline Boulevard, you will see a well-used trail going off into the tanoak-madrone forest heading up to Indian Rock. This outcrop, which rises 25–30' above the surrounding land, is a favorite of rock climbers and picnickers. On the north side the canyon drops off sharply, leaving a surprisingly precipitous rock face.

After your detour to Indian Rock, you soon come to the Castle Rock Trail crossing, where you could again depart from your route to hike on trails through Castle Rock to Saratoga Gap and Big Basin. However, if you keep to the Skyline Trail, you will soon descend to the junction from where the Summit Rock Loop Trail goes right, downhill, to reach Bonjetti Creek. This trail is described in Trip 3.

At the junction a prominent park sign points straight ahead to Saratoga Gap on the Skyline Trail, which generally follows the route

116

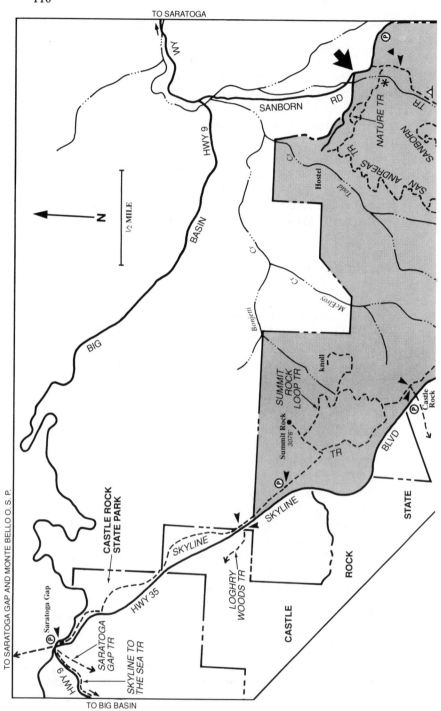

CONTINUED ON SMALLER MAP AT LEFT

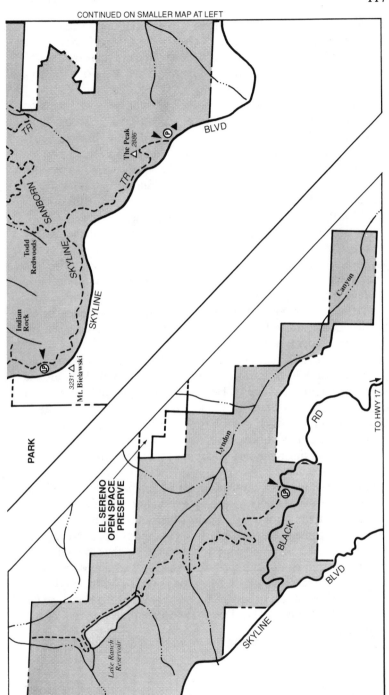

Sanborn-Skyline Park

of old Summit Road. The trail rises to the ridgetop, where small meadows alternate with groves of black oaks and madrones. There are signs of human habitation, too, along the way—the remains of a water tank, abandoned machinery. Not long ago a house stood on a knoll east of the trail.

Heading north on this stretch of the trail, you come to a junction with the north end of the Summit Rock Loop Trail. From this junction, Summit Rock and the start of the trail down to Bonjetti Creek are only a few minutes' walk away (see Trip 3). To continue on the Skyline Trail to Saratoga Gap, keep to the left through the forest. In 0.2 mile you emerge at a generous parking area which was left after a realignment of Skyline Boulevard. This parking area is the starting point for the Summit Rock Loop Trail to Bonjetti Creek.

The Skyline Trail/Ridge Trail continues just east of the parking area, going through the woods for ¼ mile to Skyline Boulevard, where you leave Sanborn-Skyline Park, cross a private drive and enter Castle Rock State Park. At this point, west across Skyline Boulevard the Loghry Woods Trail starts down to the Castle Rock Trail Camp. The Skyline Trail/Ridge Trail now descends below Skyline Boulevard to traverse the steep mountainside on a narrow path through the forest.

After veering east close to the Castle Rock Park boundary line, your trail turns back toward Skyline Boulevard and skirts around some fenced private property. Here the trail widens and you are now on the historic old Summit Road, traveled by wagons and early autos. The old toll-road station was at Saratoga Gap. More than forty years ago this part of the ridge was logged, and you will see signs of old logging roads and skid roads. Young firs are now growing up through the oaks.

For the last ⅓ mile you take a narrow footpath on a steep side slope, open to hikers only. Crossing several bridges built of wooden planks, you tread a route tight against the sandstone bank.

Soon you come to the parking area at Saratoga Gap, a staging area for many trails. Hikers and equestrians can go northward on the 7.6-mile Canyon Trail through the Saratoga Gap and the Monte Bello open-space preserves to Page Mill Road. Westward the Skyline to the Sea Trail heads down beside Highway 9 toward Big Basin and the coast and the Saratoga Gap Trail takes off south to the Castle Rock Trail Camp.

El Sereno Open Space Preserve

The mountain for which the preserve is named is the highest point on the ridge west of Los Gatos. The preserve's 1083 acres, lying at the south end of the Sierra Morena, extend almost to the cleft where Los Gatos Creek and Highway 17 cut through the Santa Cruz Mountains. Though the ridge is mostly chaparral covered, a few hardy live oaks are beginning to come up through the chaparral. Stands of oak, bay and tanoak trees fill the canyons.

Around the turn of the century the land was used for raising hay and grazing cattle and was regularly burned to eliminate chaparral growth. In the '40s a Bay Area industrialist bred horses on the site. Now this 2-mile-long MROSD Preserve is a part of the growing chain of green belts along both sides of the crest of the the Santa Cruz Mountains.

The preserve has about 4 miles of dirt roads that traverse the ridgeline. These roads, now used for patrolling the park and servicing the powerlines, act as firebreaks and make fine, wide hiking, riding and bicycling trails. Even in winter their surface is firm, though not paved. This is a place to enjoy on bright, sunny days in winter and spring or in late afternoons of summer and fall.

Jurisdiction   Midpeninsula Regional Open Space District.
Facilities   Undeveloped except for 4 miles of trails.
Preserve Rules   Open from dawn to dusk. No dogs, guns or fires.
Maps   MROSD *El Sereno;* USGS quads *Castle Rock Ridge* and *Los Gatos.*
How To Get There   From Highway 17 near Lexington Dam turn west on Montevina Road. At the end of the road, where signs mark the preserve entrance, there is a steep, roughly surfaced roadside shoulder for limited parking.

Hike to the Meadow

A wide, south-facing trail skirts the high plateau above Los Gatos and Saratoga, ending at a sloping meadow edged with spreading oaks and brightened by wildflowers in spring.
Distance   5 miles round trip.
Time   3 hours.
Elevation Loss   960'

TRAIL NOTES

From the preserve entrance the trail climbs along the spine of the ridge above Lyndon Canyon, which lies in the San Andreas Fault Zone. Looking out over this steep canyon on a clear day, you can see the Pacific Ocean over the tops of the forested western flanks of the Santa Cruz Mountains. Nearby you look down on Lexington Reservoir, where brightly colored sailboats and windsurfing craft dot the waters.

In less than ½ mile, as the trail goes through a clump of oaks and madrones, you make a right turn and start a traverse along the flanks of El Sereno. After a couple of switchbacks the trail turns sharply east. Here on a windblown shelf, you can see the bench marks made when the land was surveyed. Three points are set out in triangular form on this high hill. However, you will not need a land survey to recognize the familiar landmarks of the South Bay—the giant hangars at Moffett Field, the salt ponds along the Bay, the black Pruneyard towers and the distinctive forms of the Diablo Range from Mission Peak to Mt. Hamilton. Southeastward stretches the Sierra Azul, with the tops of Mt. Thayer and Mt. Umunhum most visible.

Now the trail begins a gradual descent along the side of Trout Creek canyon. With its headwaters in the preserve, this creek flows southeast to empty into Los Gatos Creek just below Lexington Dam. Its banks are densely wooded, making good cover for the deer who freely roam the ridge and its canyons.

About 2 miles from the entrance the trail makes a hairpin turn. After this turn watch for an opening in the bushes where a trail leads off to your left (not to be confused with the gated trail 20 feet west). This trail to the meadow is edged with small-leaved scrub oak and the white-flowered ceanothus known as deer brush. In a very short time you reach a sloping, grassy meadow where you can sit and enjoy the views. At its lower edge are several fine oaks whose spreading branches reach the ground, forming perfect perches for picnickers. Golden poppies, purple owl's clover and deep-blue brodiaea come up through the meadow grasses.

You may note a 4–5′ band of nearly bare ground skirting the grassland at the edge of the chaparral. Experiments at Stanford's Jasper Ridge Biological Preserve have shown that this band is not due, as some had thought, to a sterilizing effect of the chaparral. It is, rather, due to the nibbling of small creatures—field mice, shrews, voles—that make their home in the chaparral. They venture out only a short way from the safety of their cover. From the number of hawks often circling over the meadow, you can see this is a life-saving precaution.

In summer and early fall try this meadow for an early supper so you can enjoy the view and make the uphill return trip in the cool of evening.

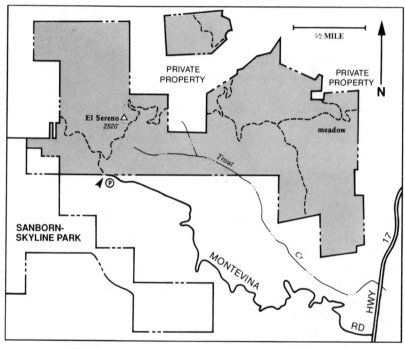

El Sereno Open Space Preserve

St. Joseph's Hill Open Space Preserve

This 270-acre site adjoining the Town of Los Gatos was formerly part of the Jesuit Novitiate. The dominant feature of the site is St. Joseph's Hill, a grassy knoll on the east boundary. The preserve lies between the Santa Clara County parklands around Lexington Reservoir and those of the Town of Los Gatos, thus forming an open-space corridor between the north and south sections of the Santa Cruz Mountains.

Jurisdiction   MROSD
Facilities   Trails for hikers, runners and bicyclists
Preserve Rules   Open from dawn to dusk. Dogs allowed on leash.
Maps   MROSD *St. Joseph's Hill Open Space Preserve,* USGS quad *Los Gatos.*
How To Get There   Take Highway 17 south from Los Gatos, turn left to Lexington Reservoir at Alma Bridge Road. Continue to designated parking areas.

Loop Trip to the Hilltop and Back by the Creek

A favorite of runners and bicyclists, this trip reaches a knoll above Lexington Reservoir, then follows the route of an old water flume to Los Gatos and returns on the Los Gatos Creek Trail.
Distance   5-mile loop.
Time   2–3 hours.
Elevation Gain   600'
TRAIL NOTES

From roadside parking on Alma Bridge Road, turn uphill on a gated road across from the boat launching ramp and begin climbing on a rough and rocky pavement. Glowing through the dry summer grasses are great drifts of magenta clarkia (farewell-to-spring) . As you climb, a chorus of birdsong greets you from the tall eucalyptus below the trail and from a mixed oak and chaparral hillside on your left. Through openings in these woods you look west to the steep slopes of El Sereno Open Space Preserve. From below, the noise of Highway 17 rises, but as you drop into a shady ravine filled with bays and oaks, the sound fades.

You are traversing Santa Clara County parklands almost until you reach a fork in the trail. Then you are in the MROSD preserve. At the fork a sign offers two destinations: the Jones Trail to Los Gatos or the climb to St. Joseph's Hill. Choosing St. Joseph's Hill, you turn right, uphill, to follow the service road along a cyclone fence. Through the fence you see the terraces where once-thriving vineyards produced the grapes from which the Novitiate wines were made. No longer in wine production, this north half of the preserve is under a MROSD and Town of Los Gatos open-space easement, but off-limits to the public at this writing.

The trails here, wide service roads, circle the preserve, and all eventually lead to a 1253' grassy knoll, the summit of the preserve. Following the fenceline trail, you come to two roads that take off right. Take the second one, which reaches a bare flat midway up the hill, leveled off years ago for a rifle range. A single oak tree is rising above the chaparral that surrounds the flat.

From this flat the views open up, but if you continue to the top of St. Joseph's Hill, you will have commanding views out to San Francisco Bay, across the canyon to El Sereno, northwest to forest-clad ridges of the northern Santa Cruz Mountains and south to the lake behind Lexington Dam. East lies the Sierra Azul Open Space Preserve, dominated by the broad, sparsely vegetated flanks of Mt. Umunhum.

On the way down, retrace you steps to the first turnoff below the top and turn right for a different route to the road along the fence

**The Jones Trail skirts an oak grove
in St. Joseph's Hill Open Space Preserve**

line, then go downhill, left, to the main trail. Here, turn right to take the Jones Trail, which follows an historic stage route that once connected Los Gatos with the towns of Lexington and Alma. Both these towns were flooded when Lexington Reservoir was built in 1952.

The Jones Trail traverses the extremely steep hillside above Los Gatos Creek, alternating between woods of oak and bay trees and chaparral where lavender pennyroyal and purple nightshade edge the trail. At a grove of widely spaced, large oaks, you veer left past tree-sized, red-trunked manzanita. Signs warn of steep side slopes and a narrow trail. No horses are allowed beyond here. Bicyclists and pedestrians must walk in the "Walking Zone", a narrow, 0.3-mile downhill stretch.

However, a slow pace will allow trail users to appreciate this most beautiful section of the trail. It skirts narrow, precipitously sheer ravines and crosses intermittent streambeds lined with ferns and bright with shade-loving flowers in spring.

This section of the trail, with its steep side slopes and narrow tread, follows the precarious route of an old wooden flume that used to carry water to Los Gatos and San Jose. The remnants of this flume were removed when the trail was built, but a section of flume is installed in the local museum.

When you leave the "Walking Zone", you enter the Novitiate Park at the edge of Los Gatos. The trail skirts the upper side of a meadow surrounded by forest, and then exits at Jones Road, in Los Gatos. There is no parking here, so return to your starting point or have a car shuttle waiting at a public parking lot off Main Street in town.

However, to make the loop trip, continue down Jones Road through residential neighborhoods to Main Street and turn west. Just before crossing the bridge over Highway 17, look for the Los Gatos Creek Trail entrance on the left. Follow this trail 1.7 miles upstream to Lexington Dam and back to your car. (See Los Gatos Creek Trail, Trip 3.)

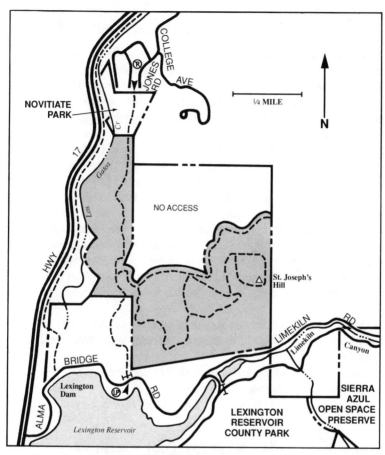

St. Joseph's Hill Open Space Preserve

Sierra Azul Open Space Preserve

The Spaniards called the southern half of the Santa Cruz Mountains the Sierra Azul. In 1983 the Midpeninsula Regional Open Space District chose this name for its collection of preserves in the Sierra Azul's northern section. At this writing the 8351-acre preserve comprises three areas; Kennedy Limekiln Area, which includes trails accessible from the east side of Lexington Reservoir and from Kennedy Road east of Los Gatos; the Cathedral Oaks Area, not yet open to the public; and the Mt. Umunhum Area, where, except for two trails on the east flank, access is not yet secure.

Within the areas open to the public, unsurfaced roads make wide trails to the preserve's high ridges. As the district augments its holdings, it expects to secure property or trail easements to join the scattered areas of the Sierra Azul Open Space Preserve. Described here are two trips to ridgetops on the west and north flanks of the Sierra Azul in the Kennedy Limekiln Area and two short hikes to destinations on the north side of the Mt. Umunhum Area.

Jurisdiction Midpeninsula Regional Open Space District.
Facilities Undeveloped, except for hiking, equestrian and bicycling trails.
Preserve Rules Open dawn to dusk. No dogs on trails.
Maps MROSD *Sierra Azul, Limekiln Kennedy Area* and *Mt. Umunhum Area*, USGS quads *Los Gatos, Santa Teresa Hills.*

Trip 1.   **The Kennedy Trail Ascent of**
                     the North Slopes

An 1800-foot climb from Kennedy Road to the heights of the Sierra Azul rewards you with sweeping views, shady canyons and a delightful picnic site halfway to the top.
Distance 7 miles round trip to fork in trail.
Time 4 hours.
Elevation Gain 1800'
How To Get There From Highway 17 take the East Los Gatos exit to Los Gatos Boulevard. Turn north and in 0.2 mile turn right on Kennedy Road. Go 2 miles to Top of the Hill Road. Entrance to the Kennedy Road Area is across the street from this intersection, where curbside parking is available.

TRAIL NOTES

This area was part of the Rinconada land grant, later owned by a Mrs. Mahoney. When the City of Los Gatos needed water for its growing population, it tapped the streams of this mountainside, but the supply was neither dependable nor plentiful. In the 1940s a road was built, now the Kennedy Trail. A camellia nursery operated at the foot of the mountain. Subdivisions were talked of, including a 200-home scheme, but the lack of a good water supply and the steep road grade finally led its investors to abandon the idea. The unsurfaced road to the former subdivision makes a wide, though sometimes exposed, trail to the heights of the preserve.

On the west side of Kennedy Road look for cement gateposts marking a driveway. Immediately beyond, go over the hiker-equestrian stile in the split-log rail fence to a dirt road going uphill through an old walnut and apricot orchard. You will see the MROSD preserve map and Wildlands sign with its familiar logo and symbols inviting hikers and horsemen but barring dogs and motor vehicles.

From here you climb steadily but gradually on an east-facing slope to walk into the first of several deep canyons. As you enter the cool shade of oaks and bays, the sound of rushing water comes to you in winter and spring.

After a few more turns around the slopes you come to another ravine with a stream still running as late as June. These intermittent watercourses dry up by late summer, but their canyons offer cooler temperatures all year.

Now you head due east again, coming out in chaparral country. Many plants of the chaparral bloom in summer after spring wildflowers have faded and gone. Chamise, that small-leaved, scrubby bush that covers so much of this hillside, produces small, creamy clusters of flowers on the ends of its branches in June and July. Yerba santa bears pale purple, trumpet-shaped blossoms on its 6–8′ stems. And all along this trail you will find the profusely blooming, apricot-colored sticky monkey flower clinging to the banks. After several rainy years its blossoms are spectacular, lasting late into fall.

In less than two hours you come to a natural bench in the mountainside where the trail enters a lovely oak forest. This flat is a good place to stop for a picnic under the trees. Leading off from your trail is a network of old side roads in the forest, laid out for a subdivision that never materialized. In small grassy clearings Indian warriors, Douglas iris and lupines bloom where the light reaches them.

To continue, you climb through a heavily wooded hillside graced by more oaks and madrones. The trail now alternates between chaparral and woodland as it rises to the 2400' level. From these heights are views in all directions. Due east and almost right below you on Los Capitancillos Ridge is Almaden Quicksilver Park. South of that ridge rise the flanks of Mt. Umunhum, Mt. Thayer and El Sombroso, where separated holdings of MROSD may some day be connected to this trail. The north half of the Santa Cruz Mountains, the Sierra Morena, stretches as far as the eye can see.

Veering sharply east across the spine of the ridge, you then descend to a fork in the trail. Take the right-hand trail to continue west and downhill to reach the shores of Lexington Reservoir. (See Trip 2). However, if you don't have a car shuttle waiting, turn back at the fork. You can make the easy downhill trip in about one hour and a half.

Trip 2. A Climb to Priest Rock and the Ridgetops Above Limekiln Canyon

Climbing a winding service road on a ridge between Limekiln and Soda Spring canyons takes you from Lexington Reservoir toward the heights of Mt. Thayer.

Distance   6½ miles round trip.

Time   3½ hours round trip.

Elevation Gain   1300'

How To Get There   From Highway 17 about 2½ miles south of Los Gatos turn east at Lexington Dam onto Alma Bridge Road. Follow it around the reservoir and across the bridge over an inlet from Limekiln Canyon until you come to the second green metal gate on the left. There is space for a few cars off the road.

TRAIL NOTES

This is a trip for the cool weather of crisp fall days or sunny spring days. Most of the chaparral-clad ridge has only occasional trees and is hot in summer.

Crawl through or over the green metal gate and take the service road—which we will now call a trail—uphill. The first mile of this trip traverses lands leased from the Santa Clara Valley Water District by the Santa Clara County Parks and Recreation Department for its Lexington Reservoir Park. The trail climbs a steep hillside, winding through an oak forest with an understory of toyon, manzanita and buckbrush. As you go up, you can, for a time, look directly down through the trees to Lexington Reservoir. When the spring wildflowers are in bloom, you will find blossoms of purple brodiaea and clumps of Douglas iris. In summer graceful, creamy white flower heads of ocean spray hang over the trail.

A shady oak grove on Reynolds Road Trail

The path now rises more steeply over chaparral-covered hillsides. When you come to a gate and an equestrian stile, you are on MROSD property. Then 1½ miles from the trailhead the trail bends sharply and comes to a brushy hilltop where a craggy outcrop, Priest Rock, stands above the manzanitas on the left of the trail. From here at an elevation of 1762' you can see south down into Soda Spring Canyon. On the other side of the ridge is Limekiln Canyon, on the sides of which you can see the scars of quarrying.

From here the trail stays on the ridgetop, heading east. Shortly there is a four-way "crossroads" where our service road/trail meets a trail coming up from Soda Spring Canyon and another from Limekiln Road. Both these trails can be explored to the edge of district property, although the north one may be overgrown in places. Our trail continues on the ridge for 1½ miles to join the Kennedy Road Trail at an elevation of 2628'. If you turn back here, the return trip is all downhill.

North beyond the Kennedy Road Trail junction is the trail described in Trip 1. Southeast are many separate tracts of MROSD land which may eventually link this Kennedy Limekiln Area with the Mt. Umunhum Area. At this writing, you can make a 9½-mile loop trip by turning southeast on the Kennedy Road Trail and returning on the service road along the south-facing slopes above Soda Spring Canyon.

To make this loop, turn southeast (right) at the Priest Rock/Kennedy Road Trail junction and follow this ridgecrest trail for 1½ miles to the present District boundary. Turn sharply right here on the powerline service road. Continue on this P.G.& E. service road along the sides of Soda Spring Canyon for 2½ miles. You rejoin the Priest Rock Trail just ½ mile east of the rock.

Trip 3.   On the Lower Slopes of El Sombroso

A short climb along an old farm road leads to a grove of evergreen oaks at the preserve boundary.

Distance   2 miles round trip.

Time   1 hour.

Elevation Gain   400'

TRAIL NOTES

To reach this 109-acre parcel southwest of San Jose, take Hicks Road south from Camden Avenue, following Guadalupe Creek as it meanders in a tree-covered corridor below the Guadalupe Reservoir. At the corner of Arnerich and Hicks roads is the restored Guadalupe Mine School House, built in the 1880s when the quicksilver mines were flourishing on the slopes north of the road. Restored in the 1980s, it now boasts a cinnabar red trim on a tawny gold base, reproducing the color of the mercury-bearing ore and the gold that brought fame and fortune to owners of the Almaden Mines. These tones are seen today in the rocks underfoot and the grasslands beside the trails in Almaden Quicksilver Park.

Past the school house and before reaching the Guadalupe Dam, look for an unmarked road on your right. (Reynolds Road on the map). Heading immediately uphill, you pass a row of mailboxes on the right, but the main road curves left. Continue around several zigzags until you reach an opening in a rustic fence with the MROSD wildlands sign just beyond. No motor vehicles are allowed beyond this point, so park under the oaks beside the road.

Now set out on the unpaved farm road, your trail, past an olive orchard on the left and around a knoll, beyond which sits a charming farm with house and barns set under old, wide-branched oaks. Enjoy the rustic site, but honor its privacy and continue uphill, taking time to gaze at the distant, tall peaks of the southern Diablo Range and the more rounded Los Capitancillos Hills just across the canyon.

Pass the side roads taking off left and continue right, south, climbing gradually . You may notice an old water tank among the trees at road's edge as you ascend under a canopy of buckeyes, oaks and a few maples. You reach a fork in the road and turn left. Just beyond here the preserve ends in a sheltering clump of oaks. This is a pleasant place to relax before retracing your steps downhill. On a summer's eve, enjoy the twinkling lights as they come on in the twilight settling over the valley. As you descend, contemplate the possibility of trail connections from El Sombroso through this parcel to Almaden Quicksilver Park. Such a trail would add another link in the Bay Area Ridge Trail along the ridges and hilltops of the South Bay.

Trip 4. Bald Mountain Ramble

This nearly level trail takes you to a grassy knoll overlooking the crest of the Santa Cruz Mountains and across to the heights of the Diablo Range.

Distance   3 miles round trip.

Time   1½ hours.

Elevation Gain   Nearly level.

How To Get There   In southwest San Jose, take Hicks Road south from Camden Avenue. South of the Guadalupe Reservoir turn west (uphill) on Mt. Umunhum/Loma Almaden Road. This road immediately veers left just after the turnoff and continues past a

View from Reynolds Road Trail
to Los Capitancillos Ridge and the Almaden Valley

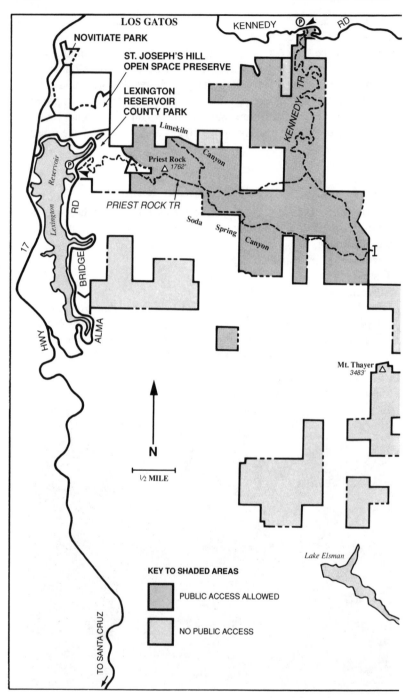

Sierra Azul

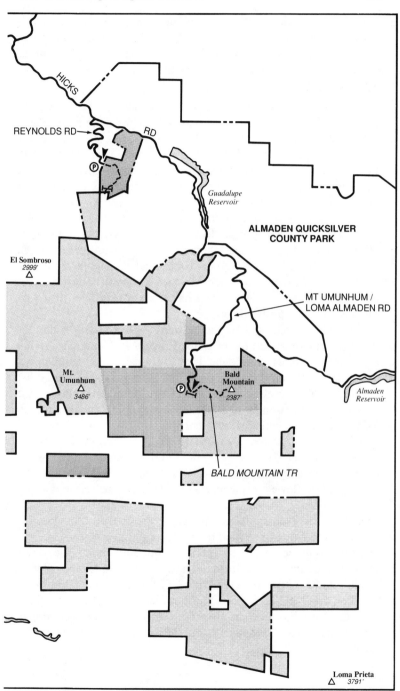

HICKS

REYNOLDS RD

RD

Ⓟ

*Guadalupe
Reservoir*

**ALMADEN QUICKSILVER
COUNTY PARK**

El Sombroso
2999'
△

MT UMUNHUM /
LOMA ALMADEN RD

Mt.
Umunhum
△
3486'

Bald
Mountain
Ⓟ △
2387'

*Almaden
Reservoir*

BALD MOUNTAIN TR

Loma Prieta
△ *3791'*

Open Space Preserve

hand-painted sign declaring it a private road. MROSD has access rights to the preserve over this road, but visitors should stay on the road, using only the trail to Bald Mountain at this time. In 2½ miles park off the road at an MROSD gate.

TRAIL NOTES

The trail to Bald Mountain, a wide fire road temporarily barred by a mound of earth, leaves the left side of Mt. Umunhum Road. Past a MROSD sign you head east on this trail which traverses a south-facing mountainside just below its 2300′ crest. There is very little tree cover, but tall chaparral shrubs overhang both sides of the trail. Although quite hot on a midsummer day, this protected trail is warm on a sunny day in winter.

A few sycamores are flourishing on the downslope, probably nourished by hidden springs. The deep canyon on your right drops off abruptly and you can see where its drainage joins Herbert Creek, which then flows east through more steep-sided canyons around the prow of Bald Mountain to reach Almaden Reservoir. These canyons are filled with stands of bay and oak trees, which also crowd the ravines on the opposite ridges.

Dominating your view on the outward leg of this trip is the flattened, antenna-covered top of Loma Prieta. Mt. Umunhum (Indian for humming bird), surmounted by its formidable, multi-storied structure, looms on the skyline on your return. Between these two peaks, two of the highest in the Santa Cruz Mountains, runs a ridge, almost as high, forming a protective rampart for the Santa Clara Valley against incoming storms and winds.

When the authors took this hike in late June, spring wildflowers— purple brodiaea, orange poppies, yellow daisies and magenta clarkia, were still blooming beside the trail. At the same time, the creamy white flowers of chaparral plants, chamise and toyon, perfumed the air.

Just before reaching the grass-covered top of Bald Mountain you cross a saddle through which the breeze can blow stiffly, once you are out from the lee of the hill. As the trail circles the mountaintop,views open up north and east to a trio of Santa Clara County foothill parks—Almaden Quicksilver, Calero and Santa Teresa.

When you have identified other familiar landmarks of the South Bay, the East Bay and the southern Santa Clara Valley, continue around the top of the mountain and then retrace your steps back to your car.

Almaden Quicksilver Park

Almaden Quicksilver Park, more than 3500 acres, takes in most of the 6-mile-long Los Capitancillos Ridge in the lower Santa Cruz Mountains, the site of the once-most-productive quicksilver mine in the world. Today on 25 miles of trails, following old roads that lead to the mines, hikers and horsemen can explore these lovely hills and imagine New Almaden's heyday when miles of tunnels pierced the hills and more than 500 houses clustered on the ridge.

On the oak-dotted ridge mine tunnels and shafts are now closed off, and at the main park entrance the furnaces of the New Almaden Quicksilver Mining Company have long since been dismantled. English Town, Spanish Town and a Chinese camp where miners lived are gone. But the hills are still strewn here and there with mine dumps. Studies by the State are underway to determine whether hazards remain in the park from mercury mining and what, if any, steps for remediation are needed.

The cinnabar ore in these hills attracted Indians long before the coming of the Spanish in the 18th century. They travelled from as far as the Columbia River to get the red ore they used to paint their bodies. A well-worn trail along Guadalupe Creek led from the Ohlone villages near the Bay to a shallow cave on top of the hill where the ore was visible.

As early as 1824 Antonio Suñol of San Jose, looking for gold in these hills, found red ore, but it was not until 1845 that a Mexican cavalry officer and engineer, Andres Castillero, filed a mining claim to this deposit, and still later the red ore was confirmed as mercury-producing cinnabar. Meanwhile, the Mexican Governor of California had made grants of two ranches on these hills, one on each side of the ridge, with boundary descriptions so vague as to give rise to violent disputes and years of litigation.

Castillero returned to Mexico, where he met Alexander Forbes, who acquired part of his interest in the mine. Forbes came to California and brought Mexican miners to construct mine workings. He named the mine "New Almaden" after the famous quicksilver mine in Spain and formed the New Almaden Quicksilver Mining Company.

When the discovery of gold in California greatly increased the demand for quicksilver, which was used in the reduction of gold ore, mine operations expanded. Miles of tunnels were built and giant ore-reduction furnaces constructed. The reduction works, known as the "Hacienda" (from one of the Spanish meanings of the term), were built at the foot of the hill near the present entrance to today's park.

By 1851 two mines were in operation in addition to the New Almaden—the Enriquita and the Guadalupe, northeast along the ridge. In 1854 the manager, Henry Halleck, began construction of La Casa Grande, a building of 27 rooms and 3 stories, originally planned as a hotel, but used as the manager's house. A village of cottages for the staff was built along Alamitos Creek. A Spanish Town for Mexicans and an English Town for Cornish miners were perched high on the hill near the mines. For a short time there was also a Chinese Camp.

New Almaden became a tourist attraction bringing eminent visitors, including an emissary from the emperor of China, who came seeking purchases of quicksilver. The emperor, pleased by the reception of his emissary, sent back an eight-sided pagoda, which stood on La Casa Grande grounds until 1920. Pillars from the tea house can be seen at the New Almaden Quicksilver Museum.

By 1870 production at the mine had peaked, but under a new manager, James Randol, mining methods were improved and new bodies of ore found at the Randol shaft, sunk at some distance from the other mines. After Randol left in 1892, the fortunes of the company declined again and by 1912 it was in bankruptcy.

Under different management the Senator Mine at the north end of the ridge, put into operation with modern reduction equipment, produced through 1926, the last large-scale production.

During the Depression the Civilian Conservation Corps demolished nearly all the early structures in a program to reduce hazards. Not a single cottage in English Town or Spanish Town remains. The two churches on Mine Hill are gone.

After a brief period of operation during World War II, the mine was shut down and the last furnace was dismantled. Although an 8-year study by the U.S. Geological Survey showed that there is still the possibility of finding ore at New Almaden, mining has ceased.

In 1974 Santa Clara County purchased 3598 acres of the mine area for a park. New Almaden is now listed as a Historic District in the National Register of Historic Places. The community of New Almaden has been placed under a County Historic Zoning District so that the integrity of this more-than-a-century-old village is protected.

Now at the main park entrance a ranger's office is in place. Here also a reconstruction of the old mine office will some day house an interpretive center.

A New Almaden Quicksilver County Park Association, a group formed in 1983, supports the protection, restoration and development of this unique site. It sponsors work parties to maintain trails and stages events to encourage community involvement in projects to benefit the park. The association conducts van tours in the park to places of special interest and into restricted areas open only on such tours. Guides familiar with the history of the fabled English Town and Spanish Town bring alive for you the park's lively past. You will hear details of the mercury mining operations. There are also occasional docent-led hiking or horseback trips up canyons to famous mining sites. For information write P.O. Box 124, New Almaden, CA 95042.

The county's New Almaden Mercury Mining Museum at 21570 Almaden Road has displays of mining equipment, models, maps and photographs which give you some grasp of the astounding scale of mining operations at New Almaden. Exhibits of household furnishings, clothing and a collection of photographs of the vanished settle-

"English Town" housed hundreds of Cornish miners and their families in the mines' heyday

ments bring to life the busy community of the late 19th century. Hours: 1 to 4 P.M. Saturday.

Twenty-five miles of trails over the hills of Almaden Quicksilver Park provide easy walks of a few miles and vigorous climbs of 10 miles or more across the 1700' summit of the ridge. For the hiker this park offers trail routes that take him quickly away from the urban scene to secluded woods and to restful vistas of the Santa Cruz Mountains. The park has long been popular with horsemen, and more recently with runners, who find the hillside trails just right for training and for competitive runs.

Of the three entrances to Almaden Quicksilver Park for the hiker, the north entrance at McAbee Road leads to a better choice of trails and to a greater variety of terrain. The Mine Hill Trail is the only one leaving the New Almaden Road entrance on the south. Although the Hacienda Trail does turn off from the Mine Hill Trail after a short way, its alignment is steep and its surface eroded in many places.

The Mockingbird Hill entrance, an equestrian staging area, offers convenient parking for the Hacienda Trail, which gains 500 feet in elevation in ¾ mile on what is dubbed "Cardiac Hill." Although this climb will not seriously affect a walker in good condition, the steepness is uncomfortable. However,this entrance also provides access for hikers to the New Almaden Trail, a route that takes off from the southwest corner of the parking lot. This pleasant path, for hikers only, follows the contours north for six miles along the lower part of the ridge, joining the Mine Hill Trail near the McAbee Road entrance. The trail goes in and out of canyons, now and then emerging on sunny meadows, traversing wooded hills without making the kind of climbs found on most of the other trails in the park.

Jurisdiction   Santa Clara County.

Facilities   Trails: hiking, equestrian. Park office at the main entrance on Almaden Road—"La Hacienda". Equestrian staging area, restrooms and the only potable water in the park at Mockingbird Hill Road entrance.

Park Rules   Open from 8 A.M. to ½ hour past sunset. Dogs on leash only. No bicycles.

Maps   Santa Clara County *Almaden Quicksilver Park;* USGS quads *Los Gatos, Santa Teresa Hills.*

How To Get There

By Car   (1) Main entrance: Take the Almaden Expressway to Almaden Road and go 1½ miles on Almaden Road to the park

entrance on the west side of the road. (2) Mockingbird Hill
equestrian staging area: From the end of Almaden Expressway go
on Almaden Road 0.3 mile and turn right on Mockingbird Hill
Lane to the park entrance at its end. (3) McAbee Road entrance:
From Almaden Expressway turn southwest on Camden Avenue,
then west on McAbee Road to its end. Roadside parking only.

By Bicycle An off-road bike path runs beside Almaden Road
from Santa Teresa Boulevard to within a mile of the Mockingbird
Hill entrance.

By Bus County Transit 64 to main park entrance.

Trip 1.   Mine Hill Trail

Climb the old wagon road past the site of New Almaden Mine and
the miners' settlements on Los Capitancillos Ridge toward the mines
at its north end.

Distance 6.5 miles one way.
Time 3½ hours one way. (Requires car shuttle.)
Elevation Gain 1200'

TRAIL NOTES

On the way to the main park entrance you pass the community of
New Almaden, a row of cottages along Alamitos Creek. This village,
which once housed staff of the mine, is described in a periodical of
1854 as ". . . a little hamlet of a row of neat houses, enclosed with
a paling fence, containing in front a small flower garden with
shrubbery." Also remaining from New Almaden's heyday is La Casa
Grande, once the superintendent's home and currently a restaurant
and playhouse. Next to the park entrance was the massive ore-
reduction works called the Hacienda, which have been dismantled.

Aside from the absence of these works, our trip up the hill cannot
be greatly different from a journey on a road somewhat west of the
Mine Hill Trail, taken by Mrs. S.A. Downer in the 19th Century. She
wrote in the magazine Pioneer in 1854, "Around the side winds the
road, constructed at immense cost and labor for the transportation of
the ore from the mountains to the Hacienda below . . . the road,
winding and turning up the mountainside, disclosed new beauties at
every foot of distance."

As you climb the road now in the spring, the hillsides are covered
with brodiaea, lupine, Indian paintbrush, shooting stars and milkmaids. The old road is an easy grade for walking. From the park
entrance, woods shade much of the way up the hill, making this a
comfortable trip on any but the hottest days. In ¼ mile you pass the

**The huge mercury-reduction works, called the Hacienda,
stood at what is now the park entrance from Almaden Road**

Hacienda Trail, then continue your winding way to Capehorn Pass, a
saddle at an elevation of 1000 feet. Here is a crossroads, where the
Randol Mine Trail and a short connection north to the Hacienda
Trail take off.

The Mine Hill Trail continues uphill on the way to settlements
where Cornish, Mexican and Chinese miners once lived. The well-
weathered banks of the old road become flower gardens in spring.
Some sections of roadside below English Town, kept moist by
springs above, blossom into delightful herbaceous borders—yellow
yarrow, blue larkspur, purple brodiaea, with accents of scarlet
Indian paintbrush against a background of delicate white flowers of
4' tall Queen Anne's lace.

After an easy walk of an hour we pass the gated entrance to
English Town, now off-limits and patrolled. We glimpse poplars,
plum trees and deodars, planted when a community of 500 houses,
with churches, school, stores and cemeteries too, covered the
hillside south of us. This community, fallen into disrepair and van-
dalized, has been torn down.

The road continues uphill past mine tailings and old side roads to
mines and shafts now tightly covered. A look at the topographic map
for this area shows many mines and shafts with names of a romantic

ring—Santa Ysabel and St. George shafts, Enriquita and Providencia mines. But there was little romantic about the hard, dangerous work of mining cinnabar, except for the hopes of riches—often realized—for those who owned the mines.

All mine shafts and tunnels have been sealed. However, the entrance to the San Cristobal Mine has been reconstructed so that visitors can look into the tunnel.

Beyond English Town's entrance a trail turns down to a brief side trip to the Alice Trestle where there is a section of railroad trestle that carried ore cars. On the way is an old brick powderhouse that stored blasting powder.

After a climb of almost 3 miles the Mine Hill Trail comes out on a high grassy meadow close to the 1700' summit of the ridge. Called Bull Run, this high pasture commands views out over the valley and up to the Santa Cruz Mountains. A picnic table under an oak looks out over the canyon of Guadalupe Creek to the Sierra Azul. There is a horse drinking trough but no potable water.

When we leave Bull Run, our trail follows the ridge as it slopes down northwest. In spring the green meadows are dotted with flowers; by May and June yellow mariposa lilies blossom through the turning grass; by late summer the pale oats are a golden contrast to blue skies and dark oaks edging the meadows.

As we lose altitude, ragged serpentine outcrops break the smooth contours of the hills. The magnesium-rich soil of this formation produces the carpets of flowers—goldfields, cream cups and more—so often found in serpentine grasslands. Serpentine is associated with cinnabar and is a common rock type in the California Coast Ranges.

As the track swings west you can see Guadalupe Reservoir below. Along the way you pass the Prospect #3 Trail going east which provides a convenient connection down to the Randol Trail. Then at a deep, sharp switchback the Providencia Trail takes off south to contour along the hill below Bull Run with fine views across the canyon to the wooded slopes of Mt. Umunhum.

From the switchbacks, the trail continues down, soon meeting the north end of the Randol Mine Trail, which you could take for a return trip. Soon after, at the Guadalupe Trail junction, we continue on the Mine Hill Trail as it veers north to traverse a wooded hillside. Easy walking on the broad trail on a gentle grade brings you to shady east slopes. The trail goes under oaks past groves of buckeyes so handsome in bloom here that in May they are worth a trip to see. Great creamy pink flowers carried on upright panicles as much as 10" long cover the buckeyes' rounded crowns.

After about a mile on this pleasant hillside our trail intersects the upper end of the Guadalupe Trail. Here also the New Almaden Trail comes in from the east and heads straight downhill to the Senator Mine Trail. The Mine Hill Trail goes east, bends left and descends for a few hundred yards on the edge of a meadow.

The rest of the way down, the trail goes in and out of woods edging small grasslands. High chaparral lining the trail includes particularly luxuriant growths of poison oak, as well as more welcome wild cherry and elderberry. This cool, northeast-facing, damp side of the hill is crossed by small watercourses and supports a fine stand of live oaks. Late in the day quail calls fill this little canyon, and you may see deer going down to the creek below, or at least hear them crashing through the brush as they become aware of your approach.

About ½ mile downhill from the Guadalupe Trail intersection, our trail veers left, following the park boundary. We cross a creek flowing down from the Senator Mine Area and come out by the McAbee Road park entrance. With a car parked at this entrance for a shuttle, you can save the long hike back.

Trip 2.   Randol and Mine Hill Trails Loop

This long trip takes the hiker past the sites of mine shafts and tunnels on the wooded east side of Los Capitancillos Ridge and returns over the summit on the Mine Hill Trail.

Distance   10.5-mile loop.

Time   6 hours.

Elevation Gain   1300'

TRAIL NOTES

You can start a loop trip that includes the Randol Mine Trail and the upper part of the Mine Hill Trail from either end of the park. However, the trip from the Almaden Road entrance is shorter by one mile, so it is the one described.

Begin on the Mine Hill Trail as in Trip 1. In a mile you will be at Capehorn Pass and the south end of the Randol Mine Trail. This is an easy trail, but with some gains and losses of elevation as it drops down into canyons and rises to ridges, losing 200 feet by the time it reaches its northern junction with the Mine Hill Trail.

We turn left, down the Randol Mine Trail through chaparral of greasewood and poison oak. In shady bends, blue nightshade blossoms luxuriantly all summer and here and there are slender stalks of cream-colored Fremont lilies in spring. Around a sharp bend ⅓ mile from Capehorn Pass we see the first tailings from the Day Tunnel spilling down the slopes below the road. The tunnel on the uphill side of the trail is now closed, as are all the tunnels and shafts at New Almaden. You will find a picnic table in the shady bend of the trail where the Great Eastern Trail takes off uphill to meet the Mine Hill Trail.

Beyond the Day Tunnel your trail becomes more wooded as it descends the hillside. Coming out on an open ridge, you see below the vast dump of the Randol Tunnel, then turn into a ravine. At a bend in the trail is the short Santa Ysabel Trail, which goes uphill under the trees, passes the Santa Ysabel Mine site and then rejoins the Randol Mine Trail, thus short-cutting a long loop east. But if you continue on the Randol Mine Trail instead, at a pleasant little flat you pass the site of the Buena Vista Shaft. Old stone and brick walls stand in a tangle of weeds and vines. Topping the walls are massive granite blocks on which was bedded the pump used to lift water from the Randol Tunnel.

The Buena Vista Shaft, built in 1881, went down to 600 feet below sea level. Its coal-fired steam-powered pump, with a 24-foot flywheel, was used to lift water from the Randol Tunnel nearby. This became an uneconomic project. About the time the shaft was put down, the demand for mercury fell, and no ore was ever hoisted from the shaft.

If the hour is right, this sunny flat is a good place to picnic while you contemplate the New Almaden mining activity of a century ago. The old road you have been following was busy with miners coming and going to shifts in the tunnel and with wagons carrying ore to the reduction furnaces at the foot of the hill.

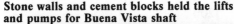

Stone walls and cement blocks held the lifts and pumps for Buena Vista shaft

From the Buena Vista Shaft our road descends to a canyon, then climbs again up a ravine to cross one of several little streams that cascade down this side of the New Almaden hills. Again descending, we traverse along the side of the ridge, the trail rising and falling in and out of ravines. Small grassy slopes alternate with groves of oaks. In spring, shows of flowers on the road banks include baby blue eyes and Douglas iris, and shady hillsides are golden with great drifts of buttercups.

Nearly a mile beyond the Buena Vista Shaft you round a broad, grassy ridge and from this vantage point you see the busy valley below, with homes, schools, shopping centers and industrial plants. For the next mile the trail winds in and out of ravines, a pleasant jaunt under the trees. Climbing through the underbrush are the vines of native clematis, with creamy white flowers in spidery clusters during the spring. By summer the seed heads are balls of fluff that remain on the plants through the fall.

The Randol Mine Trail finally turns decisively uphill to the sloping ridgetop to meet the Mine Hill Trail. Signs at the junction point to the Mine Hill Trail route that goes uphill and then down to the Almaden Road entrance, where your trip started. (See part of Trip 1 in reverse.) The north section of the Mine Hill Trail goes to McAbee Road, less than 2 miles downhill from here.

Trip 3. Hacienda Trail Loop from Mockingbird Hill Entrance

A trip to the heights of the ridge on the east side of the park overlooks Alamitos Creek.

Distance 4-mile loop.
Time 2½ hours.
Elevation Gain 1200'
TRAIL NOTES

Leave the Mockingbird Hill equestrian staging area at its southeast corner. The trail from here is broad, but steep. This section is dusty in summer and muddy after rains. However, its shady route is through a handsome oak-and-madrone woodland, first west and then south up a spur of the ridge north of Capehorn Pass. As you approach the hilltop, the trail goes along a narrow spine from which you look east over the Santa Clara Valley and west to the Mine Hill and Randol trails cutting across the main Almaden ridge. The trail dips, then makes a final rise to its 1000' summit before descending to the turnoff to Capehorn Pass.

From here you could go south to Capehorn Pass and the Mine Hill Trail, but for this trip continue on the Hacienda Trail. Yellow mariposa lilies blossom in June and silvery-headed blow-wives sparkle in the grass on their foot-high stems.

From the junction the Hacienda Trail descends gently for a few hundred feet of elevation, then makes one of several precipitous drops that make this section of the trail uncomfortable for hikers and horsemen alike. However, wide views open up toward the eastern foothills and the Diablo Range. In the foreground to the northeast are the hills of Santa Teresa Park. A trail connection one day will link these two parks.

By late May this part of the Hacienda Trail is a flowery way adorned with lemon-yellow mariposa lilies, lavender brodiaea, pink buckwheat and magenta clarkias. A few grassy flats edged with spreading oaks make good picnic places.

Your trail now rounds a hill and follows a powerline service road down the hill in two long traverses. The trail reaches into deep canyons where small streams cascade down in winter and spring. Coming out of the last traverse, the trail climbs again to the Mine Hill Trail ¼ mile above the park entrance.

To complete the loop, turn uphill on the Mine Hill Trail and follow its pleasant grade up to Capehorn Pass. (For this segment see Trip 1.) An easy half hour will take you to the pass, where you turn right (north) to meet the Hacienda Trail and return on it to the Mockingbird Hill parking area.

A good alternate loop trip on the Hacienda Trail starts from the Almaden Road entrance. Take the Mine Hill Trail, then in ¼ mile turn off on the Hacienda Trail. Continue uphill to the junction where the short trail turns south. You cross to Capehorn Pass, turn left on the Mine Hill Trail and follow it back to Almaden Road.

Trip 4. Senator Mine and Guadalupe Trails Loop

A 4-mile loop takes you from the Senator Mine across the ridge through meadows flowery in spring to Guadalupe Creek and past its reservoir, returning on the Mine Hill Trail.

Distance 4-mile loop.
Time 2 hours.
Elevation Gain 720'

TRAIL NOTES

You go through remote meadows and quiet oak woods where any number of sites invite you to enjoy a leisurely picnic. This trip may be taken in either direction, but is described here starting on the Senator Mine Trail. Much of the route is through woods, making it a good choice for warm weather.

There is room for a few cars to park outside the gated McAbee Road entrance to the park, from where a service road follows a creek canyon to the Senator Mine area. The Mine Hill Trail turns off left immediately beyond the entrance gate, but you continue along the road, which becomes the Senator Mine Trail.

Where the canyon widens, you come to two high concrete towers, a part of the furnace plant left from the days when this mine was producing as much as 10 76-pound flasks of mercury a day. After new management took over operations of New Almaden Quicksilver Mine following its bankruptcy in 1912, the Senator Mine was worked again in the 1920s. A plaque by the towers describes the new processes used then in the reduction of mercury at the mine. By 1926 this operation too had ended.

Beyond the towers, the Senator Mine Trail takes off uphill to the right of a small flat along an old road, curving up a wooded canyon to a saddle in the ridge. The Senator Mine Trail ends at a saddle where it meets the Guadalupe Trail. One end of this trail turns uphill around the east side of a ridge, but your route goes west, downhill, toward Guadalupe Creek. At the saddle are a number of places to picnic under the shade of oaks if you are only out for a short walk. The easy half-hour walk from the park entrance makes this spot a good choice for an early picnic supper in summer.

Out of sight north, just beyond the park boundary, is the site of the Guadalupe Mine, one of the three main mines operating in the mid-1800s.

Continue from the saddle down the Guadalupe Trail. Ahead the Santa Cruz Mountains come into view, topped by 3500′ Mt. Umunhum, easily identified by the tall, blocky structure on its summit, a former military installation. As you walk downhill you soon catch the sounds of Guadalupe Creek running below. Along the hillside among the sunny grasses are scattered mariposa lilies, their elegant tulip-shaped blossoms borne on tall stems. Both the intense lemon-yellow lily and the taller white lily with maroon markings are plentiful.

A few turns down the trail bring us close to the creek, which at this point is not within the park. From here it is a lovely walk past

Equestrians on Prospect #3 Trail join Randol Mine Trail

flowery meadows and through groves of wide-spreading oaks. Unfortunately, the creekside is outside the park, so you can't go down to it, but you can enjoy its sycamore- and alder-lined banks. In the other direction are glimpses from the trail of the steep heights of Los Capitancillos Ridge. During spring and summer shrubby monkey flower plants cover these slopes with their apricot blossoms.

The trail soon turns uphill away from the creek and climbs to the level of Guadalupe Dam. Below the dam and our trail is the site of the San Antonio Mine; now the only signs of it are some tailings and an old shed.

Little Guadalupe Reservoir is a narrow body of water filling the canyon for 1½ miles upstream from the dam. Its blue waters are inviting, but its steep sides do not allow any place for picnicking. However, there is space by the trail, as it climbs above the reservoir, to stop under the trees for lunch.

Then the trail veers away from the reservoir to come out on an open hillside from where you can see the Mine Hill Trail descending Los Capitancillos Ridge to meet the Guadalupe Trail at a saddle. From this saddle take the Mine Hill Trail back to the McAbee Road park entrance, an easy walk of less than an hour (see Trip 1).

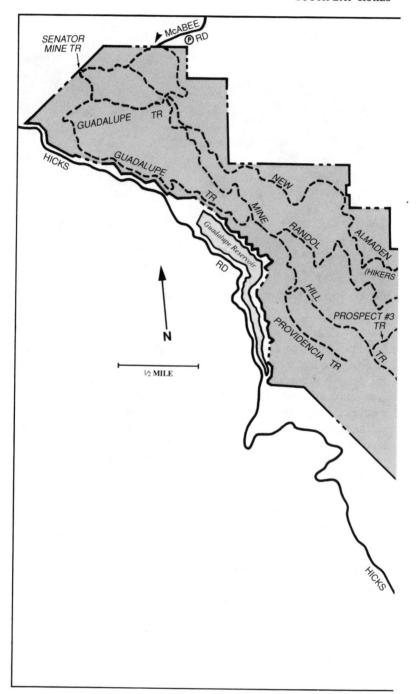

Almaden

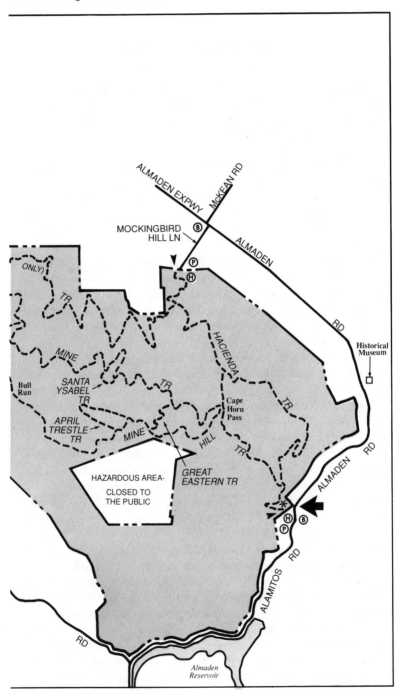

Quicksilver Park

Santa Teresa Park

The rolling hills of 1600-acre Santa Teresa Park rise from the valley floor to 1155' Coyote Peak. The low-lying northeast section is given over to a golf course and an archery range. For the rest, miles of trails lead over grasslands, past rugged outcrops and along tree-lined ravines of Santa Teresa Hills.

A broad saddle stretches across the center of the park between Coyote Peak and the hills to the west. In it are the picnic tables, barbecues, an equestrian arena and parking. Trails for hikers and equestrians leave from here. Designated for bicyclists as well as for hikers is a loop trail in the northwest section of the park. A master plan, under preparation at this writing, may suggest variations in trail use and design.

The 9646-acre Santa Teresa Ranch was granted in 1834 to Joaquin Bernal, a native of Spain, as a reward for his investigation of minerals in California on behalf of King Juan Carlos. The silver and mercury mines in the surrounding Santa Teresa Hills were not very productive, but you can still see some tailings of the Bernal Mine on the park's hillsides.

However, springs in these hills supplied plentiful water for Bernal's herds and orchards. Bernal had lived on the ranch for some years before the grant was made to him at the age of 94. He had already built four adobe houses, and his children and grandchildren numbered 87. This prolific family lived for generations on the ranch. One of the family homes, built of hand-hewn timbers, is still standing. Large orchards, vineyards and cultivated fields that once covered the lower slopes of the hills and fertile flatlands have all but disappeared, replaced by subdivisions and industrial parks.

In Joaquin Bernal's day a French saddlemaker whose work was much valued by horsemen of the time was given an adobe house on the ranch. Local horsemen must look elsewhere for saddles, but they find the trails over Santa Teresa's hills good riding. A stable on the north edge of the park provides equestrian rental facilities.

The park entrance road, realigned to provide access to an industrial plant just beyond the park's northwestern boundary, crosses the meadow west of the picnic grounds, and bisects the park and the route of the Mine Trail/Hidden Springs Trail Loop. Newly completed trails southwest of the park reach the Los Alamitos/Calero Creek Trail and will some day make connections via roadside trails to the Mockingbird Hill entrance of Almaden Quicksilver Park.

Jurisdiction   Santa Clara County.

Facilities   Trails: hiking, equestrian, bicycle. Equestrian arena. Picnic areas and barbecues: family, group by reservation. 18-hole golf course, driving range and clubhouse. Archery range.

Park Rules   Hours: 8 A.M. to ½ hour after sunset. Dogs on 6′ leash in picnic areas. Bicycles allowed on loop trail in northwest section only. Phone: 408-268-3883 or 408-358-3741.

Maps   Santa Clara County *Santa Teresa Park;* USGS quad *Santa Teresa Hills.*

How To Get There

By Car   From Highway 101 in south San Jose take Bernal Road south 1.6 miles, then continue uphill into the park. After 1 mile, turn left to reach picnic areas, parking and main trails. Or continue past this left turn to limited parking at turnout before gate to an industrial plant.

By Bus   County Transit 67 and 68 stop at Santa Teresa Expressway and Bernal Road.

Trails wind through the grassy Santa Teresa Hills

Trip 1.   Coyote Peak Climb

A loop trip takes in vistas from Coyote Peak and returns on a traverse across the north-facing hillside.

Distance   3-mile loop.

Time   2 hours.

Elevation Gain   600'

TRAIL NOTES

Leaving the east side of the Pueblo Group Area, take the Hidden Springs Trail uphill heading east. In the fall, dun-colored dry grasses are enlivened with the little starry white flowers of tarweed. In the spring some of the hillsides are transformed by wildflowers into seas of color.

The trail rounds the hill, crossing one of the park's year-round streams to meet the Ridge Trail coming in on your left. Continue on the Hidden Springs Trail bearing right (uphill). Climb up past a small pond holding waters from a spring. You come out on a high saddle where your trail meets the Coyote Peak Trail at a three-way junction. Turn right on the Coyote Peak Trail to make the ½-mile climb to Coyote Peak, the high point of the park at 1155'.

From the summit (leveled off for communications installations in World War II) one has commanding views southwest of the Sierra Azul and northeast of the Diablo Range, where the white domes of Lick Observatories mark Mt. Hamilton. On the valley floor below, subdivisions have supplanted orchards and field crops that until the 50s flourished on the rich alluvial soil. You can see the electronics plants that now extend down Silicon Valley as far as the lands that belonged to Joaquin Bernal. Today, cavalcades of horsemen wearing T-shirts with logos of computer firms canter over his hills on the trails of Santa Teresa Park.

From Coyote Peak you look down toward the southeast end of the Santa Clara Valley as it narrows between Santa Teresa Hills and the spurs of the Diablo Range foothills only a few miles away. Through this passage flows Coyote Creek, which drains the rugged ranges of vast Coe Park.

Around the peak great black turkey vultures soar on almost motionless wings, catching the updrafts. Red-tailed hawks circle high over the grasslands looking for unwary ground squirrels.

The Boundary Line Trail descends from the east side of Coyote Peak, but is steep and gravelly. So use the Coyote Peak Trail, and turn right at its intersection with the Hidden Springs Trail. This trail zigzags down through scattered trees, coyote bush, poison oak, and elderberry. At a sign that says NO HORSES BEYOND HERE turn left into Laurel Springs Rest Area, leaving the Coyote Peak Trail, for hikers only, which makes a steep descent to the lower part of the park, where it meets the Ohlone Trail.

In the rest area you cross the creek to a pleasant retreat under tall bay laurels with a picnic table and tie racks for horses. Trees meeting overhead make a cool canopy on a warm day and a good place to stop for a picnic. A stream from the spring runs in all but the driest years. Coffeeberry and elderberry shrubs grow luxuriantly. Huge burned-out bay trunks fallen by the trail are sending up sprouts to regenerate these hardy trees.

Now take the Ridge Trail, which comes out of the trees on a steep uphill pull, then makes a series of ups and downs. This leg of the trip goes in and out of groves of oaks and over grasslands, rising and falling on gentle grades. On this section of trail, we look down on the greens of the golf course, and immediately below is the little poplar-bordered pond near the Ohlone Trail.

When the Ridge Trail meets the Hidden Springs Trail, turn right and descend over undulating terrain to the picnic area where you started.

Trip 2. The Hidden Springs/Mine Trail Loop

Skirting around the park's central knoll takes you past old mine sites and into a remote oak-studded valley.

Distance   3½ miles.

Time   2 hours.

Elevation Gain   200'

Connecting Trail   Stile Ranch Trail west to Los Alamitos/Calero Creek Trail.

TRAIL NOTES

This trip can be taken in either direction, but is described here starting north on the Hidden Springs Trail. From the picnic area cross the park's entrance road and turn left on the Hidden Springs Trail. Climbing gradually to the trail's summit, you look east across the tree-filled canyons to the sloping grasslands on the east park boundary. A few deciduous oaks offer summer shade; springtime brings bright poppies and delicate lavender brodiaea.

After rounding the central knoll, the trail descends into an oak woodland, crosses the old Bernal Road, passes a turnoff to the Ohlone Trail, and drops abruptly down to the new Bernal Road. A crosswalk, flanked by stop signs in both directions, leads you to the Mine Trail on the other side. Your immediate view is of parking lots, corrals and barns of the stables downhill. But, veering left you contour through scattered oaks and past remnants of mining operations. Staying above a wooded swale, you gradually climb west to a junction with the bicycle/hiking trail that loops around the heights of the park's northwest corner. Bear left here (west), on the trail which you share with bicyclists, who are required by prominent signs to wear helmets and control their speed.

Now you are at the highest point of your trip; in the west across the valley loom the dark forested ridges of the Santa Cruz Mountains. Shortly you cross Bernal Road again. Note that there is parking at a turnout just a few hundred yards up the road, which provides an alternate entry to this trail. As you head down the Mine Trail through rolling grasslands dotted with majestic evergreen and deciduous oaks, you feel far removed from the nearby Silicon Valley scene. The Mine Trail undulates up and down the hills, then crosses a little reed-lined watercourse that flows south into Arroyo Calero on the park's south side.

Climbing up a last hill, the Mine Trail meets the Stile Ranch Trail from the west, built by volunteers in the early 1990s. Now, passing a sizeable clump of small-leaved chaparral oaks and bearing left, you descend to an old ranch road through a canyon, whose hillsides, studded with lichen-covered serpentine rock interspersed with straggly gray sagebrush, come ablaze with wildflowers in spring. The road follows a tree-lined stream, passes an old corral, and curves around beside the park's wide, west meadow. Past the horse arena you return on the Pueblo Trail to the parking areas and picnic tables where your trip began.

A spreading valley oak shades the Pueblo Group picnic area

Trip 3.   The Hidden Springs/Ohlone Trail Loop

The pleasant Ohlone Trail winds in and out of small canyons above the golf course on the east side of the park, making an easy 3-mile loop with the Hidden Springs Trail.

Distance   3-mile loop.
Time   1½ hours.
Elevation Gain   200'
TRAIL NOTES

Start this trip as in Trip 2 going uphill (north) on the Hidden Springs Trail. After passing the summit, bypass an informal trail on the right and continue downhill through the forest. Just before you reach the trail crossing over the park entrance road, the Ohlone Trail turns off right. Take this trail, which contours around the lower east side of the park. It leads into a small canyon where a lively little stream emerges from the woods during the wet winter and spring months.

Now as you bear east around the hillside, your immediate view is of the golf course fairways and clubhouse. The trail passes through a grove of spreading buckeyes and out again onto open slopes. At the next bend you look down on an oval pond, framed by tall poplars, edged with cattails and overhung by willows. Ducks paddle about, shrubs flower in the background and a weeping willow dangles its branches into the water. Unfortunately, this pond is now off limits because it is within the golf course boundaries. The Ohlone Trail, now a trail for hikers only, goes on ahead into a wooded canyon just above the pond.

If you follow this Ohlone Trail past its junction with the Coyote Peak Trail, you can continue for another ½ mile along the hillside, where there are several pleasant transitions from grasslands to wooded canyons. In spring the pathside is sprinkled with blue-eyed grass, poppies, johnny jump-ups and lupines. In summer you will want to linger in the shade of oaks and bays.

The Ohlone Trail continues to the park boundary, crossing the old Alamitos Canal, no longer used by the Santa Clara Water District, though if often holds some water in winter. On your return you will look west to the oak-studded hill in the center of the park.

However, this 3-mile loop bears right at the junction, following the Coyote Peak Trail uphill to its intersection with the Ridge Trail and the Hidden Springs Trail. Bear right (west) on either trail to return to your starting point. (These trails are described in Trips 1 and 2.)

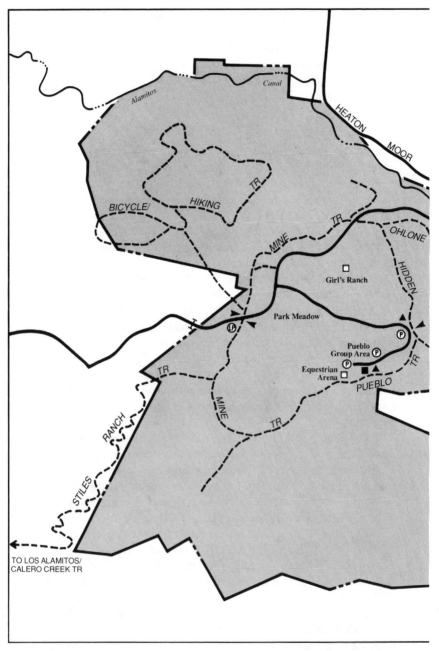

Santa Teresa

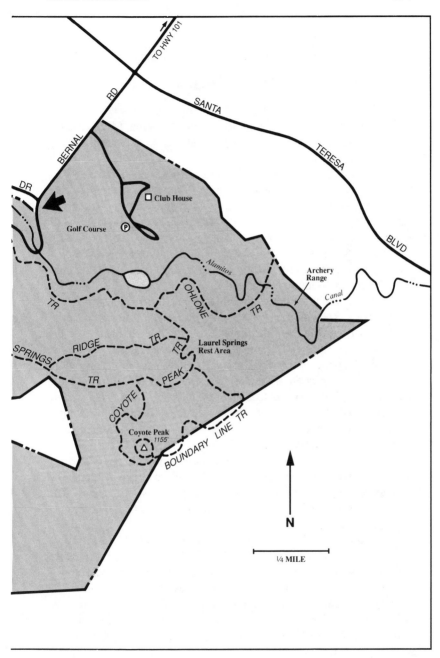

Park

Calero Park

Calero Park's 2400 acres include rolling hills and wooded ridges that are the backdrop for a reservoir open to boating. Miles of trails for hikers and horsemen lead beside creeks to sheltered valleys and to hilltops with sweeping views.

In 1935 the Santa Clara Valley Water Conservation District constructed a dam on Calero Creek, one of five dams completed that year, in a major effort at water conservation and flood control for the valley. When brimful after winter rains, the reservoir covers 349 acres. Boat-launching ramps and lakeside picnic tables make it popular for water sports. But, by the end of summer the reservoir's water level is likely to be low, especially in dry years. As of September 1990, no swimming is allowed in Calero Reservoir.

Park trails into the backcountry take you to hidden glens that seem far removed from the nearby suburbs and make fine trip destinations for any season. You can enter a world little changed over the past 150 years since cattle from Mexican ranches ranged these hills.

Within the park's boundaries are parts of two vast ranches granted in 1835 by José Figueroa, the Mexican Governor of California—the Rancho Ojo de Agua de la Coche and the Rancho San Francisco de las Llagas. Both of these ranches were later acquired by Martin Murphy, an Irishman who crossed the Sierra in 1844 and eventually came to own 50,000 acres in and around the Santa Clara Valley.

Murphy's holdings were soon broken up, and Boanerges R. Bailey bought a piece by Calero Creek where he built a house in 1865. The road to Highway 101 bears his name, and his house still stands. The house, now within the park's boundaries, serves as headquarters for the Calero Stables.

Now more than 14 miles of trails through Calero Park offer a variety of trips—easy, level strolls beside creek or reservoir, vigorous climbs over ridges, hikes to spectacular wildflower displays, walks to picnics by wooded coves and expeditions to the old Cottle ranchhouse site. Many trails that follow wide ranch roads, now park service roads through open grassland, are quite warm at midday in summer. A master plan for this park, now being prepared, may affect trail design and use.

South of the valley now filled by the reservoir, a ridge runs northwest-to-southeast, rising to an elevation of 1000'. Another ridge extends southwest toward the 1800′ heights of Bald Peaks at the south end of the park. Beyond, a succession of steep wooded ridges leads to the summit of the Santa Cruz Mountains, crowned by Mt. Umunhum and Loma Prieta, and lends a feeling of remoteness to many of Calero Park's trails.

Jurisdiction   Santa Clara County.

Facilities   Trails: hiking, equestrian. Rental and boarding stables. Equestrian staging area. Water-sports area, launching ramps and picnic tables.

Park Rules   Hours: 8 A.M. to ½ hour after sunset. No bicycles, no dogs on trails. Phone: 408-268-3883 or 408-358-3741.

Maps   Santa Clara County *Calero Reservoir,* USGS quad *Santa Teresa Hills.*

How To Get There   From Highway 101 in south San Jose go west for 1 mile on Bernal Road. At Santa Teresa Boulevard turn left and go 3 miles to Bailey Avenue. Turn right, and then at Mc Kean Road turn left. For the hiking and equestrian entrance go south 1½ miles to entrance gates on the west side of McKean Road. Parking for hikers and equestrians is at the staging and picnic area ¼ mile inside entrance gates. Just ¼ mile farther are the old Bailey house and stables.

The water-sports area is north of Bailey Avenue on McKean Road on the north side of Calero Reservoir.

Trip 1.   **Climb to the Ridge and Return along the Lake**

This loop ascends the park's central ridge, then rambles down an oak-dotted savanna with views over the lake.

Distance   3½-mile loop.

Time   2 hours.

Elevation Change   400′

TRAIL NOTES

From the staging area cross the entrance road to the signed trail that leads to the Juan Crespi Trail and turn right on it. Springtime finds these open hills thickly scattered with yellow johnny jump-ups coming through the short new grass. Pale green leaves are unfolding on the spreading valley oaks. Ground squirrels scurry through the grass searching for seeds to store against the dry seasons ahead, and overhead hawks ride the currents watching for such prey.

In ¼ mile, on a gentle rise, your trail comes to one of several small

Hikers reach the broad ridge across Calero Park

reservoirs in the park. This stock pond, used by the ranch operations below, is also frequented by great blue herons and black-shouldered kites, which comb its shores for frogs and dive into its depths for fish. A sentinel oak marks the west corner of the lake, offering shade to hot hikers.

To continue toward the ridge, stay on the trail below the reservoir's dam, then climb over a low hill and follow this old road in and out of the next small ravine. At the next outer bend in the road is the junction of the Peña and Juan Crespi trails. This trip turns left on the Peña Trail and climbs steeply for ½ mile through grasslands dotted with impressive valley oaks.

The trail veers left above a heavily wooded, steep canyon, then turns up to the ridgetop. Just before the ridgecrest you take the Los Cerritos Trail, which takes off right at an acute angle. Now on a broad grassy ridge, punctuated by stately oaks with branches sweeping the ground, you drop into little valleys, then ascend more hills. Steadily heading down, you look out over the reservoir to the boat-launching area by McKean Road. On a fine day the reservoir is blue in the sunshine. Motorboats skim the water and skiers swing back and forth in the wake of the boats.

Before reaching the lakeshore, the wide service road veers right, becoming the Juan Crespi Trail, which curves around the east side of the ridge. Wider views open up over the lake and across it to the Santa Teresa Hills. Tall blue brodiaea peek out of the grasses and the hairy roots of soap plant poke through the dust of the trail. Passing a couple of small peninsulas topped by jumbles of rocks, you wind around little coves, never very close to the lakeshore.

Back at the junction of the Juan Crespi and Peña trails, take the Juan Crespi Trail straight ahead. It goes up and down the hills above the horse stables and paddocks, past the pond and to the turnoff for the staging area.

Trip 2.   By Calero Creek to the Old Corral

A "get away from it all" trail following Calero Creek around the ridge at the south end of the park leads up to the Old Corral. This can be a short, level walk, stopping beside one of several creek crossings for a picnic, or it can be a loop trip, returning from the corral over the central ridge.

Distance   4 miles round trip.

Time   2 hours.

Elevation Gain   250′ to the Old Corral; 410′ to the ridgetop.

TRAIL NOTES

Follow the directions in Trip 1 to reach the Juan Crespi Trail, then turn left on it. In a few minutes you swing past the park entrance gates and the trail becomes the Figueroa Trail heading south. In 10 minutes more you have left behind the traffic noise from McKean Road and have passed the ranch buildings on the far side of the creek outside the park. Your trail, an old ranch road, soon reaches Calero Creek. With only the sounds of the creek you walk under oaks and through flower-filled meadows.

The trail crosses the creek several times as it follows the fenceline marking the park's boundary. In the wet season you may have to take off your shoes to wade across, but by summer crossing is easy. On the far side of the first creek crossing is a good-sized meadow. White-barked sycamores edge the creek, and the grass is filled with the johnny jump-ups so prevalent in this park. If you are quiet, you may catch sight of some of the many deer in these hills.

A quarter of a mile farther, following the creek through woodlands and small clearings, you cross the creek again and enter a broad meadow. The open grassy slopes to the right extend to the central ridge that separates us from the park entrance. The creek's head-waters are far up in the southwest corner of the park near Bald Peaks.

Leaving the meadow, we climb through an oak forest, gaining 80′ in the next ½ mile as our trail keeps close to a fenceline and a branch of the creek. Grassy clearings alternate with oak forest as the trail approaches the Old Corral. And then we reach the corral, a low point in an oak grove between hills, a trail crossroads with routes leading from it to all parts of the park.

The route you have taken is a good beginning for trips farther into the park—around and over the manzanita-crowned ridge to the south on the Javelina Loop or down the hill to Cherry Cove, an arm of Calero Reservoir, and on to the Cottle Rest Site. (See Trips 3 and 4.)

You have the choice of retracing your steps, all downhill on the Figeroa Trail by Calero Creek, or returning over the central ridge on the Peña Trail with a 160' gain in elevation. Both routes reach the parking area and are approximately the same length.

At any rate, you will want to stop awhile to enjoy the little valley by the corral, where oaks tower over grassy slopes, and you can glimpse the hills beyond the reservoir to the west.

Trip 3.   Javelina Loop Trip from the Old Corral to a Hidden Reservoir

Lunch by the reservoir, then climb past a rocky ridge for spectacular views and carpets of wildflowers in season.

Distance   2.3-mile loop plus 4 miles round trip on Figueroa Trail.

Time   3 hours.

Elevation Gain   480'

TRAIL NOTES

From the Old Corral, reached by the Figueroa Trail along Calero Creek described in Trip 2, take the Javelina Loop Trail just south of the corral, which goes up a slight rise through an oak glade. A climb of 100' in elevation past small meadows brings you to a plateau where the trail bends west. From here you see rounded, grassy Bald Peaks, which rise 1800' at the south boundary of the park. Southeast, you look down Calero Creek canyon to catch a glimpse of the summit of El Toro in Morgan Hill.

The trail continues around the bend, turning into a little valley. Rising steeply above the trail on the right is the rocky ridge around which our return trail will circle. Meadows alternate with ravines shaded by oaks and bays.

The small reservoir and its surroundings in a hidden valley cut off from the rest of the park by low hills, is known as Fish Camp. Picnic here by the water to savor the seclusion or take a trail over the dam to the shade of a wooded hillside.

When you explore the site, you will find a flaw in this little paradise. During the wet season, springs on the hillside above saturate the meadow and the trail. Then the turf is torn up and at times so muddy as to be almost impassable—the work of a herd of wild pigs who give this loop its Spanish name—javelina. A large and growing herd of feral pigs has taken a fancy to this reservoir. They are rarely in sight and will avoid you, but if you see them, leave them alone, particularly the boar, who is equipped with formidably long tusks.

Juan Crespi Trail passes stock pond on the way to the ridgetop

The road continues on the west side of the reservoir. You can escape the springtime mud by climbing the steep hillside above the road to a point where it is drier. The road leaves the reservoir, departing from this lush valley into dry sagebrush. After a steep climb of 160′ in elevation you arrive at the top of the ridge.

The Javelina Loop Trail makes a 400′ descent through chaparral on hot dry slopes, then ducks into oak-madrone woodlands before reaching a junction with the other leg of the Javelina Loop Trail. Here, in a little ravine under a dense tree canopy, you turn right for a 2-mile uphill trek to the Old Corral, described in reverse in Trip 4.

Your return to the staging area can be on the Figueroa or the Peña Trail, the former being a gentle, downhill trip. However, if you choose the Peña Trail, you will climb to the heights of the park with fine views around the compass.

Trip 4. To Cherry Cove and Alternate Destinations

After passing the Old Corral, stroll through lush meadows along wooded north-facing slopes to the western shores of the reservoir where you have choices east or west. This makes a long but lovely expedition in spring when flowers line the way.

Distance   8 miles.
Time   5 hours.
Elevation Gain   680'
TRAIL NOTES

Follow directions to the Old Corral in Trip 3. Leaving the corral on the ranch road that leads to Cherry Cove, the Javelina Loop Trail goes northwest up a slight rise, then curves west along the hillside, descending gradually toward this inlet on the south shore of Calero Reservoir. Where our trail dips into ravines, we cross small streams that are dry by late summer. Yet this trip is shaded and relatively cool, especially if you continue to the Cottle Rest Site.

About ½ hour from the corral we come to a broad meadow edged with great valley oaks. During the wet season this meadow is seeping with moisture from springs above—a muddy crossing. However, goldfields, buttercups and mallow fill the meadow, making it a flowery destination. By June the grass is drying and is speckled with mariposa lilies—pale cream with maroon markings—and lavender brodiaea. From the meadow we look across Cherry Cove, from which the sounds of motorboats reach us.

Beyond the meadow we drop down into another ravine with a running stream. Then in a grove of deciduous oaks we meet the other leg of the Javelina Loop Trail on our left. We bear right and then continue downhill toward Cherry Cove. Under the trees are the lavender-and-white blossoms of pagoda flowers and small-petalled baby blue eyes. Even in summer yellow mimulus blooms beside the trail in seeps from springs on the hillside.

After a hairpin turn to the right, we descend rapidly to the banks of Cherry Creek where it enters an arm of Calero Reservoir, Cherry Cove. White-barked sycamores overhanging the creek are sometimes standing in water when the lake floods the cove. Then it may be necessary to go upstream to cross the creek. However, at low water, it is easy to hop across on rocks.

On the other side of the creek, a broad service road, the Cherry Cove Trail, goes both east to Miner's Cove and west to the recently opened Cottle property.

Turning right takes you along the shores of Cherry Cove, a woodsy path with flower-covered banks. As you approach Miner's Cove there is no sign of mining, but buttercups turn the shady hillside gold in season, and there is an abundance of miner's lettuce. On sunny banks, tall spikes of purple lupine flourish.

The stillness may be broken by motorboats pulling water skiers who enjoy a chance to visit the inlets during spring high water, and by boaters picnicking along the shores. These coves, full of water in spring with hillsides bright with flowers and lush green grass, are a sight worth walking in to see. On banks by the roadside grow maidenhair and gold-back ferns; baby blue eyes are of the purest hue; and red Indian paintbrush accents patches of yellow buttercups. This trail does continue to the dam, but a good turnaround point is Miner's Cove.

If you choose the westward trail from the creek crossing, you follow the broad service road through grasslands enclosed by tall, rolling hills. For ¼ mile you stay on the north side of the tree-lined creek until you cross a double culvert high above the creek. Once across the rocky streambed, you go through an open gate that marks the boundary of the former Cottle property and begin to climb through oak woodlands. After crossing a tributary stream, you are under a high canopy of trees with a lush understory of ferns, poison oak and toyon, and making your way uphill and away from the creek.

At the crest of the hill begin to look on your left for an opening in the old fence that leads to a large clearing in the forest. Take the path diagonally through this meadow to the Cottle Rest Site, where the Cottle family house once stood. Now a picnic table, hitchrack and horse watering trough invite man and beast to relax—a welcome reminiscent of the hospitality early ranch families extended to wayfarers in these remote hills. Deciduous and live oaks rim the meadow and remnants of the once-domestic willows and watsonia stand near the homesite.

Above the rest site is another clearing where you can see over the treetops out across the Almaden Valley to the Santa Teresa Hills and on to the heights of the Diablo Range. Northwest are chaparral-covered hills through which the Cherry Cove Trail continues to the end of the park's property.

When you are ready to retrace your steps, take a path, left, just below the picnic table and rejoin the Cherry Cove Trail. Your return route goes right, downhill all the way to the creek crossing at Cherry Cove. At the cove, cross the creek and bear right for an uphill return. At the intersection of the two legs of the Javelina Loop Trail, you can choose the righthand one to visit the reservoir described in Trip 3. If you go left on the Javelina Loop Trail, your outbound route, you will meet the other leg at the Old Corral. Each side of the loop is about the same length, and both involve considerable elevation gains.

From the Old Corral take either the Peña or the Figueroa Trails to the park's staging area.

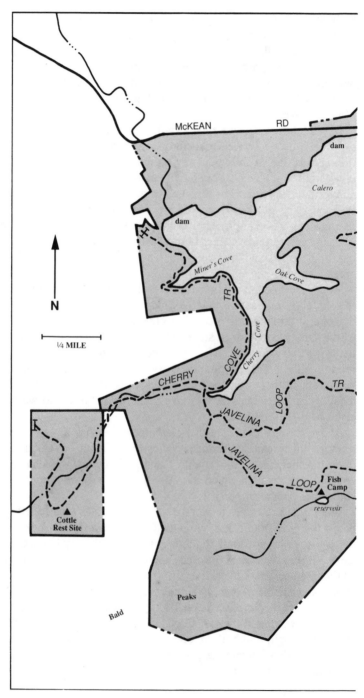

McKEAN   RD

dam

Calero

dam

Miner's Cove

Oak Cove

TR

COVE   *Cherry Cove*

CHERRY

LOOP   TR

JAVELINA

JAVELINA

LOOP   **Fish Camp**

reservoir

Cottle Rest Site

Peaks

Bald

N

¼ **MILE**

Calero

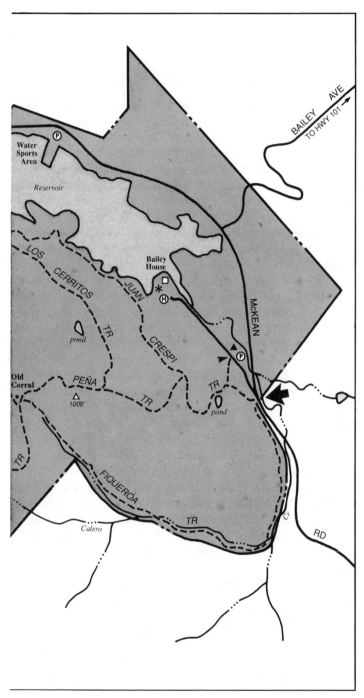

Park

Uvas Canyon Park

You reach Uvas Canyon Park by way of backcountry roads, a beautiful trip through grasslands, rolling hills and oak woodlands. Wildflowers are abundant by the roadside in spring. Going west on historic Croy Road, you follow pretty Uvas Creek, lined with alders, maples and redwoods all the way.

As you approach the park you pass Sveadal, a Swedish vacation retreat, where Swedish flags still fly and the blue of Sweden's colors trims its balconies. You enter Uvas Canyon Park in a heavily wooded canyon near the junction of Uvas and Swanson creeks. The shaded picnic grounds are close to the entrance, and campsites sit in little flats between the two creeks.

The 1100-acre park extends to the Skyline ridge over typically steep, rugged Santa Cruz Mountain terrain, cut by three creeks and their canyons. Most of the canyon of Uvas Creek is north of the park's boundary, but this beautiful watercourse runs for ¼ mile through a corner of the park.

Swanson Creek and its two tributaries descend in deep canyons from the Skyline ridge. Alec Creek enters the park from the southwest, flowing down a redwood-filled canyon. Alec Canyon, the site of logging in the second half of the 19th century, is now shaded with second-growth redwoods of good size.

South-facing sunny ridges are chaparral-covered. Here and there, stands of knobcone pines have sprung up after fires of recent years. It was the forests that attracted early settlers to Uvas Canyon, and also the plentiful water from its streams and springs. Not only was the redwood valuable, but the oak, madrone, tanoak and fir were in demand for building and for firewood. Demand for lumber of all sorts for New Almaden, only a day's drive away, sparked lumber operations that continued through the second half of the 19th century.

The Homestead Act of 1862 allowed citizens to file claims for 160 acres of land and receive ownership if they had lived on the land for five years and made certain improvements. Rich soil in the lower canyon here and ample water drew dozens of homesteaders.

But the canyon and the streams were also attractions in themselves, and nearly 30 families filed for homesteads before the end of the century. Bernt and Anna Martin, of Scandinavian extraction, settled down to farm near the confluence of Uvas and Swanson creeks. As they cleared the land, they built a rock wall which we still see by the road as we drive to the park. Their house, set back by a wide lawn, was surrounded with flower beds, vegetable gardens, a vineyard and orchards. The Martins sold lumber to New Almaden. They also ran a summer hotel, shooting game, catching fish, and raising fruits and vegetables for their guests.

It was this and neighboring properties that were eventually bought by the Swedish American Patriotic League in 1926, to become Sveadal. Crown Prince Gustav and Princess Louise of Sweden got the colony off to a royal start by attending the dedication ceremony that year. Settled by members of the league for a retirement community and summer recreation area for Swedish people of the Bay Area, it continues to serve as a favorite retreat.

The old logging roads through the hills have become park trails. This mountain park of wooded slopes has some easy creekside trails through quiet redwood groves. For the energetic there are steeper trails and a dramatic 1800' climb up a fire road to the Skyline ridge.

Spring is a favorite time to walk along Swanson Creek to enjoy its cascading waters. In summer and fall the trails under the trees appeal to hikers and picnickers as a cool retreat from the valley heat.

Jurisdiction   Santa Clara County.

Facilities   Headquarters. Trails: hiking, nature. Picnic areas: family, group. Camping: family on a first-come basis; youth groups by reservation.

Park Rules   Hours: 8 A.M. to ½ hour after sunset. Dogs on leash in picnic areas and campgrounds. No dogs on trails. No horses or bicycles on trails. Camping fee $8/car/night, $4/for 2nd car.

Maps   Santa Clara County *Uvas Canyon Park;* USGS quad *Loma Prieta.*

How To Get There   From Highway 101 in south San Jose turn west on Bernal Road. At Santa Teresa Boulevard turn left and in 3 miles turn right on Bailey Avenue. At McKean Road turn south beside Calero Park. This road becomes Uvas Road. At Croy Road turn west and drive to the park entrance.

Trip 1.   Uvas Creek Trail

A short walk from picnic and camping areas along the tree-lined banks of Uvas Creek.

Distance   0.5 mile one way.

Time   ½ hour—though you could spend all day beside this beautiful creek.

Elevation Loss   40′

TRAIL NOTES

This trail follows Uvas Creek for its ¼-mile stretch through the park. The headwaters of Uvas Creek and its tributaries are about 3 miles northwest on the slopes of Loma Prieta. From the park, the creek flows south out of Santa Clara Valley to join the Pajaro River, which empties into Monterey Bay.

This trip is described downstream from the campgrounds, although you can start this hike from either the Family Picnic area or the Family Camping area by walking toward the creek. Prominent trail signs mark the paths down to the creekside. Stay on the trails to avoid eroding the fragile banks of this canyon.

From the kiosk in the campgrounds, go down the broad Uvas Creek Trail to the creek, passing from an oak-madrone woodland to the damp, cool canyon of Uvas Creek. Tall alders, huge sycamores and big-leaved maples hug the banks and cast shadows on the waters. The trail stays above summer water level, following the creek as it cascades over boulders. Western dogwood hangs gracefully over the creek on the far side. Where a tributary pours over mossy boulders into Uvas Creek, patches of light-green-leaved thimbleberries grow on the banks.

As the canyon widens, the trail leaves the creekside to start up the steep bank. A carpet of spent leaves in hues of browns and golds covers the trail and the hillside, and in damp weather bay leaves underfoot give off their pungent fragrance.

You follow the trail uphill and step onto a wooden bridge across a side creek. Here you see Swanson Falls tumbling 10 feet into a rocky pool surrounded on three sides by high, steep banks. After heavy storms in 1986, these falls were badly eroded, reducing the vertical drop by half.

After crossing the bridge you climb along a steep vine- and fern-covered bank on big rock steps until you come to a junction. One fork continues straight along the banks of Swanson Creek back to the campgrounds; the other goes left to the Family Picnic area. This picnic site on a spacious flat is in the dense shade of large madrone trees, whose deep-red trunks contrast with the shiny green leaves.

Children enjoy the cool waters of Uvas Creek

Trip 2.　　　Loop Trip to Waterfalls on Swanson and Alec Creeks

Going up the Nature Trail, you reach three falls on Swanson Creek and then contour around to Manzanita Point and Triple Falls. Spring is the time for these falls; the little streams often disappear in summer.

Distance　3¼-mile loop.

Time　2 hours.

Elevation Gain　600'

TRAIL NOTES

Start your trip from the Black Oak Youth Group Area, which is the first picnic area on the left side of the park road. Then take the Swanson Creek Trail and head upstream. Shortly you cross a sturdy vehicle bridge built by conservation crews following the 1986 storm damage and reach the north side of the creek. In a few minutes take the steep stairway on your left, cross the creek again and follow the

Nature Trail, a narrow footpath close to the creek. Alders, tanoaks and maples provide shade in summer, and ferns line the canyon banks where the clear, rushing stream cascades over its rocky bed.

From here the Nature Trail winds upstream past numbered posts marking interesting native plants and trees. (Ask the ranger for an explanatory leaflet.) After crossing the creek several times, the Nature Trail joins the Swanson Creek Trail, a park service road, at Myrtle Flats Rest Area. Here you reach the first of Swanson Creek's tributaries. Turn right and walk along the tributary to Black Rock Falls, where the waters tumble over dark stones.

Back on the main trail near Myrtle Flats you begin to see signs of past habitation. Myrtle, the sprawling, blue-flowered ground cover, also called periwinkle, common in old gardens, has taken over the hillside. Ahead is an old cement dam and above the creek on a streamside terrace is a picnic table.

You may want to explore a path that branches west from Myrtle Flats to Knobcone Point. A homestead once stood on the hill above, one of the many agricultural enterprises scattered through these hills. Olive, fig, and cypress trees along the way were planted by the Italian family that tried to cultivate a vineyard on these hills.

Returning to Myrtle Flats, go 0.1 mile farther upstream to a wide opening in the forest. Just 200' to the right you will find Basin Falls dropping into a shallow, oval pool tucked away in a moist, rocky niche.

Still another, Upper Falls, you will find on the main channel of Swanson Creek, a few feet upstream. In 1986 storm waters swept down Swanson Creek leaving tangles of toppled trees and displaced boulders in their wake. At Upper Falls you see the impressive effects of the storm's force. A massive jumble of boulders and fallen trees lies above Upper Falls.

To continue on the Swanson Creek Trail, walk around log and boulder jams and under fallen trees. Then cross the rock-strewn creekbed to the Contour Trail. There is no bridge here, so hop across on the rocks and climb the far bank.

The first part of this trail goes out on a broad ridge, climbing gently through a young oak forest. The number of knobcone pines growing here suggests that there must have been a fire in the not-too-distant past. Before long your trail starts turning into shady ravines, winding past small watercourses where Douglas firs grow to lordly heights, making a deep, quiet forest. The stillness is broken only by scolding Steller jays.

An Eagle Scout project in 1981 built a plank bridge to take you dry-footed across the head of the third and last ravine on this trail. At the intersection with the Alec Canyon Trail you can turn left (north) on this old logging road. At an opening at a bend in the trail you can rest on a bench and look out over the valley. Then in less than ½ mile you are back at the picnic ground where you started.

By turning right on the Alec Canyon Trail, you can make a short side trip to Manzanita Point and Triple Falls. The old logging road you climb brought redwood logs from Alec Canyon to lumber mills in the flats of Uvas Canyon. Manzanitas cover this dry hillside, but at Manzanita Point you look over them to a view of the Diablo Range. On clear days you can make out Mt. Hamilton's white observatories.

From Manzanita Point the trail goes south through high chaparral, dominated by pungent yerba santa. Buckeye trees below the trail here hold their leaves late in the spring, suggesting ample underground water. At the first drop of the water table in spring, buckeye leaves dry out, then hang lifeless until blown off in the fall. You are soon in the shade of redwoods beside an intermittent creek, where second-growth trees now make a tall, handsome forest.

At the Triple Falls Trail make a right turn to see this three-tiered waterfall. Five minutes up the trail beside this tributary of Alec Creek will bring you to the 40-foot-high cascades.

Returning to the trail junction, make a right-hand turn and you will soon be at Alec Creek. A small flat on the far side makes a good destination for a lunch in the redwoods. Thick stands of virgin redwoods drew settlers and loggers to this canyon in the 1800s. At one time the hillsides were dotted with loggers' cabins and woodcutters' huts. However, a disastrous fire in the canyon in 1909 erased nearly all signs of logging activity except a network of old roads and a site upstream known as the Old Logging Camp.

For the return trip, retrace your steps on the Alec Canyon Trail back to the picnic grounds. The descent under madrones and oaks is an easy end to your trip.

Trip 3. Fire Trail Hike to Nibbs Knob and Summit Road

A steady uphill climb on the ridge between the Uvas Creek and Swanson Creek canyons takes you to views from Nibbs Knob and on to the Skyline ridge.

Distance   5 miles round trip.

Time   3 hours up; 1 hour down.

Elevation Gain   1560' to Nibbs Knob; 1760' to Summit Road.

TRAIL NOTES

Best taken in cool weather or as an early-morning summer hike from a campsite in the park, this trip gains almost 1800' elevation in less than 2 miles. The first and last stretches cling to north-facing slopes, while the middle, longer section stays just below the ridgetop on its south side. This is a good hike on which to orient yourself to the peaks and foothills of the South Bay, especially the Diablo Range from Mission Peak south.

Start your hike from the west end of Upper Bench Campground where a fire trail begins beyond a big brown gate. The admonition to carry water, clearly printed on the trail sign, you should surely heed. On a hot day the sun beats relentlessly on the mountainside. However, the first part of the trip goes up the north side of Uvas Canyon in the shade of fir, tanoak, madrone, bay and oak trees. The understory is thick with ferns, honeysuckle, ocean spray and annual flowers. From the first shining white milkmaids of early spring to the yellow blossoms of bush poppies in summer, there are flowers beside the trail.

The sound of the creek in the canyon below mingles with the laughter of children playing, the call of birds in the trees, and some-times the crashing of deer in the forest. For a while the trail takes all your attention, as it ascends steeply, carved out of this precipitous mountainside. At the second switchback, the footing is more com-fortable, and you will be able to peer over the side of the trail down into Swanson Creek Canyon to the park's campgrounds and picnic tables.

At the next switchback you can look across Uvas Canyon to the main Skyline ridge and to 3791' Loma Prieta. The tallest mountain in the Santa Cruz Mountains, its heights are crowned by an array of antennas and microwave towers.

After the fourth switchback, you begin a long, straight ascent on the last north-facing, wooded section of the trail before you come out of the woodland onto the south-facing chaparral-covered slope. From here you see the Skyline ridge, its broad shoulders stretching down to the valley below.

On the ridgetop you will see a thick growth of young pines growing up among the manzanitas; they are the new knobcone pines sprouted from seeds that the heat of a 1961 forest fire released from the pre-viously closed cones. This is one of California's three "fire pines," adapted to sprout after fires and reclothe the burned-over land.

Your trail goes steadily upward through thickets of blue-blossomed California lilac, chaparral pea, and pungent-smelling

Nibbs Knob seen from the Contour Trail

pitcher sage, topped by an occasional Digger and knobcone pine. On cool winter and early spring days the southern sun is welcome, but in summer the hiker seeks the shade of an occasional bay, scrub oak or pine tree along the way.

Overhead hawks circle lazily on the updrafts, and band-tailed pigeons fly swiftly over the hills, high above the canyons. Hidden in the chaparral, wren-tits sing their distinctive descending-scale call.

Just before the trail re-enters forest, it levels off at a saddle. Watch for a sign on your right marking the turnoff for Nibbs Knob. Don't miss this side trip. In a short 0.2-mile rise you pass the remains of an olive orchard, planted here many years ago by Henry Knibbs. Little is known about this man, other than that he was granted a patent to this homestead in 1891, and he spelled his last name with a "k".

You circle around the knob through a sparse forest of big Douglas firs, knobcone pines and madrones to emerge on the flattened top of the mountain where, quite alone in a bare clearing, sits a single picnic table. If the day is cool, this is a good place to have your picnic lunch.

Take time to explore this hilltop. Little remains but a few fences and more olive trees, but the views through small openings between the second-growth fir trees stretch north to Loma Prieta, directly west above you to the Skyline ridge and east to the Diablo Range.

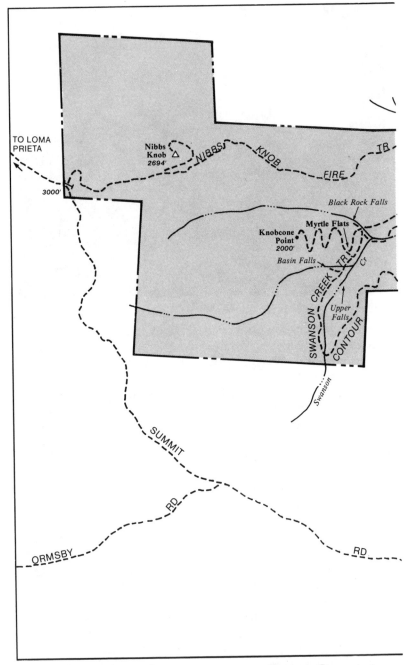

Uvas Canyon

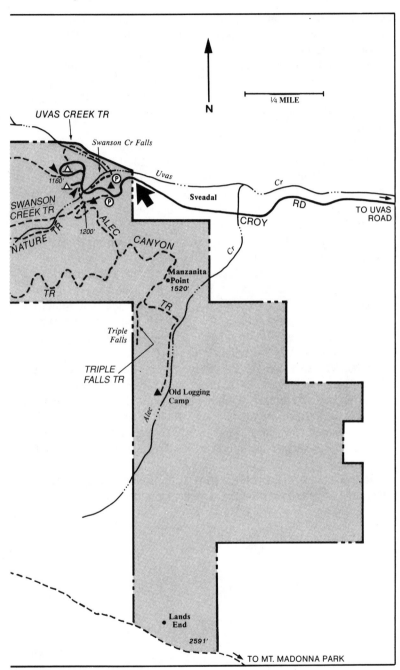

Park

On clear days one can see Half Dome in Yosemite from here. Smog often fills the summer sky now, but Henry Knibbs must have had unobstructed views.

Now retrace your steps to the junction and start the last stretch of trail up to Summit Road on the Skyline ridge. This is fine walking under a canopy of trees. The trail is covered with bay and oak leaves, only a little more golden than the fine sandstone pebbles of its surface.

You may be surprised to see grapevines climbing up the toyons and wild cherries. These vines, too, were planted by the industrious and adventurous pioneer who laid out the olive orchard in its neat circles around his Knob. From one of the switchbacks you can look back and see the cone shape of that knob, crowned with tall fir trees. Many brave souls tried their luck homesteading such high slopes in the late 1800s, only to find that water and good soil were too scarce and the climate too difficult.

You soon see the park's brown metal gate and a sign marking the limits of the park. Unpaved Summit Road is closed to motor vehicles, except for residents' cars, at this writing. But some day non-motorized traffic may be able to enjoy this mountaintop road with its 360° views. It is a direct, ridgetop route from upper Uvas Canyon Park to Mt. Madonna Park.

When you have enjoyed the shade at trail's end, start back on the Nibbs Knob Fire Trail. There is a sign NO HORSES ALLOWED. The trails in Uvas Park are for hikers only. You soon begin the steep descent back to the canyon bottom. On the upward journey you had time to look around, because you needed to pause for breath. But the return trip requires close attention to your feet on this extremely steep trail.

In less than an hour you are back at the campground, exhilarated from the hike and the wonderful views from the top.

Mt. Madonna Park

Mt. Madonna Park surrounds the 1897' southernmost high point of the Santa Cruz Mountains. It overlooks Monterey Bay and the Pajaro and Salinas River plains on the west and the Santa Clara Valley on the east. On clear days the views stretch south to the Santa Lucia Mountains and east to the Diablo Range.

In several deep canyons that crease the sides of the mountain, streams thread their way over boulders, fallen logs and tree roots. Dense redwood, madrone and tanoak forests cover the coast-facing slopes and the mountaintop. As the slopes descend toward the east, vegetation changes to oak woodlands, then dense chaparral and grassy meadows.

Bird and animal life abound in the park. You will often see Steller jays and raccoons boldly picking up remnants of picnickers' lunches. You may see a black-tailed deer on a forest trail or hear him crashing through the underbrush. The chatter of squirrels in the trees overhead is often raucous, but the shy shrew and the silent opossum are seldom sighted and never heard. White fallow deer restricted to a large hilltop pen are on view all the year.

A visit to Mt. Madonna Park in spring or early summer will reward you with sights of bright wildflowers in the grasslands and along the trails. However, at any time of year the display of fine wildflower photographs in the park office is well worth a visit to see the variety of blossoms you can find in the park. Here also are some stuffed specimens of park wildlife.

History

When Henry Miller was lord of a vast cattle domain in central California, he sought out the cool summit of this mountain for a summer retreat. Here he built a fine home and cottages for his two children. Expert craftsmen using stone quarried on the mountain constructed the foundations and the rock walls enclosing its walks. Italian woodcutters employed by Miller affectionately called the mountain "Madonna," which became its official name. He set out orchards and vineyards and planted elaborate gardens.

Serving as his summer headquarters high above his main ranch, Bloomfield Farm, in the hot valley near Gilroy, this retreat had views far out over his extensive lands in central California. It has been said that every acre of land he could see from here belonged to him. When he died in 1916, he owned one million acres of land and one million head of cattle, worth an estimated 50 million dollars. Eventually his heirs sold the land on this mountain to Santa Clara County for a park. One of the houses was removed and reassembled on the Watsonville Road and the others were sold for salvage. Now only the foundations and fragments of walls remain, further damaged by the 7.1 earthquake of October 17, 1989. Tanoaks and redwoods 12″ or more in diameter grow within the former walls.

Today, you can take a self-guided walk around the ruins and enjoy picnicking and camping on the 3093-acre mountaintop retreat of California's 19th century cattle baron. Spacious campgrounds and picnic areas, shaded by tall second-growth redwoods, the park office, a playing field, a pen of fallow deer and an amphitheater share the mile-long plateau on the ridgecrest.

Beside the Hecker Pass Road on the park's east flank is Sprig Lake, a fishing hole exclusively for children and a family picnic place. A horse-staging area in the lower park is convenient to the equestrian trails. And archery enthusiasts will find a range in mid-park.

A trail network on old logging roads, powerline service roads and footpaths covers the park north of Hecker Pass (Highway 152). On 18 miles of trails hikers and horsemen can explore its mountainsides, creek canyons and open grasslands. Some trails connect the camping and picnic areas, many begin near the park office, and several take off from Sprig Lake. A few trails through environmentally sensitive areas are restricted to foot traffic. Bicycles are not allowed on Mt. Madonna trails.

Jurisdiction   Santa Clara County.

Facilities   Park office houses small museum. Trails: 18 miles hiking, 13 miles equestrian. 100 picnic sites and 117 campsites for families; groups by reservation. Fishing at Sprig Lake. Archery range and amphitheater.

Park Rules   Hours: Open all year for day use from 8 A.M. to sundown. Fishing at Sprig Lake for children 5–12 years only, in May, June and July. Dogs and pets on 6-foot leash only; no pets on trails.No bicycles on trails.

Fees $3/car/daily, May 15th to September 15th; Camping $8/night/car; $4/night/2nd car. Call 408-358-3751 for reservations and 408-842-2341 between 3:30 and 4:00 P.M. for information.

Maps Santa Clara County *Mt. Madonna Park;* USGS quad *Mt. Madonna.*

How To Get There (1) Main entrance—from Gilroy or Watsonville take Hecker Pass Highway 152, turn north on Pole Line Road. (2) Sprig Lake entrance—on east side of park turn north off 152.

Trip 1.   Circle Trip through Banks and Blackhawk Canyons

Visit the major stream canyons on the east and west sides of Mt. Madonna's ridgetop to see flowers in spring and ferns in summer.

Distance 2-mile loop.

Time 1¼ hours.

Elevation Gain 420′

TRAIL NOTES

From the park office go west along the road a few hundred yards to the wide Blue Springs Trail and turn left. At first you are in a shallow-soil, dry zone where chinquapin, knobcone pine and manzanita thrive. In spring the manzanita's bell-shaped flowers hang in clumps from its shiny-leaved branches. In summer the tall,

Picnickers find a sunny table in the meadow near Park headquarters

yellow-flowered bush poppies and magenta-blossomed chaparral peas brighten the wide trail cut for powerline maintenance.

Keep heading downhill, staying east of the road until you come to the Redwood Trail junction. You turn right here, cross Pole Line Road, and step onto a narrower, shady foot trail which trends gently downhill through the redwood forest. After crossing the head of Banks Canyon, your woodland way dips down to the creek bed. Sword ferns grow shoulder-high along the hillside and boulders line the streambed. Although this canyon was logged years ago, some second-growth trees are now 2 or 3 feet in diameter and over 100 feet tall.

As the Redwood Trail rises out of the canyon, it meets the Bayview Trail close to the park's west boundary. Here you turn left. Through an opening in the forest you can see out to the waters of Monterey Bay on a clear day, but in summer the coastal fog at times closes in and hangs on the southwest face of the Santa Cruz Mountains. Caught by the redwood's leaves, fog drips to the ground below, watering its shallow roots.

The Bayview Trail dips down into Banks Canyon again, makes several switchbacks and then ascends to meet the Sprig Lake Trail. If you went left here for 0.1 mile, you'd come to a major trail junction at a clearing on Pole Line Road. Instead, this trip proceeds a little farther on the Bayview Trail for its sweeping vistas southwest to the Pajaro Valley and the Santa Lucia Mountains.

After continuing on this more open section of the Bayview Trail for 0.1 mile, look for the sharp left uphill turn that will take you on the horse trail and back to the trail junction at Pole Line Road.

When you reach the junction, you are at the head of Blackhawk Canyon. You can choose any of the three springs trails—Blue, Rock or Iron—that traverse the upper canyon of Blackhawk Creek. At this writing some of these trails are unmarked, but each leads back up the mountain to the park office. To take the Iron Springs Trail, follow the wide Blackhawk Trail east down a shady canyon beside the creek. In a few minutes you arrive at the Iron Springs Trail and make a sharp left turn, keeping to the trail along the right slope. The rust-colored soil to the left of the trail shows the seepage from Iron Springs.

Walking through this canyon, one might think of a spacious forest reception hall, the high, leafy roof supported by tall columns of bare tree trunks. The springs and rivulets of this canyon feed Blackhawk Creek. In 0.2 mile you meet the Redwood Trail, on which you turn left and go uphill.

Shortly you reach the Redwood/Rock Springs Trail junction. A right turn on the Rock Springs Trail, for hikers only, leads back uphill to the main road, where you turn right again. Enroute you pass the amphitheater, often the scene of wedding festivities under the trees. If the park office is open, stop in to see the exhibits of Mt. Madonna's history and its plant and animal life.

Trip 2. An Ecological Sampler

A circle trip from the Miller homesite goes through a broadleaf evergreen forest to chaparral country and into redwoods on the mountain's east slope.

Distance 3½-mile loop.

Time 2 hours.

Elevation Gain 300′

TRAIL NOTES

Go east past the park office to the old Miller homesite at the end of the road. The broad, gated Tanoak Trail leads off to the northeast. Take this trail downhill through the filtered light of a broadleaf evergreen forest. Underfoot a carpet of fallen creamy pink and tan leaves from madrone and tanoak trees makes pleasant walking. Wild honeysuckle vines and poison oak compete with red-berried toyon shrubs for light and space under the trees. In early spring the upper leaves on foot-high Indian warrior plants turn deep red at the base of the trees.

At the Loop Trail you turn left and continue through the forest for a short stretch. As you approach the Merry-Go-Round Trail, the woods thin out, and you turn right, downhill, on it. Soon you are out in chaparral, where manzanita, chamise, toyon and ceanothus predominate. Hiking here is best in winter or very early on a summer day.

The chaparral, a miniature forest, supports many birds, including the scrub jay, easy to recognize by his bright blue feathers and his raucous call. You may also see a small gray bird with a black hood hopping into the bushes. This bird—the Oregon junco—is quite at home in California too.

In about ½ mile you'll find the junction with the Tie Camp Trail, where you turn right. In the railroad's heyday, redwood ties were made at Tie Camp, south of here. For the next 1.1 miles the trail goes through chaparral and oak woodlands, with some Digger pines here and there on the hillside. Then as the trail turns into a ravine, it enters a deep redwood forest.

The trail has been following an old road on a gentle grade. At a second ravine you leave the road for a narrow trail and begin switchbacks up the mountain through open woods. The trail widens as it meets the Ridge Trail, where you turn right and continue uphill through oak woodland for ½ mile. You are now on an old logging road under second-growth redwoods that clothe the hillside.

Still in the woods you pass the Contour Trail intersection and, continuing on the Ridge Trail, veer right toward the Iron Springs and Loop trails. You head uphill through the trees, where now madrones and oaks meet overhead. Perhaps you will notice spiral ridges on the limbs of some madrones. The tree twists toward the light as other trees grow above it, blocking full sunlight. When you reach the Loop Trail, turn right. Steadfastly bear north uphill on this wide trail. Now out in open brushy country, only scattered eucalyptus trees and electric powerlines rise above you. After 0.4 mile on the Loop Trail you turn left to wend your way uphill through remnants of overgrown orchards, vineyards and gardens that circle the hillside below Miller's summer home. The empty stone-and-cement pool you pass was the estate's old fountain, once graced by a statue.

When you reach the wide carriage road below the basement foundations, all that remain of Miller's house, turn right and walk to the park road where you started. If you have time, an historical and nature-trail guide, available at the park office, will help you explore more of this hilltop site, which once looked out over the vast domain of cattle baron Henry Miller.

Trip 3. Round Trip from Sprig Lake to the Ridge

This circle hike climbs up the ridge south of Blackhawk Canyon and then descends gradually beside its stream back to the lake.

Distance   4.2 miles round trip.

Time   3 hours round trip.

Elevation Gain   1100'

TRAIL NOTES

On hot days start this trip early, even though the Sprig Lake Trail goes through forest all the way. You will gain 800' in the first ¾ mile. After that the grade becomes gentler as you approach the east knob of the ridge near the Valley View Campgrounds. If you took the Blackhawk Trail up the mountain, the elevation gain would be more gradual, but the trail climbs unremittingly for 1.6 miles.

From the Sprig Lake parking area, go across the bridge to the lake's west side where a gate bars a service road. Beyond, a footpath circles the lake, but the Sprig Lake Trail goes sharply uphill on the left, climbing quickly through oak woodlands on the east side of the

**Young fishermen under 12, coached by parents,
try their luck at Sprig Lake**

ridge. Before long it crosses several ravines where intermittent streams run briefly after rains. However, there is enough underground water to sustain a variety of moisture-loving plants the year around. As late as July the authors found little purple-throated white violets here. In spring the purple iris stand in thick clumps beside the trail, and the showy, bright-pink Clintonia blossoms reach upward on tall stems. If the deer are not too hungry, you will find bright blue berries on the Clintonia flower stalks in summer. Even when this plant has neither blossoms nor berries, you can recognize it by its broad, strap-shaped basal leaves.

Many switchbacks take you ever upward around to the north-facing side of Blackhawk Canyon. As you near the ridge, the large multi-trunked canyon oaks are interspersed with tall redwoods. When you begin to see outcroppings of buff-colored rock above the trail, you are approaching the ridgecrest. At this point the steep climb is over and you are close to the Valley View Overlook. This is a good destination for a shady picnic lunch among the rocks, or a short way along a trail to the left for open, sunny space and valley views.

From here the trail contours around the hill below the Valley View Campgrounds on a more gentle grade. In about ½ mile bear right on a narrow, somewhat overgrown trail. After the long, forested climb

you find yourself in chaparral on the sloping plateau of Mt.
Madonna. Huckleberry bushes are plentiful in the chaparral, and in
late summer deer and hikers vie for their fruit.

Not so plentiful are the chinquapin, a near relative of the oaks, and
the knobcone pine, a tree found occasionally on the east slopes of
the Santa Cruz Mountains. You can tell the chinquapin by its gold-
backed leaves and prickly burrs. The knobcone pine has whorls of
short, stubby cones that remain closed and on the tree until a fire
comes along. Then the cones open, letting the seeds fall.

When you pass the trail to Giant Twins (two redwoods) on the left,
you leave the chaparral and enter woods, skirting pleasant, tree-
canopied Valley View Campground I and contouring around the
hillside above Blackhawk Creek. For the last ¼ mile of your trail you
pass tall redwoods dripping with a feathery moss. From this shady
forest you suddenly drop down to a sunny clearing, a junction of
many trails beside Pole Line Road, at the head of Blackhawk
Canyon.

After reading all the trail signs with destinations to far corners of
the park, turn down the broad Blackhawk Trail to begin your trip
back to Sprig Lake. This trail, over a wagon road used for hauling
logs, goes beside Blackhawk Creek. Park vehicles now bump down it
to the springs, while hikers and horsemen enjoy its winding, shady
route among the redwoods. Big pools have formed where boulders
and fallen trees interrupt the creek's flow. Tall woodwardia ferns line
the banks, and bright white milkmaids blossom in early spring.

1989 earthquake damage to Miller house

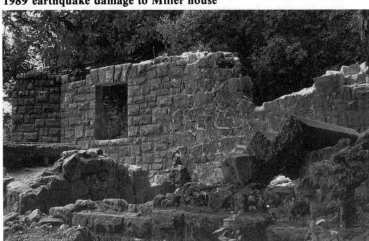

After you cross the creek several times, you come to the big sand filters and pumphouse, once part of the park's auxiliary water supply, fed by the springs you pass on the last leg of Trip 1. Where the creek makes a big curve north, you come to a fork in the trail. A left turn would take you on the Contour Trail heading up to the Ridge Trail, but you continue on the Blackhawk Trail, crossing the creek above a tangle of fallen logs. The Blackhawk Trail through the redwoods and firs is cool as it follows the year-round stream. Pink-blossomed sorrel carpets the ground and tall ferns grow by the creekside. The trip down the canyon is pleasant and easy, though in stormy winters there may be downed trees and mud underfoot.

On some bare banks in the forest you may find little "villages" of 3–6-inch "skyscrapers," known as hoodoos by geologists. These occur when large raindrops fall from the trees and erode away soil, leaving little columns protected by a hard capstone.

About ¾ of the way down the mountain, the trail veers away from the stream to climb up the hill and join the Ridge Trail. Through small grassy openings in oak-madrone woodlands it wanders down for about ¼ mile. Fluffy panicles of creambush overhang the trail in early summer, and blue-eyed grass puts out its yellow-centered, deep-blue blossoms in shady places beside the trail. Rounding a bend, you descend quickly to the horse-staging area. From here, arc to the right and in five minutes you are back at Sprig Lake.

This vigorous, 1100′ climb followed by the long creekside descent is a good stimulus to a hearty picnic supper at the lakeside tables.

Trip 4.   Downhill Hike from Redwoods to Lakeshore

Skirting the park's northeast boundaries on the Loop and Merry-Go-Round trails, this gentle hike traverses dense redwood forests, crosses grassy knolls and terminates at Sprig Lake—if you have a car shuttle.

Distance   3.4 miles one way.

Time   1½–2 hours.

Elevation Loss   1080′

TRAIL NOTES

Some of your party could do this hike on the last day of a camping trip in Mt. Madonna Park, arranging to be picked up at Sprig Lake as your car heads back to the valley.

Starting from the ridgecrest at the Summit and Old Mt. Madonna roads intersection, drive 0.3 mile north on the unpaved section of

Old Mt. Madonna Road. Once the main road from Gilroy to the Pajaro Valley, now this seldom-used backroad winds quietly through a shady redwood canyon. You could safely walk down this road to the beginning of the trail. However, there is room for several cars to park near the trail entrance.

Walk around the logs barring vehicular traffic and begin your forest walk on the Loop Trail. The forest is very quiet, except for the song of birds and the chatter of squirrels. First the trail dips into a little ravine where a stream flows into summer in wet years, and in five minutes you come upon some of Henry Miller's work—a big water tank and pumphouse backed by a 15′ moss-covered stone wall. Miller dug back several hundred feet into the steep hillside here to tap the spring and then piped its flow into the tank, from which he pumped it with a steam engine hundreds of feet uphill to his home. Today this water is used as a backup water supply for fire suppression.

From the water tank your way continues on a gentle grade, curving back into canyon heads, rounding little knobs or going far out on a mountain shoulder. Always in the shade, this is a delightful, cool leg of the trip. In spring the blooms of the shade-loving forest wildflowers—deep-rose trillium and yellow-green fetid adder's tongue—punctuate the shadows of the tree-covered slopes.

The stumps of some very large redwoods have notches where the lumberjacks inserted boards to stand on while sawing the tree. The loggers always felled a tree uphill, because the longer fall downhill would have splintered the tree.

Now that logging has ended, the redwoods are growing large again. Redwood needles and tanoak leaves carpet the trail, making pleasant underfooting. The rivulets and streams from the steep sides of Mt. Madonna's north slope feed charming Little Arthur Creek in the valley below.

At the junction of the Loop and Merry-Go-Round trails, you could turn right and follow the Loop Trail 0.8 mile back to the park office. However, with a shuttle arranged you continue downhill to more open country on the Merry-Go-Round Trail. The trail is on sandstone, and as the forest gives way to chaparral the grade becomes steeper.

In ½ mile you come to a turnoff to the Tie Camp Trail, but your walk continues through scrub oak, ceanothus and manzanita country to the grasslands just 10 minutes down the trail. Here the views are lovely. On a clear day you can see across to the ridges of the southern Diablo Range. Above you to the south lie the forested flanks of Mt. Madonna. Bands of dark-green trees mark the major canyons where Blackhawk and Bodfish creeks flow eastward through the park. These boulder-strewn, grassy meadows with their long views would make delightful picnic stops on a sunny winter or early spring day. Even in summer, the authors found the shade of occasional oaks, tall elderberries or toyons comfortable places to enjoy the open meadowlands.

Turning south, the trail swings away from the park boundary and drops into an oak woodland, where it crosses a creekbed several times. Back out on a ridge with woods on either side, the trail then winds down into a deep redwood-and-bay-tree forest with an understory of tall wood ferns, wild blackberries and poison oak. The creek is joined by several tributaries on its journey to Sprig Lake. When you come to the horse-staging area, go around the log gate and head down the hard-surfaced road to the popular picnic and fishing area.

The little lake is stocked by a Gilroy's sportsman's club and the Santa Clara County Fish and Game Commission. Fishing is restricted to children between 5 and 12 years, with a limit of 5 fish per day. Eager youngsters line the lakeshore, while parents and older children applaud the catch.

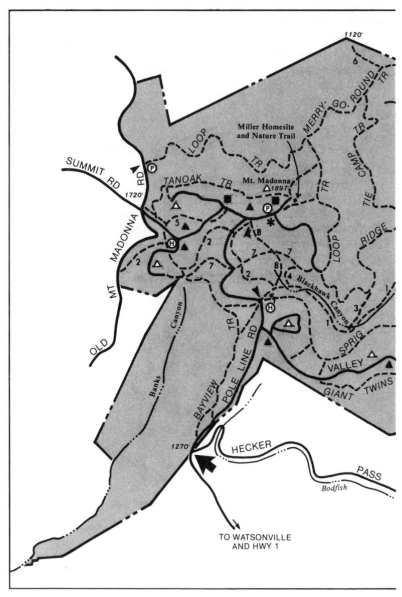

Mt. Madonna

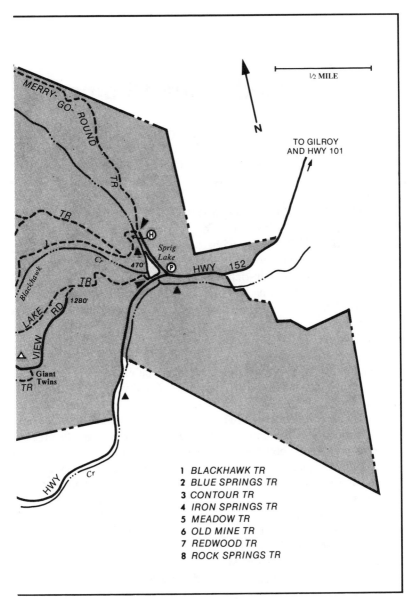

MERRY-GO-ROUND TR

TR

TO GILROY
AND HWY 101

N

½ MILE

Ⓗ
*Sprig
Lake*
470'
Ⓟ HWY 152

Cr

Blackhawk

TR

LAKE RD 1280'

VIEW

△ Giant
Twins
TR

HWY Cr

1 BLACKHAWK TR
2 BLUE SPRINGS TR
3 CONTOUR TR
4 IRON SPRINGS TR
5 MEADOW TR
6 OLD MINE TR
7 REDWOOD TR
8 ROCK SPRINGS TR

Park

Creekside Park Chains

Coyote Creek

Coyote Creek, the longest of Santa Clara County's watercourses, flows year-round, still relatively untrammeled for most of its tree-bordered 31 miles to San Francisco Bay. From its headwaters in the rugged Diablo Range it flows through Coe Park, then is impounded at Coyote and Anderson dams. Then, flowing north on the east side of Santa Clara Valley, it is held back in percolation ponds at Metcalf Road. It passes through central San Jose, is joined by Penitencia Creek and flows through rich agricultural lands. At historic Dixon Landing the creek turns west and enters the San Francisco Bay National Wildlife Refuge, where it is joined by a network of sloughs and marshes at the south end of the Bay.

At Dixon Landing Coyote Creek trails will meet the Bay Trail on a route from San Francisco Bay Area National Wildlife Refuge.

Nearly all of the creekside land is in public ownership from Anderson Dam to downtown San Jose. County parks border the creek for nearly 20 miles and then San Jose's Senter, Kelley and William Street parks preserve large sections of land on both sides of the creek. From there until it reaches the Wildlife Refuge, the creek passes by a public golf course, an airport, and three small parks.

Long-range plans envisage trails along Coyote Creek from Anderson Dam to San Francisco Bay in a creekside park chain. Paths along Coyote Creek are considered a short-term route for the San Francisco Bay Area Ridge Trail crossing from Santa Teresa Park on Bernal Road. At this writing paths border the creek in Kelley Park and 17 miles of trail extend southeast from Coyote Hellyer Park to Burnett County Park below Anderson Dam. Described here are two trips in parklands beside this beautiful creek.

Trip 1. **Kelley Park Paths**

Stroll through a San Jose creekside park to picnic areas, a zoo and a historical museum.

Jurisdiction City of San Jose.

Facilities Japanese gardens, miniature railroad, zoo, picnic areas, historical museum. Wheelchair accessible. Phone: 408-277-4192.

Map City of San Jose *Kelley Park.*

Park Rules Hours: 8 A.M. to ½ hour after sunset daily. Japanese Friendship Gardens 10 A.M. to sunset. Happy Hollow 10 A.M. to 5 P.M. Monday—Saturday, Sunday 11 A.M.–6 P.M. (last admission 5 P.M.). Phone: 408-277-4193. San Jose Historical Museum 10 A.M. to 4:30 P.M. Tuesday through Friday, 12 to 4:30 P.M. Saturday and Sunday. Admission fees for Happy Hollow, San Jose Historical Museum. Parking $2/car.

How To Get There

By Car From Highway 101 take Story Road west to Senter Road. Turn southeast to the park entrance on the northeast side of the road.

By Bus County Transit 83.

TRAIL NOTES

The first formal trail upstream from downtown San Jose begins at Kelley Park, where the city's 156 acres beside Coyote Creek offer entertainment for the whole family as well as trails enough for an hour's stroll. Children find fun and adventure at Happy Hollow, with its Baby Zoo, puppet shows and a scaled-down railroad.

After a quiet walk through the flowery Japanese Friendship Garden past carp-filled ponds and over zigzag bridges you can stop at the teahouse for a cup of tea and a snack. Picnic tables and

A small replica of the tower that once lit the downtown area stands near the reconstructed Pacific Hotel in Kelley Park

barbecues are scattered under the trees throughout the park.
Adults and children as well take pleasure in San Jose's Historical
Museum, where old homes and businesses are restored or
authentically reconstructed. O'Brien's Candy Store, for fifty years
an institution in downtown San Jose, awaits with ice cream sodas to
end your trip.

For the next 3½ miles from Kelley Park upstream to Coyote
Hellyer Park, Coyote Creek flows through a broad band of publicly
held lands. Only a few creekside areas remain in private ownership.
However, except in San Jose's Senter Park, which borders the creek
for ¼ mile, there are no established trails.

**Trip 2.   Coyote Hellyer Park Trails South
                   to Burnett Avenue**

In 223-acre Coyote Hellyer Park, on the banks of Coyote Creek,
an 8-foot-wide paved trail starts from the northern picnic areas and
extends upstream through the park all the way to Burnett Avenue. In
the park near the trail, set among tall cottonwood and sycamore
trees, are picnic tables and barbecues on little knolls beside the
creek. At the Visitor Center is a small natural-history exhibit. A velodrome for bicycle races and a stocked fishing lake are added
attractions.

Jurisdiction   Santa Clara County; Shady Oaks Park, City of San
Jose.

Facilities   Trails: 17 miles hiking and bicycling, and 7 miles
equestrian at this writing; wheelchair accessible in part. Visitor
Center. Picnic areas and barbecues: family, groups by reservation. Children's playground. Volleyball court. Velodrome. Fishing,
boating.

Park Rules   Hours: 8 A.M. to ½ hour after sunset. No swimming.
Dogs on 6-foot leash; not permitted on trails. Fees: $3/car.
Seniors free. Phone: 408-358-3751

Maps   Santa Clara County Coyote Hellyer Park, USGS quads
Morgan Hill, Santa Teresa Hills, San Jose East and Milpitas.

How To Get There

By Car   From Highway 101 southeast of Freeway 280 inter-
change take Hellyer Avenue west ½ mile to park entrance. Silicon
Valley Boulevard access: Turn east off Highway 101, go ¼ mile.
Metcalf Road access: Turn east off Monterey Road (Highway 82).

Distance   17 miles one way.

Time   On foot, 7 or 8 hours. By bicycle, 2 hours.

Elevation Gain   Relatively level.

TRAIL NOTES

The trail from Coyote Hellyer Park to Metcalf Road is a dedicated short-term segment of the Bay Area Ridge Trail. You can enter it from several locations within Coyote Hellyer Park as well as at Silicon Valley Boulevard and Metcalf Road south of the park. The trip is described here in three sections: through Coyote Hellyer Park, from the highway undercrossing in the park to Silicon Valley Boulevard, and from Silicon Valley Boulevard to Burnett Avenue. The Coyote Creek Trail will continue another mile downstream to Capitol Expressway with the completion of Yerba Buena Road across the creek.

1. Through Coyote Hellyer Park (2¼ miles).

Leave your car at one of the northern picnic areas in the 223-acre park and walk over to the creek's edge. A hiking trail is on the east side of the creek here, although informal trails wind along its banks on both sides. The paths generally stay close to the water, passing picnic areas shaded by tall cottonwood trees.

Where the park road crosses the creek near the velodrome, all the trails come together. The paved bicycle and hiking path starts here and continues through the park on the east side. Although there is no formal equestrian trail until after Metcalf Road, certain sections are used by local equestrians.

Waterfowl like Cottonwood Lake in Coyote Hellyer Park

Going upstream past picnickers and well above the creek level, the trail parallels the creek's meanders. At Hellyer Avenue the trail goes under the bridge, squeezed between a cyclone fence and the bridge abutments, high above the creek. Shortly it returns closer to creek level, skirting the parking and picnic areas. At low water you can hop across the creek. But after winter rains, this stream can be a deep, racing watercourse, to be treated with respect.

Now the trail leaves the creek and heads around Cotton-wood Lake, where more picnic tables and barbecues are placed under newly planted trees. Fishermen line the shores of the lake, often bringing in catches of trout and bluegill. On the far side of the lake is a children's playground and nearby a parking area.

2. From the Park to Silicon Valley Boulevard (4½ miles).

If you want to walk the midsection of the trail, you can use the southernmost parking area in Coyote Hellyer Park and find the trail as it dips under the concrete span of Highway 101. Now you enter a woodsy stretch where the gravelly creek bed is wide and wild black-berry bushes grow in mounds on the banks. This is the coolest section of the trip. In summer you can leave the trail to find shady stopping places under the cottonwood and sycamore trees.

As the trail heads south, passing a new industrial park on your left, you come to the end of Coyote Hellyer Park. For the next mile the trail lies in a narrow strip of publicly-owned park land by the creek.

As you continue, you find that the tree border changes to oaks with an understory of toyon, poison oak and elderberry bushes. Some of the oaks must be two hundred years old, their huge branches arching over the trail to make a leafy green canopy. If you pause for a while in their shade, you can hear woodpeckers hammering on dead tree trunks or quail calling in the bushes.

One and a half miles from the highway undercrossing a handsome bridge arches over the wide riparian corridor. Cross it to Shady Oaks Park, where acres of turf and benches under ancient oaks make a pleasant rest stop.

Then return to the trail and continue upstream past a few farms now being replaced by an industrial park. In ½ mile you reach a new bridge on Silver Creek Valley Road. The trail passes under the new bridge and then bears right on the old Fontanoso Avenue bridge to the west side of the creek. Use caution during the rainy season; the trail could be flooded.

Continuing southward, you stay close to the creek where there are a few orchards between you and the freeway. Passing a section where new houses fill the former farmlands, the creek makes a wide

Along the bicycle path beside Coyote Creek

arc to the left. The paved trail also bends left, but borders a percolation pond next to the creek.

Now scattered farms, an old fruit orchard and a few houses fill the land between the trail and the freeway. The wide band of public land beside Coyote Creek, preserved for public use, is welcome open space amid burgeoning housing developments and the busy freeway. The creek and trail wind through this open land before coming to the Silicon Valley Boulevard crossing.

3. From Silicon Valley Boulevard south to Burnett Avenue (10½ miles).

One could park a car at this trail entrance and walk along the creek in either direction for several miles, a pleasant stroll on a sunny winter day. In summer, it is a delightful late afternoon or early evening walk, since there are some fine big oak trees shading the way.

From Silicon Valley Boulevard southward, the trail follows the creek closely, often in sight of the freeway. In fact, the trail goes right under the freeway where it bridges the creek. You find a pleasant stream here, with alders and willows growing on the creek banks and reeds, blackberries and poison oak forming a dense undergrowth. Where the trail is high above the creek, the grandeur of the giant oaks reminds us that these may be the same magnificent trees Captain George Vancouver described so glowingly when he travelled through this valley from Monterey in 1792.

Here begins a series of percolation ponds extending all the way to Metcalf Road. This is the largest freshwater marsh in the county,

CONTINUED AT RIGHT, BOTTOM

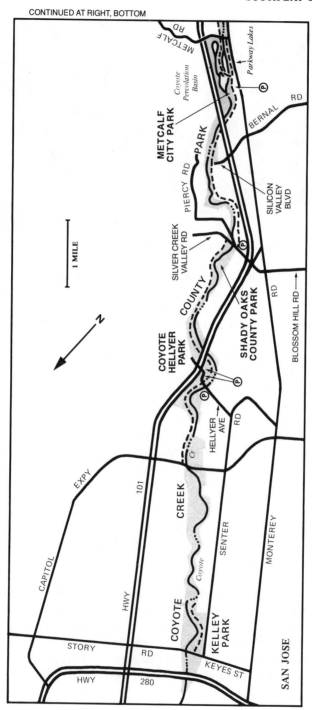

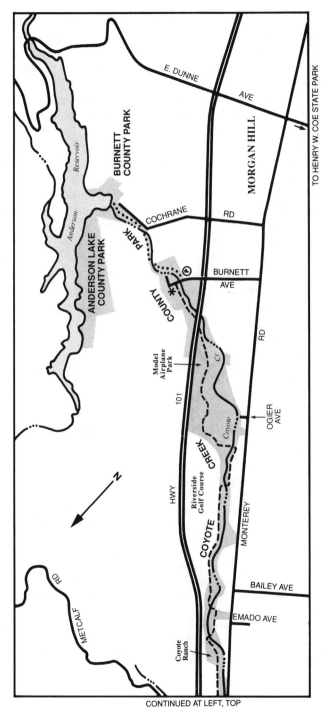

CONTINUED AT LEFT, TOP

attracting a great variety of birds—grebes, cormorants, kestrels, kingfishers and, of course, seagulls.

To the west of the ponds the trail passes a large subdivision and then winds through a new City of San Jose park. Though the trail is quite exposed now, newly planted trees bring promise of shade some day. A fresh expanse of turf, picnic tables and play areas, as well as public parking accessible from Monterey Road, make this a convenient, pleasant destination or a place to pause for lunch on your way upstream.

For a short open stretch you have views of the Santa Clara Valley foothills. Westward you can see the rounded hills of Santa Teresa County Park, where eventually an existing 6-mile segment of the Bay Area Ridge Trail will be connected to this trail. Southeast lies the low range of hills where Coyote Creek's waters are impounded behind Anderson Dam before they resume their journey to the Bay.

From the last half-mile of trail you can look out over the ponds where fishermen line the banks and members of a water-skiing club practice jumps and fancy maneuvers. Ducks and coots search the waters for food, while hawks patrol the skies for rodents that venture from their holes.

The trail ends just short of Metcalf Road, but Santa Clara County plans a single-span pedestrian/bicycle bridge to reach the east side of the percolation ponds and the next segment of the Coyote Creek Trail.

Trip 3.   Metcalf Road to Burnett Ave.

A new, 7-mile paved hiking and bicycling path and parallel equestrian trail continues upstream from Metcalf Road to Burnett Avenue. It is accessible from Monterey Road (Highway 82), in south San Jose, at Metcalf Road (Parkway Lakes) and at Burnett Avenue, its southern terminus. Officially dedicated in May 1992, this southern leg of the Coyote Creek Parkway meanders through public lands where the lush creekside environment of evergreen oaks, rangy sycamores, graceful willows and an understory of berries and shrubs is preserved. At three rest areas you can enjoy this quiet scene while eating your lunch at one of the picnic tables. A pause to watch the model airplanes take off and land at their own airport will add variety to the day's outing.

At the Anderson/Burnett Ranger Station on the east side of the creek the paved trail ends. Across the creek is a staging area for hikers, bicyclists and equestrians at the end of Burnett Avenue.

Penitencia Creek

Penitencia Creek originates high in the hills east of Alum Rock Park. Its waters are impounded in Cherry Flat Reservoir, then flow down to enter a steep-sided canyon near the park's east boundary. After cascading over falls, the creek is joined by the smaller Arroyo Aguague to become the centerpiece of Alum Rock Park. Leaving the park, it flows through residential neighborhoods, still retaining much of its stately tree border.

Long recognized as one of the county's loveliest watercourses, recent public acquisition of creekside lands now makes it possible for us to walk by its waters downstream from Alum Rock Park. Santa Clara County and San Jose City plans call for a Penitencia Creek Park Chain from Alum Rock Park to the Coyote Creek confluence at Berryessa Road.

A Stroll or Spin on the Penitencia Creek Trail

Follow the tree-lined creek for 3 miles to Alum Rock Park.

Jurisdiction   Santa Clara County.

Facilities   Trail: 3 miles hiking, bicycling. Penitencia Creek Park: picnic tables and play area. No restrooms. Some sections wheelchair accessible.

Park Rules   Hours: 8 A.M. to ½ hour after sunset. No dogs on trail.

Maps   Any street map; USGS quad *Calaveras Reservoir*.

How To Get There

By Car   From Freeway 101 in east San Jose take McKee Road east 1 mile to Jackson Avenue. Turn left and go ¾ mile to Penitencia Creek Park at Mabury Road.

By Bicycle   From bike lanes on Berryessa Road and Capitol Avenue enter the midsection of the trail and go east or west on the trail.

By Bus   County Transit 74 on Jackson and Mabury streets.

Distance   6 miles round trip.

Time   3 hours.

Elevation Gain   220'

Connecting Trail   The Creek Trail in Alum Rock Park.

TRAIL NOTES

Try this walk or bicycle ride on a sunny winter day or in the late afternoon in summer. Old sycamores, oaks and walnuts shade your way on the banks of Penitencia Creek. This trip is described going upstream from Penitencia Creek County Park at Mabury and Jackson streets to Alum Rock Park. Although some sections of the trail are not yet complete, sidewalks along Penitencia Creek Road fill in the gaps for the moment. Along the way the trail passes through small parks, beside several public schools and on top of levees by percolation ponds.

The Santa Clara Valley Water District manages the creek from Alum Rock Park west. Weirs and valves divert the water to percolation ponds, impound it behind small check dams or release it to flow freely down the creek.

Starting at Penitencia Creek County Park at the corner of Mabury and Jackson streets, you take the paved path that follows the creek upstream under tall cottonwoods, sycamores and oaks. Past a scatter of tables that offer places to picnic in sun or shade, you see a large turfed play area.

At the Jackson Avenue end of the park, go across the street to a center-striped path that meanders above the creek by Mossdale Way. At Gateview Drive the paved path veers left and ducks under the 680 Freeway. (A sign warns that the maximum clearance is 7 feet, plenty for hikers and bicyclists.) You emerge on the other side of the underpass where highway construction re-channeled the creekbed. Reeds and grasses now cover the banks, but you see the route of the old channel marked by a line of tall sycamores and valley oaks curving off to the south.

Now continue along the fenced bicycle and pedestrian trail above the creek to Capitol Avenue. Turning left on a bridge sidewalk and crossing the street takes you to a wide, paved trail winding through broad fields that alternately border an old orchard and the local streets. Never far from the creek, this path is well-used by local residents on foot, by bicycle and on roller skates.

From here you cross a footbridge to the north side of Penitencia Creek Road at Viceroy Way and continue on the levee trail under tall shade trees past the spacious playing fields of a city/county park adjoining a school.

From Piedmont Road to Noble Avenue, land acquisition along the creek for the public trail is almost complete, but a formal, paved, separated path was not finished at this writing. However, you can use the sidewalks on the south side from Bard Street to Toyon Avenue. From Noble Avenue to Tallent Avenue a levee trail follows

**Penitencia Creek in east San Jose
is impounded for groundwater recharge**

the north side of the creek, close to the neighboring houses. Then
pick up a southside creek path all the way to Poppy Lane.

The path beside the stream ends at Poppy Lane. You can retrace
your steps back to Penitencia Creek Park where there are picnic
tables by the creek with views of the eastern foothills. Or you can
continue to Alum Rock Park, by making your way 0.1 mile along the
edge of Penitencia Creek Road to the park's west entrance. There the
Creek Trail takes you in ½ mile to the Quail Hollow Picnic Area.

Back at the park at Mabury Road, downstream (west) sections of
paved trail alternate with informal paths through undeveloped park
lands and on top of levees as far as King Street. Or you might want
to cross Mabury Road to the East Side Union High School District's
Educational Park. Adjoining the school on the far side are the 33-
acre Overfelt Gardens.

Miss Mildred Overfelt gave this land in honor of her parents, early
San Jose pioneers. In the tradition of two other women benefactors
of the people of Santa Clara County, Josephine Grant and Sada Coe,
Miss Overfelt wanted her gift to become a place where one could
find peace and solitude. The lovely gardens can be viewed from
paths that meander past lakes, an amphitheatre, a Chinese Cultural
Center and a camellia garden. The gardens are open daily from 10
A.M. to sunset.

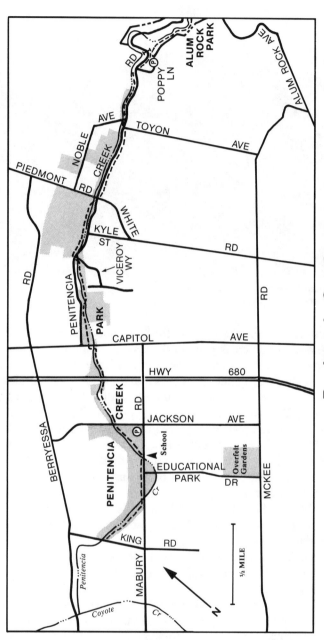

Penitencia Creek

Guadalupe River

From Mt. Umunhum to San Francisco Bay this year-round stream threads its way down steep hillsides, over gravelly flats, past suburban housing, through downtown San Jose and along the industrialized Bayside to the marshes and sloughs of the Bay.

Indians had three large villages beside the Guadalupe, and they followed it upstream to dig cinnabar in the Almaden Hills. They ground this red ore to paint their bodies and to barter with tribes up and down the Coast.

The first Spanish settlers built the Pueblo de San José close to the river banks, but they were flooded out and had to seek higher ground. Their final site for the pueblo, near today's downtown, proved to be more desirable. The Anglos extended the town to both sides of the river. In 1850 San Jose became the first capital of California.

The waters of the Guadalupe irrigated the early orchards in the Santa Clara Valley, but they flooded homes too. In 1935 the Guadalupe Dam was built to protect farmlands, and small dams and percolation ponds served to build up the groundwater storage. Although tamed by the dam upstream, the Guadalupe still flows in its tree-bordered riverbed relatively free of concrete and riprap.

Santa Clara County plans recognize the recreation potential of the Guadalupe River and recommend trails along its banks from the Almaden Hills to the Bay. Today the City of San Jose's Guadalupe River Parkway plan, now in its initial construction stage, calls for a three-mile linear park chain through the heart of downtown San Jose.

A river trail corridor from Virginia Street just south of Freeway 280 will connect with the Guadalupe Gardens, a regional park planned for open space uses in the vicinity of the airport approach zone. Then parkway trails will join the existing trail from West Mission Street to Highway 101.

The Guadalupe Parkway project will enhance the riparian habitat and emphasize the river as a natural resource to be enjoyed by citizens of San Jose and other communities. There will be places for recreation, from small lunchtime gatherings to large events at a riverside amphitheater.

The parkway plan incorporates flood control needs while fulfilling a need for open space and recreation areas in the urban environment of downtown San Jose. It will provide a continuous riverwalk with access to the river, passing under street bridges to avoid street crossings. A combination of gardens, terraced plazas, natural landscaping and unique water features is provided in the plan.

Portions of the riverwalk exist from Woz Way by the Children's Discovery Museum to Park Avenue. It is hoped that the parkway project from Freeway 280 to Freeway 880 will be carried out by the mid-1990s.

Eventually these paths for pedestrians and bicycles will be a part of a riverside trail system from the Guadalupe Dam to San Francisco Bay, creating a recreation facility worthy of this beautiful river.

Riverside Jogging Trails in Downtown San Jose from West Mission Street to Freeway 101

A path on the east bank of the Guadalupe River provides a convenient opportunity for runners from nearby offices.

Jurisdiction   City of San Jose.
Maps   San Jose street maps.
How To Get There
By Car   From Highway 17 near the San Jose Airport take the North First Street exit and go south on it to West Hedding Street. Turn right to Guadalupe Parkway and park in one of the public lots at the County or City government center or along the creek banks at West Mission Street.
By Bus   County Transit 62, 64, 75.
Distance   5 miles round trip.
Time   2½ hours.
Elevation Change   Nearly level.
TRAIL NOTES

Along the tree-lined Guadalupe River, the City of San Jose owns a broad corridor through which runs a path from West Mission Street to Bayshore Freeway. This path is popular with joggers from the office buildings nearby.

The trail on the east bank of the river starts from the vicinity of the government centers. Cross Guadalupe Parkway and step onto the informal path above the creek. Turn right and head downstream under trees that still grow along these once-heavily-wooded riverbanks. Under the bridge carrying Highway 17 there is enough headroom above the water except during flood conditions. Beyond the bridge the trail widens, following a levee service road, and continues past palm and pepper trees planted near early riverside homes. Beyond Brokaw Road the path continues to the freeway, where you must turn back. It is hoped that this trail will someday continue to the Bay on levees of the Santa Clara Valley Water District.

Beyond Bayshore Freeway the Santa Clara Valley Water District levees along the Guadalupe River, rebuilt in 1983 for flood control, could provide a trail route to Alviso and connections with Baylands trails and those of the San Francisco Bay National Wildlife Refuge near Alviso. There are as yet no formal trails on these levees, but the Water District allows recreational use of these routes if some governmental body takes the responsibility for operating and maintaining them.

The river north of Bayshore Freeway passes through industrial parks and small subdivisions. Historic buildings along the way—James Lick's Mansion and John Wade's house and barns—are close to its banks. North of Montague Expressway the river passes Agnews State Hospital and a municipal golf course. And a few bends before the river reaches the Bay in Guadalupe Slough it is bordered by a trail in Sunnyvale Baylands.

Marsh along the Guadalupe River near Sunnyvale Baylands

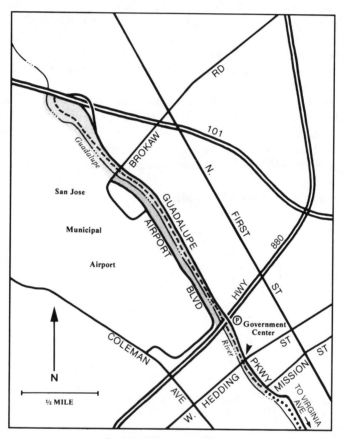

Guadalupe River

Los Alamitos and Calero Creeks

In the Almaden Valley the Los Alamitos Creek Trail south of the popular 54-acre Almaden Lake follows levees upstream to the confluence with its tributary, Calero Creek, and continues almost a mile beyond to Harry Road. Upstream along Calero Creek are trails as far as Harry Road, where a path continues up the creek and into Santa Teresa Park.

These trails will some day be important links in a continuous trail system that will join Almaden Quicksilver, Calero and Santa Teresa county parks. The Los Alamitos Creek Trail will be extended downstream around Almaden Lake to join the Guadalupe River Park Chain. This Almaden Valley trail will thus be a link in the City and County regional trail system.

Jurisdiction   City of San Jose, Santa Clara County.
Facilities   Paths for pedestrians, bicyclists and equestrians.
Maps   USGS quad *Santa Teresa Hills.*
How To Get There   From Almaden Expressway turn east on Winfield Drive, right on Cross Springs Dr, and left across the Mazzone Drive bridge. Trails on levees east of the Graystone Lane bridge are reached from Camden Avenue.

TRAIL NOTES

At this time only an unpaved path exists on the levee on the north side of the creek from south of Almaden Lake to the confluence of Calero Creek, and it is not a continuous route. The first access is from the north side of the Mazzone Drive bridge. You can walk up and down this lovely creek for about a mile. Ancient sycamores grow by the water's edge, their twisted white limbs hang over the creek and shade your way. On the banks are willows and maples, and live oaks line the creek corridor.

The grassy Santa Teresa Hills rise steeply above the northeast banks of the creek. Immense boulders at the base of the hills are outcrops of the same sandstone cut from quarries here to build Stanford University and the San Jose Hall of Justice. Near the trail the historic little Pfeiffer Stone House, built in 1875, housed tools for the quarry. As the creek meanders along its tree-bordered course, it widens into ponds, then narrows.

The City of San Jose's plan for development of this park chain emphasizes the natural riparian habitat, using native plantings. For Almaden Valley residents the parallel pedestrian, bicycle and equestrian paths will link small parks, playgrounds and community facilities along this winding year-round stream. Interpretive programs will highlight the values of such creek systems.

Beyond the confluence of the two creeks at Villagewood Drive, trails continue upstream. By Los Alamitos Creek are existing parallel paths, an asphalt path for bicycles on the levee and an unpaved pedestrian and equestrian path on a shelf above the creek. At Harry Road a proposed equestrian trail will go west to the Mockingbird Hill entrance to Almaden Quicksilver Park.

By Calero Creek are an existing equestrian trail and a bike/pedestrian trail at street level. Santa Clara County's unpaved trail continues upstream past Harry Road for 1½ miles, passing handsome sycamores and willows and lush creekside undergrowth. It then joins a trail into Santa Teresa Park. These trails through the Almaden Valley are expected to become links between the Bay Area Ridge Trail and the Bay Trail.

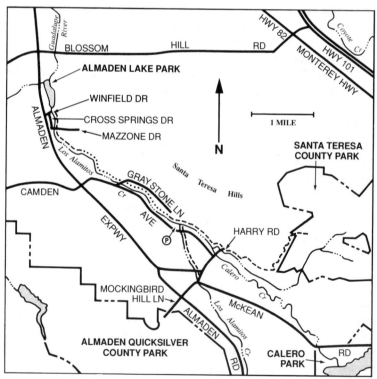

Los Alamitos/Calero Creeks

Los Gatos Creek

Los Gatos Creek originates on the south side of Loma Prieta, drains the western flanks of the northern Sierra Azul, and flows northwest in a beautiful canyon to Lake Elsman, a San Jose Water Company dam. After escaping the dam, it travels several miles in a deep canyon to its impoundment at Lexington Reservoir. From the spillway of this reservoir it continues through parks, percolation ponds, and residential and commercial areas to its confluence with the Guadalupe River in central San Jose.

The Santa Clara County Trails and Pathways Plan proposes almost 20 miles of trails along Los Gatos Creek's banks. Existing trails on the banks of Los Gatos Creek extend 4½ miles upstream from Campbell Park, through Los Gatos Creek Park to Vasona Lake Park in Los Gatos. From there a short stretch is missing, but the trail continues from Main Street in Los Gatos 2 miles to Lexington Dam. From Campbell Park the creekside trail continues downstream 2 miles to Leigh Avenue. Most of these trails are paved, and well-suited for bicycling, hiking and jogging. Many jurisdictions have cooperated to create this linear recreational parkway, including the cities of Los Gatos, San Jose and Campbell, Santa Clara County, the Santa Clara Valley Water District, and the State of California.

Jurisdiction   Parks, City of Campbell, Santa Clara County; Trails, Santa Clara County, Town of Los Gatos, City of San Jose.

Facilities   Trails: hiking, jogging, bicycling, skating. All parks—picnic and barbecue areas: family, groups by reservation; playgrounds; restrooms; parking. Other facilities: (1) Campbell Park—parcourse. (2) Los Gatos Creek Park—lake for windsurfing, model-boat sailing, fishing; observation tower. (3) Vasona Lake Park—lake for sailing; fishing pier; turfed activity area; miniature railroad; Youth Science Institute Museum.

Park Rules   (1) Campbell Park—Hours: 7 A.M. to 10 P.M. Group reservations for picnic areas at City Hall. Dogs on leash. (2) Los Gatos Creek and (3) Vasona Lake Park—Hours: 8 A.M. to ½ hour after sunset. Dogs on leash in designated areas only. No swimming. Fees: $3/car on Saturdays, Sundays and holidays. Seniors free. Phone: 408-356-2729 or 408-358-3751.

Maps   City of Campbell, *Campbell Park*, Santa Clara County, *Los Gatos Creek Trails, Vasona Lake Park;* USGS quads *San Jose West* and *Los Gatos.*

How To Get There

By Car (1) Campbell Park—From Highway 17 take the Hamilton Avenue exit and go west on it to Winchester Boulevard, where you turn left. At Campbell Avenue turn left and then turn right at Gilman Avenue and go to the park entrance on your left. (2) Los Gatos Creek Park— From Highway 17 take the Camden Avenue/San Tomas Expressway exit and go west on it. In less than ¼ mile turn right at the first exit onto Dell Avenue. Dell Avenue curves around south under Camden Avenue/San Tomas Expressway past Sunnyoaks Avenue to a small lane on your left which leads to the park. (3) Vasona Lake Park—From Highway 17 take Lark Avenue west to University Avenue and south to Blossom Hill Road, where you turn left to the park entrance.

By Bicycle   Bicycles can enter the parks' trails from several city streets.

By Bus   County Transit (1) Campbell Park—26; (2) Los Gatos Creek Park—38; (3) Vasona Lake Park—27, 38.

**Trip 1.   Upstream from Campbell Park
                              to Vasona Lake**

Join hikers, joggers, bicyclists and bird-lovers on 4½ miles of creekside trails. Convenient trail entry points at parks and major street crossings allow for short loops or trips of any length.

Distance   4½ miles one way with shuttle.

Time   2½ hours.

Elevation Gain   A slight rise upstream—150′

TRAIL NOTES

Try these paved level paths upstream from Campbell Park on a sunny winter day with the creek a torrent of storm waters, with winter-migrating waterfowl bobbing at its edge, and with a few dark clouds gathering over the distant mountains. You will have plenty of company—joggers, serious walkers, bicyclists and even some roller skaters. The busy scene is reminiscent of promenades on the banks of European rivers.

The native trees, alders, oaks and sycamores, planted when the trail was new, now branch overhead and the shrubs screen adjoining businesses and Highway 17. Wild fennel, willows and cattails grow along the creek banks.

Fishermen arrive early at a stocked percolation pond

Starting at Campbell Park on the west side of the creek a parcourse invites you to add a series of exercises to your walk or run. Prescribing stretching and bending movements at 18 stations, the course uses the trail on both sides of the creek.

Heading southwest, you are soon at the first dam. When the creek is running full, water pours over in a glistening sheet to break with a mighty roar below. From a convenient bench you can watch the spray and let the sound of falling water mask the presence of the nearby freeway. In summer, a limited amount of water goes over the spillway, and the stream, much tamed, is only inches deep.

If you are following the parcourse or ready to return to Campbell Park, a bridge crosses the stream just below the spillway. Wooden benches on the other side invite the casual stroller to pause and watch the ducks that fly up and down the stream. When you reach Campbell Avenue, cross the bridge and go down the stairs to Campbell Park's picnic tables and green lawns under the trees—a pleasant finish to a 3½-mile round trip.

If you continue upstream past the dam, the trail goes under Camden Avenue and in ¼ mile you reach the hub of Los Gatos Creek Park. This county park is especially appealing for its water-oriented sports. If the breeze is up, the wind surfers' brightly colored sailing craft on the percolation ponds will catch your eye.

Fishermen lining the banks of the pond near the parking area actually catch fish, and nearly tame ducks and geese paddle up for bread thrown out by excited children. If you plan to fish, look into the licensing requirements, as a State Fish and Game warden patrols the area.

Continuing upstream, take the paved path on the levee between the creek and the three large western ponds. You look across the creek to other percolation ponds edged with plantings of native shrubs that give food and shelter to many birds. Reportedly 100 species have been counted here.

To make best use of your bird book to identify the waterfowl, come during the spring nesting season when their plumage is brighter and more like the pictures. In winter, you will find migrating and resident ducks. But in any season you will recognize the handsome 20–30-inch-tall white egrets as they fly above you, their long legs stretched out behind.

Near the end of the third percolation pond you can cross the creek to the Observation Tower by taking the path to the left. (A wooden ramp makes the covered hexagonal deck wheelchair-accessible.) From here you have a long view east to the Diablo Range and west to the Santa Cruz Mountains. On a clear day you can see the observatory buildings on Mt. Hamilton. And on the creekside paths below, joggers, strollers and bicycle riders provide an almost continuous passing parade.

Retrace your steps to the main paved trail south to Vasona Park. The stream banks, though rock-lined against floods, support blackberries, coyote bushes, alders, willows and some ancient sycamores. On your right the urban scene encroaches. However, new development ordinances in the towns of Los Gatos, San Jose and Campbell required installation of trail segments according to an adopted plan, with plantings to grace the way.

Where the path forks, take the left path to follow the meandering creek to Lark Avenue, then cross the creek on the Lark Avenue bridge to a paved path on your right. Now your way passes close to backyards but borders the creek where alders, sycamores and cottonwoods line the bank. In ½ mile you will hear, especially in the rainy season, the sound of water thundering over the dam that impounds Vasona Lake. At the foot of the dam immense alders and oaks spread their roots out over the creek bank. The 30-foot-high dam, completed in 1935, was one of a half dozen conservation dams constructed at this time for flood protection and for restoration of Santa Clara Valley's rapidly falling water table.

When you have taken in the splashing waters of the spillway in winter or enjoyed the cool, leafy creekside in summer, follow the trail to the top of the dam. You will see Vasona's lakeside trails curving around to the picnic tables scattered through the park. The authors' favorite spot is on a slight rise under some of the park's magnificent oaks.

Boating on the lake, fishing piers, playgrounds for children and turfed activity areas attract large weekend crowds to this park at all times of the year. If children have accompanied you, a sure-fire treat is the miniature railroad that leaves from Oak Meadow Park on the northwest corner of Vasona Lake Park. A visit to the Youth Science Institute will intrigue nature-lovers, both young and old.

Your return to Campbell Park is a gentle downhill trip.

Trip 2.   Downstream from Campbell Park to Leigh Avenue

This newly completed, wide, paved trail attracts local residents and park visitors.

Distance   4 miles round trip.

Time   1 hour.

Elevation Loss   A small loss.

TRAIL NOTES

From Campbell Park you can make a 2-mile trip downstream along Los Gatos Creek. Leave the parking area at Campbell Park, cross the Campbell Avenue bridge and go right, down the ramp. Turn right again and walk under the bridge on a cantilevered wood-plank

Strollers downstream from Campbell Park

path with a yellow center stripe. This elaborate and expensive structure hanging over the creek demonstrates the City/County commitment to a continuous regional creekside trail system.

On this reach the trail passes inns, industrial and office buildings, with side trails leading to neighborhood streets and major shopping areas. The one to the Pruneyard, on a steep pitch, slows downcoming bicyclists with a maze of zigzag fencing. Up and down the path go rollerskaters, bicyclists young, old and just learning, skateboarders, joggers and of course those on foot. The traffic is heavy and it pays to be observant.

All the while the creek is just below the trail, flowing steadily between its banks to join the Guadalupe River. From the fenced trail are varied vistas of the creek corridor—sometimes a narrow channel enclosed by high side walls, sometimes a tree-canopied watercourse, and elsewhere a subdivision-lined creekside, where the path is bordered with fledgling trees and native shrubs.

Crossing under Highway 17, Hamilton and Bascom avenues, you finally come to Leigh Avenue, at this writing the end of the paved path. Between Bascom and Leigh avenues, the creekbed is wide, edged with subdivisions set back from the banks. Here are parallel paths, one paved for bicyclists, skaters and baby strollers, and another unsurfaced for joggers, pedestrians and dogs. Strict rules apply to dogs—they must be on leash at all times and their owners must pick up after them—so says the prominent sign at trail entrances.

Beyond Leigh Avenue, the creek continues its course toward the Guadalupe River and their combined passage to the Bay. As development occurs along this stretch, new creekside trails will be built. Someday we will be able to hike, bike, or skate our way to the Bay.

In the meantime, turn around at Leigh Avenue and retrace your steps with the multitudes of recreational travelers along this popular creekside trail.

Trip 3.   Forbes Mill to Lexington Dam

A wide trail through Los Gatos Creek's narrow canyon follows part of a historic route to the coast. Now modern joggers and strollers frequent the way used by Indians and early settlers.

How To Get There

By Car (1) Forbes Mill entrance—From Highway 17 take the East Los Gatos exit and go to Los Gatos Boulevard. Turn right. This becomes Main Street. Turn right on Church Street and go past shops and condominiums downhill to Forbes Mill Museum and parking. (2) Lexington Dam entrance—From Highway 17 2½ miles south of Los Gatos turn east on Alma Bridge Road to the dam, park at first building on left and find the trail entrance on the left.

By Bicycle Bike lanes on Los Gatos Boulevard and Main Street lead to Church Street and Forbes Mill Museum. Bike over-crossing of Highway 17 from Lundy Lane in West Los Gatos terminates at museum.

By Bus County Transit 62 and 76.

Distance 3.4 miles round trip.

Time 2 hours.

Elevation Gain 300'

TRAIL NOTES

Take this trail midday in winter months, when you can enjoy the creek racing down its channel, or in early spring, when you can look out over the delicate greens of budding alders and sycamores lining the canyon. In summer the sun makes the trail warm for much of its length, so walk it in early morning or in late afternoon when the sun is behind the hills.

Though this trail is accessible from either end and combines with trails in St. Joseph's Hill Open Space Preserve, starting the round trip from Forbes Mill takes advantage of a downhill return. First-time walkers should plan a trip when the attractive museum at the mill is open—Tuesdays through Sundays, 10 A.M.–4 P.M.

The old Forbes Mill was built by James Alexander Forbes in 1855, when he brought water to his grinding stones in a wooden flume from a mile up the creek. Photographs in the museum show an imposing four-story building of gray sandstone. After years of disuse only one story remained. Now rebuilt as a museum, it contains well-displayed photographs and artifacts of Santa Clara Valley history.

Scottish-born Forbes, who came to California already fluent in Spanish and experienced in business, became mayordomo for Mission Santa Clara. He took out Mexican citizenship and was granted Rancho Potrero de Santa Clara.

In 1850 Forbes acquired 2000 acres of Rancho Rinconada de Los Gatos on the creek and beside the mission trail between Santa Clara and Santa Cruz. When he built his mill with machinery ordered from New York, a delay in delivery resulted in losses that led to his bankruptcy. Although the mill eventually proved successful, he lost his mill and his fortune. Forbes then turned to horticulture, planting orchards in the valley.

Through this narrow canyon beside Forbes Mill centuries of
travelers have passed. Undoubtedly it was an Indian route to the
coast. Then it became the Mission Trail between Santa Clara and
Santa Cruz. Later, a stage line ran through the canyon, meeting
morning trains from San Francisco at the San Jose station, stopping
for lunch at the Lyndon Hotel in the Town of Lexington and then
going on to Santa Cruz.

Next, the Southern Pacific Company completed a railroad in
1888. Soon after the building of the Los Gatos/Santa Cruz Highway
in 1935, the railroad was abandoned. Now, on a modern four-lane
road, routed around Lexington Reservoir, a torrent of cars and
trucks pours over the summit of the Santa Cruz Mountains, linking
populous San Jose and Santa Cruz. Today, on foot, we have come
full circle—we walk here for pleasure and exercise.

To begin this walk take the marked trail entrance left of the
museum. This Town of Los Gatos trail goes under Main Street and
out between the concrete-channeled creek and Highway 17. The

Runners on the trail to Lexington Reservoir

sounds of traffic will lessen as the highway climbs above and away from the creek. Soon oak trees spread shade over the trail and alders grow by the creek, no longer confined to a trapezoidal ditch. Beside the trail under arching oaks is a huge pipe carrying water to thirsty San Jose from Lake Elsman. On shady banks bright yellow buttercups bloom by the path in spring, contrasting with the various blue blossoms of Douglas iris, larkspur and lupine.

As the trail gains elevation, the canyon opens up. Around a bend, Lexington Dam comes into view, rising nearly 200' above the creek bed. This rolled-earth dam, completed in 1955, flooded the little communities of Lexington and Alma and a lovely valley.

Soon the trail bears left and comes out at a bridge crossing the spillway. Far below you see the remnants of the old road, reached now by a path that takes you down to the stream. This is not recommended when winter rains swell the lake behind the dam and water pours out in torrents from the 50-inch outfall pipe.

The last push up the steep side of Lexington Dam is challenging. Downhill bicyclists who fail to heed the signs to walk their bikes may also be a challenge—be wary!

From the dam's crest you are rewarded by views of the reservoir and the heavily wooded hills of the Santa Cruz Mountains. The 1½-mile-long lake is popular for windsurfing, fishing and boating, but swimming is not allowed. You can watch the action at the lake or take Alma Bridge Road to the lakeside Oak Knoll Area for a picnic under the trees.

If you are going to take the loop trip, walk along Alma Bridge Road ¼ mile to St. Joseph's Hill Open Space Preserve and take the Jones Trail to Main Street in Los Gatos. The trail entrance is on your left. (See page 122.)

The trip back on the Los Gatos Creek Trail is an easy one, downhill all the way. If you have time, take the pedestrian overcrossing by the museum to Old Town Los Gatos with its antique stores, shops, and old buildings. With Phyllis Butler's *The Valley of Santa Clara—Historic Buildings, 1792–1920,* you can spend a fruitful day discovering the old town built around Forbes Mill, Forbestown, which was eventually renamed Los Gatos.

220

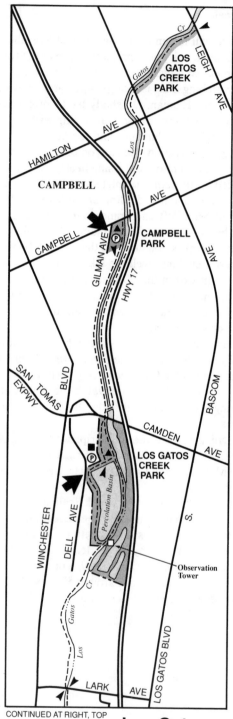

CONTINUED AT RIGHT, TOP

Los Gatos

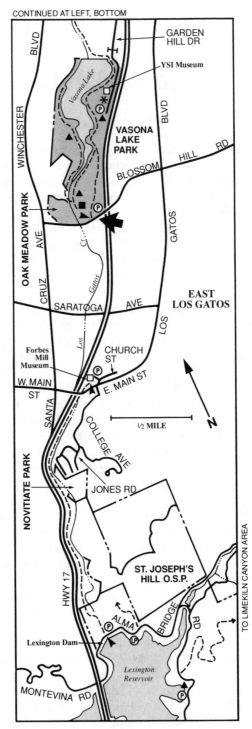

BLVD

GARDEN
HILL DR

YSI Museum

Vasona Lake

WINCHESTER

VASONA
LAKE
PARK

BLVD

HILL RD

BLOSSOM

OAK MEADOW PARK

GATOS

EAST
LOS GATOS

CRUZ

SARATOGA AVE

Los

Gatos Cr.

Forbes
Mill
Museum

CHURCH
ST

W. MAIN
ST

E. MAIN ST

SANTA

½ MILE

N

COLLEGE AVE

NOVITIATE PARK

JONES RD

ST. JOSEPH'S
HILL O.S.P.

HWY 17

ALMA

BRIDGE RD

Lexington Dam

Lexington
Reservoir

MONTEVINA RD

TO LIMEKILN CANYON AREA

Creek

The Baylands

Introduction

Over millennia San Francisco Bay has gone through many cycles of change. During the ice ages, when sea level was some 300 feet lower than it is now, the Bay was a valley. As the last ice age ended, the Bay was flooded until it reached approximately its pre-fill outline about 5,000 years ago.

As sediments from the surrounding mountains filled the depths of the South Bay during the past 200 years, the salt marshes, once narrow strips, broadened. In 1850 Bay marshes covered over 300 square miles. Now 80 percent of this area has been lost by filling and diking.

The South Bay, as Spanish explorers found it, was a narrow body of water bordered by broad salt marshes through which meandered sloughs carrying waters from the surrounding mountains.

When Gaspar de Portolá's expedition of 1776 approached the southern arm of San Francisco Bay, it had to keep inland to skirt impassable marshes. The next year Juan Bautista de Anza, Pedro Font and José Joaquin Moraga, setting out to explore the east side of the Bay, left camp on the Guadalupe River and met with a network of sloughs and marshes. Along Coyote Creek where it turns west, they were forced "to twist their way to higher ground at the foot of the hills." Traveling in late March, they went past level country "green and flower-covered," crossing five arroyos before coming to Alameda Creek.

Just upland of the marshes, these explorers came across Indian villages near sloughs where fish, shellfish and water fowl were plentiful. In canoe-like balsas made of bundles of tules, Indians traveled down the sloughs and out into the Bay to spear fish and to net waterfowl.

Soon after the founding of Mission Santa Clara and the Pueblo of San José, Alviso became the main port at this end of the Bay. During the next 100 years landings ringed the South Bay at the head of navigable waters on its sloughs. After completion of the railroad from San Francisco to San Jose, in 1864, these ports diminished in importance.

Sweeping changes in the South Bay came later, with the diking of its broad marshes to make salt-evaporator ponds, which began in the last century. By the 1940s much of the cordgrass had been eliminated by construction of salt ponds. Only a small fraction of marshland remained—along sloughs and in patches near their outlets. The value of the extraordinarily productive cordgrass is now recognized, and the remaining areas of it are protected. The shallow salt ponds do serve a function for wildlife, having become feeding grounds for myriad resident shorebirds and migrants. Some levees are now important nesting grounds for several bird species.

Here and there South Bay marshes were filled in the first half of this century. Only since World War II, however, have our marshes, tidelands and flood plains in the South Bay come to be viewed as real estate, to be filled to make acreage for industry and houses to serve the surging population of Santa Clara and Alameda counties.

The Bay's edge has been used not only for salt ponds but more recently for dumping garbage and sewage and also for industry. As more creeks were dammed, spring runoffs decreased and so was their flushing action in the Bay.

By the 1950s public clamor against pollution, degradation and filling of the Bay grew into a campaign to "Save the Bay." Biologists, naturalists, ornithologists and botanists who had long recognized the damage being done were joined in the 1960s by a groundswell of conservation activists. Led by such crusaders as Lucy Evans and Harriet Mundy in the South Bay, the indomitable Helen Kerr and Sylvia McLaughlin and Esther Gulick in Berkeley, the Save the Bay organization was born. Legislation passed in 1968 created the Bay Conservation and Development Commission, which has controlled development within 100 feet of the shoreline.

The commission has had considerable success in reversing the trend of pollution and fill. Parks, preserves and wildlife refuges around much of the South Bay now allow frequent public access to the shoreline. Regulations of the Army Corps of Engineers now afford some protection to seasonal wetlands.

Today, in parks and preserves around the Bay trails draw hikers, bicyclists, runners, birdwatchers and nature buffs to the marshes, sloughs, and salt ponds by the Bay. At visitor centers and museums and through workshops and conducted tours, the public is learning about the ever-changing tidelands, marshes, mudflats and sloughs that were once out of sight and out of mind.

For a deeper understanding of the South Bay, its natural history and its wildlife, the authors heartily recommend Diane Conradson's *Exploring Our Baylands,* the revised and expanded second edition of 1983. It will enrich any trip by the Bay. The Santa Clara Valley Audubon Society's *Birding at the Bottom of the Bay* gives novice and expert alike a good idea of what birds are found in our Baylands.

The Bay Trail

After many years of planning and effort, a system of trails around the South Bay is taking shape. The concept of a Bay trail was included in Santa Clara County plans as early as 1973 and by 1983 Palo Alto had a Bayfront Trail.

Further impetus to Bay trails came from the Bay Trail legislation of 1987, requiring the Association of Bay Area Governments to prepare a recreation trail for hikers and bicyclists ringing San Francisco and San Pablo bays. A Bay Trail plan, prepared with advice of citizen committees and local officials, is now being implemented with the cooperation of federal, state and local government agencies.

Today many miles of trail are open to hikers and bicyclists from Palo Alto to Alviso, and more miles down the eastern shores from Coyote Hills to Newark are now in place. Palo Alto's Bayfront Trail continues past its flood-control basin and joins Mountain View's Shoreline and Bayfront Trail. A bridge across Stevens Creek to the Midpeninsula Regional Open Space District's Stevens Creek Nature Study Area takes the trail down to Moffett Field.

Although Moffett Field still presents a trail-routing problem, an easement runs south of there through industrial land to Sunnyvale's Baylands. The City of Sunnyvale opened nearly 4 miles of trail around levees bayward of its water-treatment plant. The adjoining Sunnyvale/Santa Clara County Baylands will have a wetlands preserve with trails at its perimeter.

An extension of the Bay Trail is planned for the next few miles to Alviso, and thence, by an as yet undecided route, to Dixon Landing. Just north is a 2-mile stretch of existing Bay Trail through marshes and Coyote Slough Lagoon. From there routes are under discussion, at this writing, for a link to the San Francisco Bay National Wildlife Refuge at Newark. Refuge trails join Coyote Hills Regional Park trails, reaching all the way to Alameda Creek, thus completing the part of the Bay Trail around the South Bay.

The plan for this regional Bay Trail also provides for connections to existing parks and creeks and to existing and proposed transportation facilities. Public agencies are making progress in filling the gaps in the South Bay. Persistent trail enthusiasts and planners from four counties, a half dozen cities, the National Wildlife Refuge and the Midpeninsula Regional Open Space District, with the cooperation of flood-control districts, public-works departments and special districts, have already put together miles of Bayside trails. It may be some years before you can bicycle or walk completely around the South Bay, but an impressive start has been made.

Coyote Hills Regional Park

SEE MAP ON PAGE 234

In this park are a thousand acres of gentle hills, fresh-water and salt marshes, and the site of an Indian village and its 2300-year-old shell mounds. The park is a sanctuary for wildlife, which the visitor can observe at close hand from park trails and boardwalks.

The Coyote Hills are a rocky miniature range, rising from an alluvial plain. Juan Bautista de Anza's party, when exploring this side of the Bay, looked out from the lower East Bay hills and mistook these hills for islands, perhaps seeing some of the surrounding land and marshes flooded at high tide.

Both fresh-water and salt marshes attract a great variety of birds. The upland meadows provide habitats for songbirds, small animals and even a herd of deer. Bayward of the park are the salt ponds, levee trails and marshes of the San Francisco Bay National Wildlife Refuge, where you can walk at the edge of the Bay by one of our largest remaining natural salt marshes. The salt ponds are haven to a multitude of water birds, both resident and migrant.

This fertile site was home to Ohlone Indians. Their village by the Willows Marsh is gone, but their shell mounds are still visible. Through archeological investigations of the site facsimiles of Indian structures have been built. Programs centered on the Indian village site bring to life the culture of those who lived here for thousands of years.

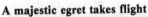
A majestic egret takes flight

The Spanish grant of these hills and surrounding lands was known as Potrero de los Cerritos—"Pasture of the Little Hills." Since that time, dairy farming, truck farming and commercial duck hunting have been carried on here. At one time a thousand ducks a week were shipped to San Francisco restaurants. More recently military installations and research laboratories have occupied the hills. Today a quarry is fenced off on the southern hilltop. The East Bay Regional Park District acquired this site in 1967.

TheVisitor Center, refurbished in 1990, offers handsome displays of the Indians, the plants and animals they used, their tools, and a diorama of the site where they lived. Here too is a full-scale reconstruction of a tule boat like those they paddled in the sloughs for fishing, hunting and trading.

Children and their parents can learn through doing with the "Discovery Boxes", which contain Indian games, tools, as well as nature exploration kits. Weekend programs by the park's naturalists will add to the pleasure of your visit. You can even join a weekend work party and take part in the reconstruction of the Indian village. A fine introduction to Coyote Hills is a 14-minute videotape, shown on request, highlighting the park's features. Videos on the Indians and marshes are also available. For information on park programs call the center at 415-795-9385.

More than 16 miles of trails take visitors through the park's hills, marshes and salt ponds. There is a connection for hikers and bicyclists to the Alameda Creek Regional Trail, which extends 8½ miles to Niles and 3 miles to the Bay. You can continue on the San Francisco Bay National Wildlife Refuge's Shoreline Trail, on an outer levee, to the Dumbarton Bridge approach. Now the Apay Way joins Coyote Hills to trails at the Wildlife Refuge Visitor Center.

Jurisdiction   East Bay Regional Park District.

Facilities   Visitor Center. Trails: hiking, bicycling, equestrian, nature. Picnic areas and barbecues: family and group. Group camping, day and overnight, by reservation. Many of the trails and programs are suitable for the physically limited. Phone: 415-795-9385.

Park Rules   Hours: 8 A.M. to posted closing hour. Visitor Center hours: Thursdays to Sundays, 9:30 A.M. to 5 P.M., . Dogs must be on leash at all times. No dogs allowed in marsh areas or on levee trails. Fee: $2/car on weekends and holidays. Dog fee: $1.

Maps   EBRPD *Coyote Hills Regional Park;* USGS quad *Newark.*

How To Get There

By Car From Highway 84, turn north on Paseo Padre Parkway and left on Commerce Road. Then proceed west on Patterson Ranch Road for 1.1 mile to park entrance gate.

By Bicycle Take the Alameda Creek Regional Trail from the east and Dumbarton Bridge bike lanes from the west.

Trip 1. Bayview Trail

Hikers and bicyclists circle a hill for a bird's-eye view of the park and its surroundings.

Distance 3.5-mile loop.

Time 2 hours.

Elevation Gain 50'; 200', if you go to the hilltop.

Connecting Trails Shoreline Trail south to Dumbarton Bridge approach. Apay Way to Wildlife Refuge Visitor Center, Alameda Creek Regional Trail east to Niles.

TRAIL NOTES

Start through a gate on the road north of the Visitor Center parking lot and continue out around the north end of Coyote Hills. The Bayview Trail goes along the hillside through open grassland. Looking east over the fresh-water marsh, you will usually catch sight of some white egrets. You will easily identify this large, long-legged wading bird, over 30" tall, which hunts fish, frogs and other small animals in the marshes. In flight its neck forms an "S" curve; its cry is a low croaking sound. As you go up the hill, you may startle a ring-necked pheasant into noisy, whirring flight. This spectacular bird, with its long, pointed tail, was introduced from China as a game bird, and now is spreading over much of the western U.S.

Continuing around the hill, the trail keeps to an elevation about 50 feet above the Bay. Below, where once was marsh, are the salt-evaporator ponds in the San Francisco Bay National Wildlife Refuge. The Alameda Creek flood-control channel flows along the northern boundary of this park. A short trail joins the bicycle and hiking trail on the south side of the channel. Just opposite this trail you can go uphill (south) and walk the length of Red Hill for broad views of the Bay. But the Bayview Trail continues around the bend, where you can take the stairs down to the Pelican Trail which skirts a marsh and continues to the Shoreline Trail. (See Trip 4.)

Returning to the Bayview Trail, we can enjoy the view over the salt ponds to the far levee and its fringe of marsh and, beyond, the Peninsula hills. Birds fill the shallow ponds, particularly in fall and winter when resident birds are joined by migrants. Stop a while to listen to the fine chorus of their calls and cries.

Where the trail starts to turn away from the Bay you pass the No Name Trail which follows a levee to the Shoreline Trail at the Bay's edge. The Bayview Trail now turns east through a low saddle toward a fresh-water marsh on the east side of Coyote Hills. The Meadowlark Loop Trail turns south here, but we veer toward the Visitor Center and go around a bend above Dairy Glen, a reservation camping and picnic area.

The Bayview Trail continues east but we turn off left on the Soaproot Trail. After ¼ mile we are over another saddle and looking down on the lawns, trees and tables of the picnic grounds at the Visitor Center—and the end of our trip.

Trip 2.   Boardwalk and Muskrat Loop Trail

Take a walk over ponds of a fresh-water marsh and along the tule-bordered Muskrat Trail to one of the finest birding areas around the Bay.

Distance   1.5-mile loop.

Time   1 hour; more if the birding is good.

Elevation Change   Level. Wheelchair access.

TRAIL NOTES

From the Visitor Center walk across the main entrance road and veer right to the boardwalk. Here you enter the special world of a fresh-water marsh teeming with life. The boardwalk, following a labyrinthine course, crosses small ponds and takes you down narrow passages through shoulder-high cattails and past openings to larger bodies of water. You can look down into algae-rich shallows where decomposing reeds are a nourishing breeding ground for myriad insects and microorganisms and darting schools of tiny fish. Dragon-flies skim the surface, and waterfowl in great variety feed here.

Convenient benches let you rest and take in the scene around you. The boardwalk is a birder's delight—from it many a rare bird can be sighted. If you take one of the naturalist's bird walks here, you will soon be checking off species on the park's handy bird list.

Soon after the boardwalk ends, you turn south on the Muskrat Trail, which leads through the higher and drier parts of the marsh. During winters of heavy rainfall this whole marsh area can become a vast lake, sometimes submerging the trail. As the water level drops in spring, new growth comes out on the tules and cattails. Binoculars and bird books are available for loan at the Visitor Center desk.

Turn to look over the expanse of cattails and tules, and you can understand what an inexhaustible supply of material they offered the Indians, who used them to make mats and thatching for their houses and to build the boats (balsas) that carried them out into the Bay.

The Muskrat Trail continues through seasonal wetlands, crosses the park entry road and then turns north back to the Visitor Center. On the way back you pass Castle Rock, an imposing outcrop of chert, formed from minerals and the shells of tiny marine animals and uplifted from an ancient sea floor.

Trip 3. Chochenyo Trail

A walk into the past takes you through marsh uplands to the site of an Indian village.

Distance 3-mile loop.

Time 1½ hours.

Elevation Change Level. Wheelchair access.

TRAIL NOTES

This trail extends north from the park entrance on Patterson Ranch Road to the fenced-off village site, circles it, and turns down to the Visitor Center. You can start from either the park entrance or the Visitor Center.

Starting from the Visitor Center, you can use the boardwalk through the marsh or go due north on the Chochenyo Trail, turn east on the D.U.S.T. Trail, then make a short jog south to continue east on the Chochenyo Trail. When you come to the village site, on a small rise surrounded by willows, go around to the far side, where you can look through a chain-link fence at some of the village reconstruction. For a better view, most Sundays at 2 P.M.—weather permitting and by reservation—you can meet the park naturalist and join in a walk to the village. Sitting by the excavation, you can hear about the Ohlone Indians who lived here. Or you can take part in one of the park's programs on Indians at the Visitor Center learning some of the skills the native Americans used in their everyday lives. You have a chance to try your hand at making string or shaping an arrowhead, and to see how a fire is made without matches or flint and steel. For information call the Visitor Center.

As you walk this trail in summer or fall, you can make out tracks of many small animals in the dust of the path. You may even catch sight of a deer bounding through the tules. It is not hard to imagine how easily this land could support the Ohlones of this village. When they lived here, there were water birds and game animals in vast numbers. Fish filled the creeks, and free for the gathering were little spiral-shelled California horn snails, which grew abundantly in mud flats and on rocks. The shells of this snail, a staple of the village diet along with oysters, fill the mounds that have been excavated at the park.

Trip 4.   Meadowlark Loop Trail

This trip takes you to high grasslands where meadowlarks sing and along remote inland fresh-water marshes.

Distance   3-mile loop.

Time   1 to 2 hours.

Elevation Gain   200'

TRAIL NOTES

Start off on the foot trail west of the Visitor Center and go south over the rise ahead and downhill for about ¼ mile. Veer right on the Bayview Trail and pass the Dairy Glen day camp. When you reach the saddle between Red Hill and the southern ridge of Coyote Hills, there are several trails. This trip starts on the level trail closest to the marsh, for hikers only, and returns on the ridgetop trail.

Walk a few paces due south, then veer left on a wide trail that lies in the lee of the ridge. This is a good hike for those windy days in spring, when you and the birds seek the warm, protected grasslands. Watch the red-winged blackbirds fluttering from cattails to reeds, catching insects for their young.

Winding along beside the marsh on this unpaved trail, you may come across one of the huge black-tailed jackrabbits that live in the grass. It may try to escape your notice by lowering its long ears and huddling close to the ground or it may bound away in 10-foot leaps.

Listen for the meadowlarks. These robin-sized birds, bright yellow beneath and mottled brown above, nest in the grass. Hearing their loud and lovely flute like song is one of the pleasures of walking over open hills. As their grassland habitat is reduced by encroaching development, however, their song is becoming rarer.

In about ¾ mile you meet a gravelled road turning sharply uphill toward the top of the ridge. Go right on it and follow it past fields of fennel and remnants of former military installations. At the ridgetop you meet the paved Meadowlark Trail, the return leg of your loop. But first take in the commanding views of the Bay and the sweep of East Bay hills. From here too, you look down on the bright blue waters of the many sloughs, hidden behind the reeds as you walked by earlier. From these heights you can grasp the extent of these

Meadowlark Loop Trail winds beside the south marsh

marshes and seasonal wetlands, once home to the Ohlone Indians.

Turn right and head downhill past chert outcrops, a few scattered shrubs and flowers blooming in the grasslands. The way is lined with a veritable forest of fennel that lends an aromatic flavor to Bay breezes. The miles of paved trails in this park, accessible to nearby city-dwellers by off-road trails, are ideal for bicyclists.

At the bottom of the hill turn right to retrace your steps to the Visitor Center.

Trip 5. The Apay Way to the Wildlife Refuge

Walk the route of the Bright Moon to reach the San Francisco Bay National Wildlife Refuge. Or ride your bicycle and pedal the levee trails beside the salt ponds.

Distance 3½ miles.

Time 2 hours.

Elevation Gain Nearly level.

TRAIL NOTES

Start this trip as in Trip 4, but go through the saddle and turn south on the bayside trail. You skirt the ponds, winding in and out of little coves close to the water.

On one of the windless, warm days by the Bay that sometimes come in spring and fall (and occasionally throughout the year), this is a choice route that will tempt you to linger and picnic along the way on a small peninsula extending out into the water. The grassy hillsides blossom in spring with poppies and mustard. Here and there small eucalyptus groves mark the sites of early homes.

There are deer here, too, that find cover in the scant brush or the tall stands of fennel growing so plentifully. At the south end of the hill, a quarry is still in operation. Past its excavations, fenced off from the trail, you veer right to reach the overcrossing of the Dumbarton Bridge toll plaza, which makes it possible for us to cross safely. Then take a trail that winds through toyon, ceanothus and fremontia to the base of the hill where you see the Refuge Visitor Center.

Trip 6.   Shoreline Loop Trail
(Operated by San Francisco Bay
National Wildlife Refuge)

A bracing walk on the levees to the edge of the Bay and to the Ideal Marsh gives you open views of the North Bay and its bird life along the salt ponds.

Distance   7.5-mile loop, plus 1.5-mile trip along Ideal Marsh.
Time   4 hours.
Elevation Change   Level, except for small rise from levee.
Connecting Trails   Alameda Creek Regional Trail east to Niles and continuation of Shoreline Trail south to Dumbarton Bridge.

TRAIL NOTES

Start your trip from the Visitor Center on the Bayview Trail, leaving it for the Pelican Trail as it rounds the northern tip of Coyote Hills. Stop at the overlook, from which stairs lead down to the levee. Explanatory panels here introduce you to the life in salt ponds and marshes. Since the levee trail must be rebuilt at intervals it becomes rough and impassable for a year or two at a time.

The Pelican Trail jogs around a stretch of marsh by the channel of Patterson Creek, then joins the outer levee trail by Coyote Slough and the Alameda Creek flood-control channel. This gravelled path on the levee takes you past salt ponds that change color as the evaporation process increases salt concentration. Growth of algae turns the water greenish; then, as brine shrimps proliferate, the water becomes pinkish.

Fall and spring bring flocks of migratory birds along the Pacific Flyway, but any time of year there are great egrets and great blue herons. A novice will have no trouble identifying both of these long-legged birds, standing 3–4' tall. Fall finds the ponds lively with more varieties of ducks than the inexpert can distinguish. Distinguish

Looking across Ideal Marsh to Coyote Hills

them or not, anyone can take pleasure in watching the flight patterns, plumage and distinctive gaits and feeding habits of the many species of visiting and resident birds. Join some of the weekend bird walks with a bird field manual and your binoculars, and you will soon be telling a canvasback from a pintail and an avocet from a godwit.

When you reach the western side of the levee, about 2 miles from shore, the outboard side of the trail is edged with a remnant of natural marsh. Tall cordgrass, green in spring and brown in fall, is washed by daily tides. The changing edge of marsh erodes in heavy winter storms but tends to build up again with deposits of dead cordgrass.

As our trail comes to the Ideal Marsh, it turns back east. This is the largest area of original marshland left in this part of the Bay. Even if you do not want to take the 1.5-mile side trip, it is worth going down this marsh a little way before you turn back to the hills. A century ago more than 300 square miles of tide-washed cordgrass marsh like this fragment ringed the Bay. Today 80% of it has been filled or diked. Sloughs from creeks and streams draining into the Bay meandered through these vast green expanses, their muddy banks at low tide a rich source of food for myriad shore birds.

On the levee trail south of Ideal Marsh, you can continue to the Dumbarton Bridge approach, about 2 miles past the marsh. You can also reach this trail from the south side of the bridge approach, where a paved road, the continuation of Marshlands Road is open to vehicles for access to a popular fishing pier. Here, too, is the beginning of the bike lanes that span the Bay on the Dumbarton Bridge.

To return to Coyote Hills, retrace your steps to the north end of Ideal Marsh, then turn east for a 1.5-mile walk on the No Name Trail beside the salt ponds to the Bayview Trail.

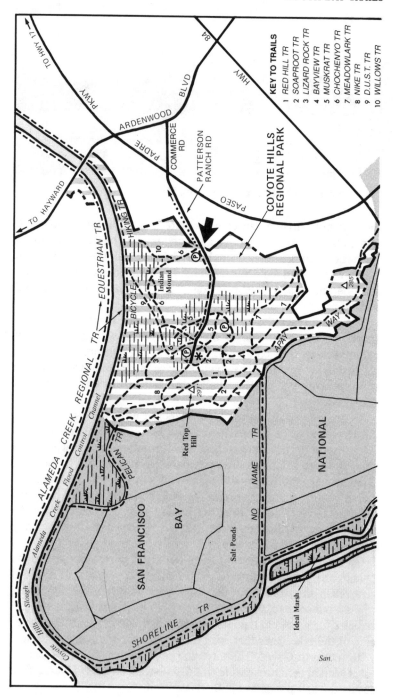

KEY TO TRAILS
1 RED HILL TR
2 SOAPROOT TR
3 LIZARD ROCK TR
4 BAYVIEW TR
5 MUSKRAT TR
6 CHOCHENYO TR
7 MEADOWLARK TR
8 NIKE TR
9 D.U.S.T. TR
10 WILLOWS TR

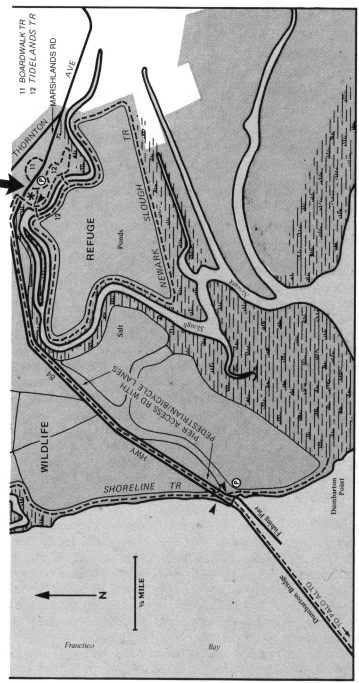

11 BOARDWALK TR
12 TIDELANDS TR

MARSHLANDS RD

THORNTON AVE

REFUGE

Ponds

NEWARK SLOUGH

TR

Salt

Slough

Newark Slough

WILDLIFE

84

PIER ACCESS RD WITH
PEDESTRIAN/BICYCLE LANES

SHORELINE TR

HWY

Dumbarton Point

Fishing Pier

Dumbarton Bridge

TO PALO ALTO

N

½ MILE

Francisco Bay

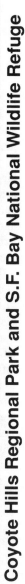

Coyote Hills Regional Park and S.F. Bay National Wildlife Refuge

San Francisco Bay National Wildlife Refuge

SEE MAPS ON PAGES 234-35 AND 250-51

The 18,000-acre San Francisco Bay National Wildlife Refuge encompasses many of the South Bay's marshes, salt ponds, sloughs, mud flats and open waters and provides a unique opportunity to experience this bayland environment on many miles of trails. The largest urban refuge in the National Wildlife Refuge system, it was established "for the preservation and enhancement of highly significant wildlife habitat . . . for the protection of migratory waterfowl and other wildlife, including species known to be threatened with extinction, and to provide an opportunity for wildlife-oriented recreation and nature study."

The handsome Visitor Center building on a promontory on the south end of the Coyote Hills, near the eastern approach to the Dumbarton Bridge at Newark, houses lively displays of Bay natural history, including a boardwalk trip simulating the mudflats and marshes you can visit across Marshlands Road. A book sales area and an information desk at the entrance to the center offer maps and information about interpretive programs. These programs, planned to interest visitors of all ages, range from elementary bird walks to slough trips by canoe. A docent program enlists and trains volunteers who assist the refuge in expanding its information and education programs. A trip to the Visitor Center at refuge headquarters will open your eyes, challenge your mind and entertain your children.

Miles of trails will take you on levees beside marshes and sloughs. A new half-mile boardwalk trail over bridges and levees takes visitors through the sloughs east of the Visitor Center. The Refuge has developed a "do-it-yourself" trip around its headquarters, with information panels explaining the dynamics of tidelands, their wildlife and some local history. In addition, more than 30 miles of trails along the Bay shore and out onto levees surrounding salt ponds are currently open to hikers and bicyclists. From these trails visitors can see tidal action at close hand in the marshes, watch shore birds feeding in the salt ponds and look for birds migrating along the Pacific Flyway.

The trails around refuge headquarters now connect with a trail at the south end of Coyote Hills Regional Park by a foot-and-bicycle bridge over the Dumbarton Bridge toll plaza. (See Coyote Hills Trip 5.)

Down the Bay at Station Island the Refuge conducts tours, by reservation, into the historic town of Drawbridge. A new section of the Bay Trail goes through the Refuge's Coyote Slough Lagoon near the Warm Springs District of Fremont.

At Alviso the Environmental Education Center on the edge of a marsh carries on research and teacher-training programs in its laboratories, library and observation tower. The center is open free to school classes and organized groups. Nearby 9 miles of trail circle salt ponds and marshes.

The refuge owns 12,000 acres of salt-evaporator ponds that are still in use for salt production. By agreement, the Leslie Salt Company can continue its salt operations as long as it wants if it uses its present methods of solar evaporation and does not fill in any open water areas. The levees, made of dredged mud, deteriorate and must be rebuilt at intervals, a process that leaves them rough for a year or two. Because most of the refuge's trails utilize levees, trail routes will change from time to time as levees are closed for repairs. Trails are rerouted until the surface has consolidated. And some levees are closed during the season when waterfowl use them for nesting grounds.

**New trail on bridges and levees
through restored marsh east of Refuge Visitor Center**

Fishing is permitted from the outer levees north and south of the Dumbarton Bridge east approach and from fishing piers at both ends of the old Dumbarton Bridge. These piers also provide good bird-watching. Waterfowl hunting is allowed on some levees and from boats in some of the refuge's salt ponds, sloughs and open waters. Although you may see boats with hunters and their dogs near the Visitor and Environmental Education centers, hunting is forbidden in these areas.

For recorded information on current activities at the refuge, call 415-792-3178.

Jurisdiction   U.S. Department of the Interior, Fish and Wildlife Service.

Facilities   Visitor Center, Environmental Education Center. Trails: hiking, bicycling, self-guided nature. Picnic tables. Hunting and fishing in designated areas. Handicapped facilities: Call or write for further information.

Refuge Rules   Stay on the trails to protect yourself and the refuge resources. Pets, allowed only on the Tidelands Trail, must be leashed at all times; not permitted elsewhere in refuge. Hours: Visitor Center, daily 10 A.M. to 5 P.M.; closed on Thanksgiving, Christmas and New Year's Day. Trails open every day during daylight hours. Parking lot locked at 5 P.M.

Maps   SFBNWR *Wildlife Refuge;* USGS quad *Milpitas.*

How To Get There

By Car   From Highway 84, go south on Thornton Avenue, turn right on Marshlands Road to Refuge Visitor Center.

By Bicycle   Bike lanes on Dumbarton Bridge from west and trail from Coyote Hills Regional Park over the bridge toll plaza.

Trip 1.   Tidelands Trail

On this short, self-guided nature trail you can walk beside a marsh and tidal slough, stop for a picnic in a former salt company pumphouse, hide in an old duck blind to watch the birds and, along the way, learn about the plant and animal life of the South Bay.

Distance   1⅓ miles.

Time   1 hour allows time to read the information panels.

Elevation Gain   Generally level, except for a 150' climb from the marsh to the Visitor Center, and on to the hilltop.

TRAIL NOTES

This trail, designated a National Recreation Trail by the Department of the Interior, begins opposite the main entrance of the Visitor Center. It takes you to a hilltop for a view of the Newark Slough and the Bay and down to a salt pond levee where a series of information panels describes the scene around you.

From the parking lot take the path to the Visitor Center and start your trip at the overlook opposite the main entrance. Information on the Bay and its tides is here. Then go left, uphill to a knoll, the high point of the hill. Be sure to stop at the crow's-nest observation platform, fenced against strong Bay winds, for a commanding view of the salt ponds and the Bay. You will be able to trace the course of Newark Slough first north, then west around the salt pond, then bending south to meander out to the Bay. On a clear day you can see ships and sailboats against the backdrop of the Santa Cruz Mountains on the far shore.

By the crow's nest is a picnic table protected from the breezes, with views toward the East Bay hills—a good place for an early lunch at the start of your trip or for an early picnic supper on a warm summer evening some other time.

Harbor seals are often seen in the South Bay

From here the trail leads downhill past other enlightening information panels to the level of the marshlands. An overlook at the edge of
the marsh bears an account of the busy water traffic that once
headed up Newark Slough. A landing here was the embarcadero of
Mission San José, 8 miles east. In the mid-1800s travel across the
Bay by boat was easier and more direct than long journeys over bad
roads. Hay barges and schooners loaded at what became known as
Jarvis Landing. However, in the late 1800s railroads and improved
roads began to take the place of water traffic, and a severe land subsidence due to pumping water from nearby wells caused flooding of
warehouses at the landing. The landing was not used after World
War I.

Along the trail, in a craggy chert outcrop, grow century plants and
aloes possibly left from the garden of a house that once stood on this
hill. Around the bend at another overlook you learn about marshland
inhabitants and their adjustment to the ebb and flow of tides.

From here a short trail continues northwest on this level back to
the picnic tables below the Visitor Center, but the Tidelands Trail
descends on a switchback down to a handsome bridge crossing
Newark Slough.

At the far side of the bridge, you come to the levee trail. Keep
right. The trail going left is the 5-mile Newark Slough Trail. Along
the levee trail you have marsh and a tidal slough on your right, a salt-
evaporator pond on your left.

A salt marsh, an intricate natural system converting the sun's
energy to plants and animals, is a place of incredible productivity,
sustaining a rich variety of life. Salt ponds, though designed to produce salt, have become adopted homes for many bird species that
feed on the brine flies and brine shrimp living in the shallow waters.
Some levees have become nesting grounds for resident and migrating species.

As you continue along the levee, you come to an old duck-hunter's
cabin, at the edge of the slough, left much as it was in former duck-
hunting days. The story of waterfowl hunting is told here, from the
life-sustaining ways of the Indians and early duck shooting by the
Anglos through the destructive mass commercial hunting at the turn
of the century to today's controlled sport hunting. At a nearby duck
blind you can crawl inside and shoot birds with your camera.

Just beyond is a former salt company pumphouse, built on piles
over the water, now converted to a picnic shelter equipped with
tables where you can lunch in the sun or under cover.

Your trail back goes on a bridge over Newark Slough. Note the landing for boats and canoes halfway across the bridge. Refuge personnel lead an occasional canoe trip on a "bring your own canoe" basis. A short trail up from the bridge leads to more picnic tables and to the last of the information panels. Above you is the Visitor Center and the end of your trip.

Trip 2.   Newark Slough

The loop trail around the slough is an invigorating walk for birdwatchers and all who enjoy open marshland and salt ponds in the Bay's many moods.

Distance   5-mile loop.
Time   2½–3 hours.
Elevation Change   Level.

TRAIL NOTES

From the refuge parking lot take the path around the north side of the headquarters building and find the gravel trail to your right, heading downhill to the bridge that crosses Newark Slough. The Newark Slough Trail, on a salt-pond levee, follows the slough around north, then west to the far side of the pond, then south where the slough meanders out to the Bay.

At the far side of the bridge are two old buildings. The one on the right, an old pumphouse converted to a picnic shelter, offers a fine place to stop for birdwatching or lunching. Our trail passes the pumphouse, turning right by the marsh-edged slough. This is a place of open sky, wide horizons and seemingly limitless space, offering a serenity undisturbed by the flow of the tides. The subtle colors of salt ponds and marsh change with the seasons. The muted pinks of the ponds are accented by pickleweed as it turns reddish in the fall; in the winter the cordgrass and salt grass in the marsh are brown. The ponds reflect clouds on still days, and the dark skies of winter make a dramatic contrast with white gulls resting on the ponds.

Old hunting blinds remodeled into birdwatching blinds, useful to photographers and birders, are welcomed also by those who just like to sit by the trail and enjoy this lovely expanse of water. From fall to spring the ponds are filled with migrant birds stopping on their way up or down the Pacific Flyway. Throughout the year a large population of gulls, avocets, stilts, willets and many others is in residence. Flocks of stilts far out in the pond stand with only their feet under water, a gauge of how shallow and level the pond is.

You may be startled by the flap of a northern harrier hawk's great wings as it flies out of the marsh. Formerly called a marsh hawk and recently renamed, this brownish bird with a black-and-white striped tail and a white rump patch soars with its wings (spanning almost 4') in a shallow V like those of the British fighter plane named for it.

In contrasting scale, a scampering of sandpipers busy themselves in the mud along the pond's edge, searching for food. Out in the pond a flotilla of gulls turn and move away a little at the approach of hikers on the levee, but do not take flight.

Between the 2-mile and 3-mile posts an expanse of marsh by the Newark Slough broadens as the levee trail turns south. At high tide the marsh floods, making pools here and there that attract common egrets searching for fish and rodents. It does not take an expert to recognize these stately creatures, standing 3' tall on their long legs. With slow dignity they stalk their prey of insects, small animals and fish. Head moving forward, long neck outstretched, they advance one foot with deliberation and gather their bodies forward. Then, with a swift dart, they catch a fish or mouse with their long beak.

Less frequently you will see the much smaller snowy egret, with a black bill and yellow feet, and in nesting season tufted plumage on its head and breast. Also less frequently seen is the great blue heron, which stands 4' tall and flies with slow sweeps of its great wings. Halfway around the loop a small bird blind for photographers and birdwatchers looks out over the marsh to the west—a good place for two or three people to sit for lunch while watching ducks landing in a pond and egrets looking for food.

Beyond this point our trail turns east to return to the Visitor Center. We are now close to railroad tracks that carried freight across the Bay. On this side of the tracks runs the 10'-diameter Hetch-Hetchy pipeline, carrying water from the Sierra to Crystal Springs Lakes. East in the distance, steam rises from the stacks of chemical plants at the head of Newark Slough.

As we continue east, the low hills at the refuge headquarters loom larger, and we finally come to the east end of the salt pond. Going through a stile by a gate across the levee, we turn back, left, toward the Visitor Center. Our path now follows a bend in Newark Slough, and soon we meet the upstream reach of the slough, close to the site of the old Jarvis Landing. We go through a second stile and follow the slough to the left until we come to a bridge. Here we can cross the bridge and complete our trip along the hill back to the Visitor Center, or we can continue on the levee trail to the northern bridge from which we started. As we cross the slough, we can check the difference 3 hours has made in the tide level.

Drawbridge

There are no connecting trails from the Visitor Center to the Alviso Slough Trail 20 miles south by road. The only point of access between these locations is the ghost town of Drawbridge on Station Island. Drawbridge was once a small vacation community of hunters and anglers. But diking the marshes to create salt-evaporator ponds reduced the number of ducks, pollution ruined the fishing and poisoned the shellfish, and the town was abandoned. Although it has suffered much vandalism, Drawbridge is the destination of popular conducted tours on Saturdays during the dry season. Access to Drawbridge is by guided tour only. Trespassers are subject to a heavy fine if found in Drawbridge without official guide.

Fremont/Warm Springs Bay Trail

A two-mile segment of the Bay Trail takes bicyclists, fishermen and bird watchers out to tidal marshes and wetlands and along flood-control channels from a small Bay access park at Fremont Boulevard near West Warren Drive in Fremont. The trail goes through the 300-acre Coyote Slough Lagoon, recently acquired by the San Francisco Bay National Wildlife Refuge.

At a small landscaped Bay access park are a few tree-shaded picnic tables and parking. Just past a massive industrial building a gravel-surfaced levee trail takes off, heading out along a channel lined with cord grass, arcing toward Coyote Slough's meanders. In summer the vast expanse of breezy marsh is a refreshing contrast to the sun-baked East Bay hills that rise abruptly from the Bay plain.

The levee trail veers south passing below the bulk of the Newby Island landfill. As the trail turns back to the east is a fishing spot popular with anglers who catch sturgeon, bass and salmon here.

At the southern end of the trail is another little access park at Fremont and Lakeview boulevards. You find young trees, a stretch of lawn, parking and a ramp for wheelchair access to the trail. Picnic tables offer a dramatic view of 2500' Mission Peak that will tempt you to overlook the usual marsh breezes and stop for lunch here.

A proposed section of Bay Trail continues south, skirting the Fremont Airport for a few miles to Dixon Landing.

Alviso

SEE MAP ON PAGES 250-51

Adjoining the refuge is the historic town of Alviso, named for Ignacio Alviso, the mayor-domo of Santa Clara Mission, who was granted the 6352-acre Rancho de los Esteros by Governor Alvarado in 1838. He took up residence at Alviso two years later. The port of Alviso soon supplanted Santa Clara Mission's embarcadero, nearby on Guadalupe Slough.

A flourishing trade in hides and tallow exchanged for goods from Yankee vessels made Alviso an important port. After the discovery of gold, trade with San Francisco so increased that regular steamer runs from Alviso carried produce and manufactured goods. Stagecoaches coming from San Jose met the steamers at Alviso. The town prospered, and docks and warehouses were soon built by the Alviso Slough.

Completion of a railroad from San Francisco to San Jose in 1864 diminished Alviso's importance. However, such families as the Wades and the Tildens remained, and so have their houses, which you can see today. The modest house of Henry Wade and his more impressive brick warehouse, built in the early 1860s, stand in the center of town. The handsome Italianate Tilden house, still occupied by members of the same family, is near the marina on Elizabeth Street, beautifully kept up, as always.

An attempt to revive the port in the 1890s by building a "New Chicago," which was to be the port for the South Bay and the largest city of the West, was a failed dream. The current hope for the site of the "city," which is just east of the town of Alviso and adjacent to the refuge's Environmental Education Center, is to return at least some part of it to a live marsh for research, study and public enjoyment.

Another flurry of activity at Alviso came in 1906, when Tom Foon started the Bayside Cannery, which processed food crops from the fertile lands nearby and from the Sacramento River Delta. The cannery operated through the Twenties.

The town is now bypassed by industrial activity, although many buildings of the early days remain. The port of Alviso is included in the National Register of Historic Places. This designation gives some legal protection to some of the town's historic buildings. The largest remaining old cannery building is owned by the Fish and Wildlife Service. Its wall are now covered with murals by local artists, depicting Alviso's past and present.

Santa Clara County is building a launching ramp for sculls and rowboats at its marina.

The Wildlife Refuge's Environmental Education Center, about 2 miles east of the town, is open to classes and groups by reservation. Boardwalks and an observation platform extend over the marsh. Some marshland trails from the center are open to visitors. For information call 408-262-5513.

Today Alviso is busy on weekends with history buffs, shutterbugs, birders, hikers and bicyclists—and people just seeking a good seafood dinner at one of its restaurants. This old port itself is well worth a stroll, to see the record of its past that still stands in a half dozen of its buildings. Among the earliest are Wade's brick warehouse on Hope Street and his modest house next door.

Walk south on Hope Street to the South Bay Yacht Club, built in 1905, now facing a levee. It once looked out on the slough, and a measure of land subsidence here is the height of the levee now needed to keep out Bay waters. On the way back to the marina, turn at the cannery down Elizabeth Street for a look at the Tilden-Laine house, the grandest of a number of spacious houses of Alviso's heyday.

The well-kept Tilden House stands near the marina

Mural on old cannery building depicts life around the Town of Alviso

Jurisdiction   Town of Alviso: City of San Jose. Alviso Slough
Trail: SFBNWR.
Facilities   At the Santa Clara County marina, picnic tables,
restrooms, boat launching dock. SFBNWR Environmental
Education Center. Observation platform, trails on SFBNWR
levees.
Maps   SFBNWR map. USGS quad *Milpitas*.
How To Get There
   By Car   From the Alviso/Milpitas Road (237) turn north on
Taylor to Hope and Elizabeth streets. Park at Alviso Marina.
   By Bus   County Transit bus 58

Hike or Bike on the Alviso Slough Trail

From this historic town a 9-mile trip along Alviso Slough and
Coyote Creek takes you to one of the finest birding opportunities and
one of the largest bits of natural marsh in the South Bay.
Distance   9-mile loop.
Time   4–5 hours.
Elevation Change   Level.
TRAIL NOTES

This trail uses levees to circle a group of salt ponds between
Coyote Creek and Alviso Slough. Reaching the end of the Bay, it
passes Triangle Marsh, one of the largest bits of natural marsh left in
this area. The trip on the west side of the loop beside Alviso Slough
is the most rewarding part, if the whole 9-mile loop is longer than

you wish to take. For birders, a morning trip here at low tide during fall or winter, will yield the highest bird count.

Start from the east end of Santa Clara County's marina, where a Wildlife Refuge sign points the way through a hiker/bicyclist gate. Take the first trail to the left (west) around the marina and down the levee by Alviso Slough. Another levee trail heading north is the returning end of your loop trip.

Fragments of the marsh remain along both sides of the slough. At low tide you will find avocets, stilts and dowitchers picking their way on the muddy banks, searching for food. Ruddy ducks and coots paddle in the water. You may startle into flight from the cordgrass one of the northern harrier hawks, identified by its 4' wingspread and the white patch on its rump. At high tide look for the shy, big-footed, chicken-sized clapper rail, an endangered species now making a comeback in the protected marshes.

A brisk walk down the levee trail is breezily invigorating. The characteristic northwest wind blows down the Bay in summer. Winter days are often still and mild. On clear days, when smog has been blown off by a storm, this trip brings into view the East Bay hills—emerald green or golden, according to season. West are the dark, wooded Santa Cruz Mountains. This is a good place to get the feel of South Bay geography.

Northeast of the levee is a salt pond stretching almost as far as the eye can see. You pass levees on your right that dike off salt ponds but are closed to hikers for habitat protection. Some of these are resting areas for egrets and pelicans. In migrating season the ponds are often dotted with thousands of birds—many species of ducks and gulls.

After about 4 miles you come to the mouth of Alviso Slough and the open Bay. The trail turns east along Coyote Creek, paralleling a narrow band of marsh for another mile. On the opposite bank of the creek is Station Island, crossed by the Southern Pacific Railroad. Here the little town of Drawbridge thrived in the early 1900s.

From the mouth of Coyote Creek, the trail may follow a levee close to Triangle Marsh or take a more winding route somewhat inland, depending on which levees are open to hikers. The marsh along the creek is brackish, where salt water intrudes on the fresh water flowing from the creek.

When the trail reaches the railroad, you are headed toward Alviso. Looking back, you can see directly up the Bay to the gleaming piles of salt at Newark. This is the end product of the process you have seen in the evaporator ponds beside you. It begins at Leslie Salt Company's number-one pond off Mountain View's

Shoreline, where water is admitted from the Bay at the time of its highest salinity, in summer. From there brine flows by gravity down a succession of ponds, each an inch lower than the previous one. As water evaporates, the color of the pond changes, first becoming greenish with algae growth, then pinkish with the growth of a red bacterium and the tiny brine shrimp that take on this color.

At the lower end of the Bay, water still at its greenish stage is then pumped for further evaporation to a series of ponds up the East Bay shores. As the concentration increases, the water becomes almost purple. These are the colorful ponds one sees from the air. In late spring, as a final stage, a heavy concentration of brine called "pickle," is pumped into cystallizer ponds to a depth of 1—2'. By fall a 6" layer of sodium chloride crystals has formed at the bottom. Then the top layer, called "bittern," rich in magnesium, bromine and potassium, is drained off, and the salt is ready for harvest. Before the rainy season it is piled in the white pyramids you see up the Bay.

As you continue on the trail by the railroad tracks, you are on the last leg of this trip and only about 1½ miles from Alviso. The marsh by the tracks has been drained, as has much of the nearby marshlands that were to be the "New Chicago". The route we follow is subject to some change because of trail closings for levee repair and for habitat protection during nesting. After a few bends in the trail you complete the loop and are back at the marina. The last part of your way blooms with yellow daisies of *grindelia,* a shrubby, salt-tolerant plant that brightens marshlands above the tides.

The South Bay Yacht Club, at slough level in 1900, must now be protected by a 12-foot levee

Sunnyvale/Santa Clara County Baylands Park

SEE MAP ON PAGES 250-51

The 220-acre Baylands Park when completed early in 1993 will feature a protected seasonal wetlands preserve with interpretive displays, nature trails, picnic areas, and recreation areas, in addition to the existing softball complex.

Jurisdiction   Santa Clara County.

Facilities   Recreation areas, commercial softball diamonds and clubhouse, group and family picnic areas, nature areas, restrooms, children's play area, ranger station and parking.

Park Rules   Entrance fee for Twin Creeks Softball Complex $1/person.

Maps   USGS quad *Mountain View.*

How To Get There   From Caribbean Drive just northeast of Highway 237.

TRAIL NOTES

The existing commercial Twin Creeks Softball Complex in the northwest corner of the park includes 10 baseball diamonds available for club games and a clubhouse. The rest of the park emphasizes the natural setting, featuring seasonal wetlands and interpretive displays. Along nature trails interpretive signs explain the unique dynamics of wetlands. A state-of-the-art creative play area gives children a hands-on experience in this Baylands world.

In upland areas native grasses and shrubs provide habitat for such creatures as burrowing owls and the rare harvest mouse. An open water bird preserve will attract local and migrant species. Major picnic areas for large groups and families are sheltered by plantings. Nearby are play areas and large meadows. Parking is ample.

This park will serve as an important trailhead for the Bay Trail already circling much of the South Bay. A connecting trail south to Alviso is underway, and a short connector is planned north to adjacent Sunnyvale Baylands.

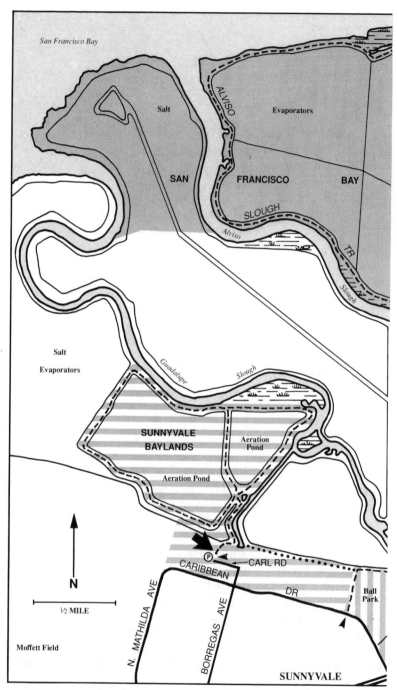

Sunnyvale/Santa Clara County Baylands,

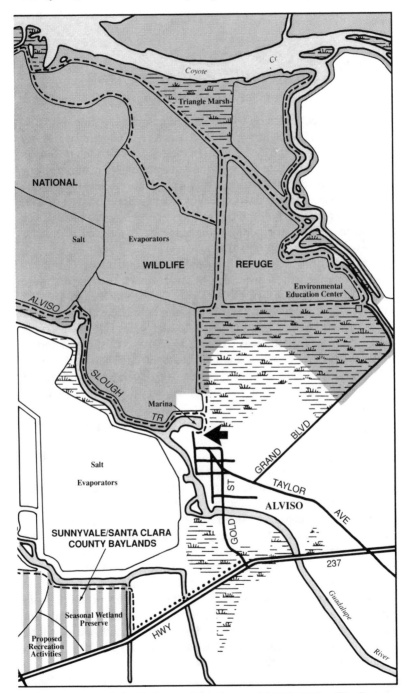

Alviso and S.F. Bay National Wildlife Refuge

Sunnyvale Baylands Trail
SEE MAP ON PAGE 250

A striking combination of natural and man-made elements makes this levee trail into Sunnyvale's Baylands a vivid experience. Nearly 4 miles of trails reach the marshes in the bends of Guadalupe Slough and circle the 455-acre ponds of the water-treatment plant. In spring 1984, to provide public access to the Baylands as required by the Bay Conservation and Development Commission, the city opened up nearly four miles of trail on the levees bordering its ponds. Close to the industrial parks along Caribbean Drive, the trail is popular with workers enjoying runs on the levee.

Two centuries ago these busy industrial lands along Caribbean Drive were the lambs' pasture of Mission Santa Clara. Beyond were vast salt marshes through which curved Guadalupe Slough. In 1842 the Rancho Pastoria de las Borregas ("lambs' pasture") was granted to a Spaniard named Estrada. After United States rule in California began, part of the land was patented to Mariano Castro and part to Daniel Murphy. Castro's holdings centered on what we know as Castro Station; Murphy's land empire soon covered a good part of Santa Clara Valley. What remains of the lambs' pasture is the name of Borregas Avenue.

At the height of Bay commerce, McCubbins Landing, on a bend of Guadalupe Slough that borders the levee trail, was one of many landings on the navigable waters of sloughs around the South Bay. But when schooners and steamers could no longer compete with the railroad, which stopped at nearby Castro Station, the landing was abandoned. Early in this century the Leslie Salt Company diked the marsh and operated salt evaporators west of Guadalupe Slough. In the mid-1960s, the City of Sunnyvale bought the ponds for aerating waste water before its final, tertiary treatment.

Today the trails around the ponds provide exceptional views of Guadalupe Slough as well as being a fine track for runners. The western segment of the trail is designated as a part of the regional Bay Trail for hikers and bicyclists. North, a connection will cross an easement on private land to reach Moffett Field. South, a trail will be constructed in the early 1990s to connect with the Bay Trail in Sunnyvale/Santa Clara County Baylands.

Jurisdiction   City of Sunnyvale.

Facilities   Trails: hiking, jogging, with measured mileposts. Benches and information plaques.

Park Rules   Open dawn to dusk.

Maps   USGS quad *Mountain View.*

How To Get There

By Car   From Highway 237 turn north on Lawrence Expressway to Caribbean Drive. Turn right on Borregas Avenue and then left on Carl Road and drive a short block to parking area and trailhead.

By Bus   County Transit 20, 60, 70 with stops on Caribbean Drive.

A Levee Loop Trail past Guadalupe Slough

This trip takes you to a healthy marsh in the company of flocks of birds and armies of runners.

Distance   4-mile loop.

Time   2 hours.

Elevation Change   Level.

TRAIL NOTES

From the parking area follow the signs to the levee trail. Turn right (east) along a salt-water channel. You can see the Sunnyvale water pollution control plant effluent after tertiary treatment flowing out into the channel leading to Guadalupe Slough.

After another bend the trail heads bayward by one of the oxidation ponds. Salt evaporator ponds are to your right. Ahead an orange radar screen turns slowly. In the oxidation ponds the water is artificially stirred by brush aerators, which are the mechanisms you see extending from the levee across the pond to your left. After about 30 days in the ponds, water is pumped back to the plant for tertiary treatment, which removes ammonia, then chlorinates and afterwards dechlorinates the water before its release into the slough.

Algae growth in the ponds is being studied with a view to encouraging the most productive types. And algae farming is being considered to recover algae which could be used to provide some of the energy to operate the plant. At present as much as 25 percent of the energy used in the plant is derived from methane gas produced here.

At almost any time of day a line of runners is circling the ponds. At noon and early evening the course is popular with employees from nearby industrial parks. A runner can complete the loop in less than an hour; some can finish three loops during the noon break. Water birds in numbers have adapted to these ponds, the largest fresh or brackish ones in the South Bay. You will find birds by the thousands and of many species, arriving, departing, riding the water, or congregating on the levees.

Now, on your right, you approach the oxbow bend of Guadalupe Slough, bordered by a broad band of marsh. You may see a great blue heron flying out of the reeds with slow sweeps of its wings. In the slough, pintail ducks dip for food. Coots, black-bodied with white bills, dive under the water for fish. Willets take off and land with flashes of their black-and-white wings. Anyone can enjoy the sight of the many birds feeding here, each in its own manner dabbling, diving, dipping or picking its way along the muddy banks. On the levee trail are benches at intervals. Knowledgeable birders find these marshes particularly rewarding, and they welcome a place to watch the engrossing activities of the birds.

Due north on a clear day the East Bay hills seem close. Mission Peak and Monument Peak rise abruptly from the Bay plain to 2500' heights, their tawny reflections filling the pond on the still days of fall. In spring the green slopes seem a continuation of the marshes in the foreground. A half mile beyond the radar, the levee turns east, passing marshes extending out 1000' in the curve of Guadalupe Slough. This corner of the levee trail is of particular interest to serious birders and to those who have discovered the fascination of changes in marshland with the tides and with the seasons.

As Guadalupe Slough curves back landward, the levee follows close to its banks. Here you can watch the movement of the tides, whose mean range is approximately 5 feet in the South Bay. The slough begins to deepen here; down the levee are the dock where Moffett Field's fuel barges unload and, next to it, a small boat-launching dock. It is about at this point where McCubbins Landing would have been.

As you turn landward from the docks, Moffett Field's massive installations of hangars and NASA's Ames Research Station wind tunnels stand out in pastel shades against the dark background of the Santa Cruz Mountains. The air and ponds are filled with gulls that challenge you to work at identifying them. The most numerous species is the western gull, a Bay Area resident that appears in great numbers at refuse dumps; adults are snowy white with dark gray wings and back. Many other species visit at certain months or alight on their way up or down the Flyway.

Looking away from the ponds to the shore, you see the Sunnyvale Baylands refuse mountain. When the pile has reached 80', it will be sculptured into a parkland with a view over the Bay.

Your trail returns to join the outgoing trail at the radar screen. You are now on an eventual segment of the Bay Trail. From here retrace your steps past the outflow back to the trailhead.

**Aeration ponds attract clouds of birds;
their levees are favored by noontime runners**

Mountain View's Shoreline
SEE MAP ON PAGE 261

In the summer of 1983 the City of Mountain View opened its Shoreline. By the early 1990s the yearly attendance had reached a million people. Strollers, hikers, runners and bicyclists enjoy over 7 miles of paved paths along bayfront, sloughs and marshes. Observation platforms and benches attract birdwatchers. A 50-acre lake for canoeing, small boating and wind sailing now has a boat house. Shoreline offers picnicking on meadows by its shores and an 18-hole golf course and clubhouse.

Shoreline's 544 acres, built on gently rolling terrain over mountains of revenue-bringing sanitary landfill from San Francisco, have been sculpted to create meadows, the lake and the golf course. Fittingly, methane gas is now piped back to San Francisco, providing further revenue.

Trail connections north to Palo Alto's Bayfront Trail and the trail along Charleston Slough expand opportunities for hikers, runners and bicyclists to explore more of the bayland scene. Two boardwalks south over the Shoreline's tidal marshes and a bridge over Stevens Creek bring bird enthusiasts and ecologists to the Stevens Creek Nature Study Area of the Midpeninsula Regional Open Space District (MROSD).

As you drive in the main entrance along Shoreline Boulevard, you pass an 18-hole golf course and pro shop and parking. Past the golf course on the left stands the historic Rengstorff house, now being restored for use as a museum and quarters for park administration. Henry Rengstorff built this handsome 16-room house in 1866, with pillared portico and classic pediment over its doorway. Rengstorff came to California during the Gold Rush but chose instead of mining to work on a steamer plying between San Francisco and Alviso. He soon had money to buy a farm and build a warehouse at his pier at the end of Shoreline Boulevard.

The main parking lots are in the center of Shoreline near the lake and golf course. Trips are described from there. The route of the regional Bay Trail follows the Bayfront Trail through Shoreline. Bicycle trails on Shoreline Boulevard and along East Bayshore to Adobe Creek also give access from the cities nearby.

Jurisdiction City of Mountain View.

Facilities Trails: hiking, bicycling. Wheelchair access. Lake for small boats, windsurfing, canoeing, boat rental. Marshland nature-study area. Golf course.

Park Rules Hours: gates open sunrise to dusk. No dogs.

Maps City of Mountain View *Shoreline.* USGS quad *Mountain View.*

How To Get There

By Car From Bayshore Freeway (101) turn east on Shoreline Boulevard and go 1 mile to park entrance. Parking lots on main road near lake.

By Bicycle Bike lanes on Shoreline Boulevard. Palo Alto's Bayfront Trail along East Bayshore Road enters the north end of Shoreline at Adobe Creek.

Trip 1.   Shoreline Walk South to the Marsh

For a breath of salt air and birdwatching, walk past Mountain View Slough at the edge of a salt pond to a marshland nature-study area by Stevens Creek.

Distance 3½ miles round trip.

Time 2 hours round trip.

Elevation Change Level.

Connecting Trail Bridge east to MROSD Stevens Creek Nature Study Area; Palo Alto Baylands trail north along Charleston Slough.

TRAIL NOTES

This short trail goes east past marshlands to Shoreline's edge along a salt pond and to a vista point at the marsh. Along the salt pond, the trail lies about 20′ above Bay level on a low plateau created by landfill. Adjacent salt ponds extend to a dike almost out of sight.

Imagine the scene as it was a hundred years ago. Then you would have been standing at about the edge of the Bay's upland marsh, where cordgrass gave way to pickleweed and salt grass. Up sloughs through marshes like this came boats from the Bay to Rengstorff's Landing. Grain and hay from fields nearby and wine from Cupertino vineyards, loaded from Henry Rengstorff's warehouses, sailed on schooners and steamers for San Francisco.

Earlier still, Indians harvested shellfish and netted birds from these sloughs. The site of the largest of their shell mounds in the South Bay is a few miles away, at Castro Station. Further back in time, during the Pleistocene Epoch, mastodons, sloths and camels roamed the valley that was here before ocean waters flooded it. Their fossils have come to light in excavations nearby.

Returning to the present, continue on the trail for about ½ mile. On a breezy day that blows away smog, the East Bay hills look close, and the dark Santa Cruz Mountains fill the western skyline.

Our trail then turns south along a saltwater marsh. Two boardwalks cross the marsh and its ponds to the edge of Stevens Creek. Cross on the first boardwalk for the view southeast, dominated by the huge hangars of Moffett Field.

Turning to the marsh below, which is currently being restored, you will find in any season shore and water birds that rest and nest in the marsh and ponds. Wintering coots, slate-colored with ivory-white bills, bob as they swim in the pond, diving for vegetable matter in the shallow water. Resident ducks will be joined in winter and spring by the many migrant species.

A bridge over Stevens Creek leads to the Stevens Creek Nature Study Area. Presently undeveloped, it is used mainly for research and education.

Trip 2.   Shoreline's North Bayfront Trail to the Charleston Slough Forebay

A walk by Mountain View Slough to the water's edge by a salt pond and along Charleston Slough forebay with a loop trip back by the lake.

Distance   3-mile loop.

Time   1½ hours.

Elevation Change   Nearly level.

TRAIL NOTES

From the parking lot near the lake, find the Bayfront Trail heading bayward along the west side of Mountain View Slough, where you can watch the ebb and flow of the tides, and the avocets, dowitchers and willets feeding on the muddy banks. On the other side of the trail are grassy meadows for picnicking and playing.

Our trail turns west away from the slough, following the edge of the salt pond below. Short trails lead through the meadowlands back to the lake from our trail, but we continue ahead toward Charleston Slough.

The expanse of water we look out over is the Leslie Salt Company's number-one salt-evaporator pond, where water is admitted in summer at its highest salinity. San Francisco Bay is one of the few places in the country suitable for making salt by solar evaporation. (See Alviso Slough TRAIL NOTES for a description of the process.)

A few duck blinds, still used, dot the salt pond. Their ownership has been handed down in families for 80 years. All blinds are at least 500 yards from shore, so you are safely beyond range of buckshot. Duck hunting, under state and federal license, is permitted during three winter months.

After a half-mile stroll along the path where you look across the pond to the levee bordering Charleston Slough, you turn down to its forebay on Shoreline's boundary. The path circles the forebay and its fresh-water marsh and islands. Along the path information panels describe the great variety of birds resting and nesting here.

Returning to the main trail, continue toward Charleston Slough and Palo Alto's 6-mile loop trail around the city's flood-control basin and Charleston Slough. At this point, also, is a junction with Palo Alto's Bayfront Trail, which heads down to East Bayshore Road and then turns north.

You will find good birdwatching in the marshes. Stately egrets often pick their way along muddy banks or search through pickleweed for small animals. Avocets sweep the shallow waters with their upturned bills. Meadowlarks, blackbirds, burrowing owls, song sparrows and many others find enough dry land in the nearby flood-control basin for nesting.

To return to the parking lot, complete the circle around the forebay. Retrace your steps to the first turn away from the Bay, then take one or the other of the pleasant, winding trails along either side of the lake. Young trees frame lake vistas, and green lawns invite picnickers. On weekends bright-sailed windsurfers skim the waters.

Where Shoreline's path around the forebay nearly completes its circle, note a short connnection to Terminal Boulevard off the end of San Antonio Road. There is ample parking on the block-long boulevard, making it another entrance to Shoreline.

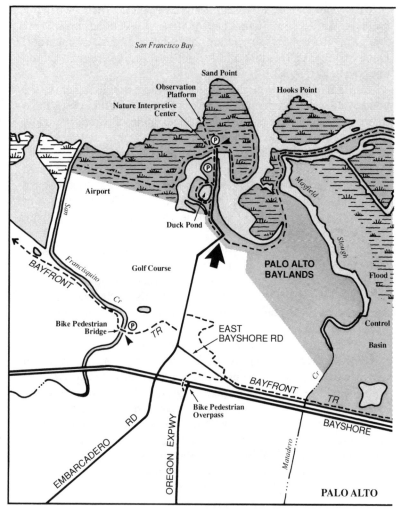

San Francisco Bay

Sand Point

Observation
Platform

Hooks Point

Nature Interpretive
Center

Airport

Duck Pond

Mayfield

Slough

PALO ALTO
BAYLANDS

Flood

San

Francisquito

BAYFRONT

Golf Course

Cr

Control

Basin

Bike Pedestrian
Bridge

TR

EAST
BAYSHORE RD

BAYFRONT

Cr

TR

Bike Pedestrian
Overpass

BAYSHORE

EMBARCADERO RD

OREGON EXPWY

Matadero

PALO ALTO

Palo Alto Baylands,
and Stevens Creek

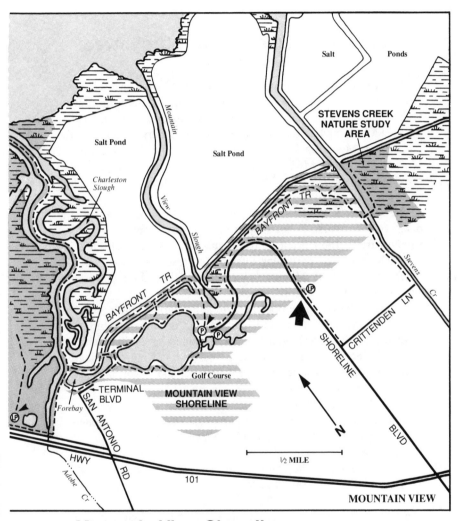

Mountain View Shoreline
Nature Study Area

Stevens Creek Nature Study Area
SEE MAP ON PAGE 261

The narrow strip of marshland along the east side of Stevens Creek set aside as a nature-study area has kept much of the character of such Baylands before the South Bay was diked and filled. The 54-acre Midpeninsula Regional Open Space Preserve lies across the creek from Mountain View's Shoreline at the northwest corner of Moffett Field. The MROSD acquired the preserve in the 1970s to provide public access to this unique marshland for study and research.

The Crittenden Marsh occupies about three fourths of the preserve. The marsh is not subject to tidal flow from the creek but receives fresh-water drainage from adjacent Moffett Field, making brackish marsh of particular interest for research. However, the nearby wetlands at Mountain View's Shoreline do receive tidal waters in channels from the creek.

Although the preserve does contain salt-tolerant plants, some of its vegetation is that of a fresh-water marsh. Consequently, birds and other wildlife of a fresh-water marsh are found here, along with the array of species that frequent the ponds and salt marshes nearby. The preserve is a nesting area for waterfowl and shore birds and a resting place for migrating birds in winter.

Jurisdiction MROSD.

Facilities The study area has a compacted surface trail along the creek levee but is otherwise undeveloped.

Preserve Rules Hours: 7 A.M. to dusk when Mountain View's Shoreline is open. Stay on the trail. No dogs. No hunting.

Map USGS quad *Mountain View.*

How To Get There

By Car Access to the study area is through Mountain View's Shoreline, reached from Highway 101 on Shoreline Boulevard. From a parking area by the golf course, walk bayward on a path to the Bayfront Trail. Go right for about a mile. Then turn right, away from the Bay, to the boardwalk that reaches the bridge over Stevens Creek to the preserve. There is also access from Crittenden Lane by turning right off Shoreline Boulevard just before the main entrance. Then cross over the bridge and turn north. Parking is possible weekdays in the lots of industrial plants along the lane, which leads to the preserve.

By Bicycle As above. Shoreline's trails and the trail in the preserve have compacted surfaces.

TRAIL NOTES

A levee trail out Stevens Creek takes you about ½ mile, ending at the cross levee bounding a salt evaporator. A MROSD sign marks the preserve boundary; visitors must not trespass on the levee system of the salt ponds to the north and east.

When you cross the bridge, look up to Black Mountain on Monte Bello Ridge in the west, behind which are the headwaters of this creek. High in MROSD's Monte Bello Preserve, Stevens Creek begins its circuitous 25-mile journey to the Bay. After flowing southeast in a linear earthquake-fault canyon, it bends north around the end of the ridge through Stevens Creek County Park, where it is dammed. Continuing north through percolation ponds and past subdivisions, it reaches the Bay here between levees of the salt ponds. A continuation of a pedestrian/bicycle trail west along Stevens Creek to Highway 101 and El Camino Real and beyond is proposed.

Environmental study groups find these marshes fruitful for their investigations. The area is a birder's paradise for finding species whose habitat is fresh-water marsh. A patient birder with a scope might add a new species to his list. Ducks in variety are here, as are migrating waterfowl in season. There are always resident egrets and great blue herons to be seen. And above, the northern harrier hawks find perches high in the utility towers that cross the preserve.

White pelicans in formation near Moffet Field

Palo Alto Baylands
SEE MAP ON PAGES 260-61

Palo Alto's Baylands preserves 120 acres of salt marsh and slough as a wildlife sanctuary. The adjacent 600-acre flood-control basin extends to Charleston Slough and Mountain View's Shoreline.

The striking Lucy Evans Nature Interpretive Center in the Baylands, designed by William Busse, stands on pilings by a levee at the edge of the marsh. A glass wall looks bayward to changing scenes of marsh and water. Timely displays, meeting rooms, a library and an open laboratory make this building a lively focus of activity for visitors. Programs on Bay ecology, slide shows, movies and children's workshops are scheduled throughout the year. Weekend walks conducted by the center's naturalists are an inspiring introduction to the special world at the edge of the Bay. The Lucy Evans Nature Interpretive Center and the Harriet Mundy Marsh surrounding it honor two women who crusaded for Baylands preservation and were instrumental in securing this sanctuary for our education and enjoyment.

Restoration of marshland near the former yacht basin is planned and a pier will be built into the Charleston Slough channel for launching windsurfing boards. Trails along levees and boardwalks over marshes take you through a representative sample of Baylands environments.

Jurisdiction   City of Palo Alto.

Facilities   Nature Interpretive Center, observation platform, boardwalk and pier for launching windsurfing craft. Trails: hiking, bicycling. Naturalist programs. Wheelchair access to Interpretive Center, one boardwalk and some trails.

Park Rules   Hours: trails, sunrise to sunset; Interpretive Center, Wednesday through Friday, 2–5 P.M. ; Saturday and Sunday, 1–5 P.M. Open Ecology Workshop: 3–4 P.M. Wednesday through Sunday. Dogs must be on leash at all times. Phone: 415-329-2506.

Maps   *Palo Alto Baylands Nature Preserve.* USGS quad *Mountain View.*

How To Get There

By Car   From Bayshore Freeway (101) turn east on Embarcadero Road 0.7 mile to sign for Baylands; turn left to parking lots at end of road.

By Bicycle (1) Bicycle and pedestrian crossing over freeway from Oregon Avenue and Embarcadero Road and (2) Palo Alto's Bayfront Trail from Mountain View along East Bayshore Road leads to bike lanes on Embarcadero Road going east to preserve.

Trip 1.   Boardwalk and Catwalk Loop

A short exploration of the Baylands takes you on the boardwalk to an observation platform on the edge of the Bay, and on a catwalk over a marsh.

Distance   1¾-mile loop.
Time   1 hour.
Elevation Change   Level.

TRAIL NOTES

If this is your first trip to the Baylands, be sure to allow at least an hour to visit the Interpretive Center. Pick up the informative blue-covered booklet describing plants and animals of the marsh and the green-covered self-guided Nature Trail for a boardwalk tour. Now, armed with your guides to tidelands, binoculars at the ready, start from the Interpretive Center. Walk around the deck to the bayward side of the building and follow the wide boardwalk across the marsh. Cordgrass, pickleweed and salt grass are right below you, just waiting to be identified. The colors of the marsh vary by the season, changing from the fresh green of cordgrass in spring to gold and brown as it dries in fall, then enlivened by an edging of the rusty red of pickleweed in winter. On boardwalk benches you can pause and watch for birds feeding in the marsh.

If the tide is very high, the water may be up to the middle of the pickleweed, but at low tide even the stems are out of water. The different plants of the marsh are adapted to varying degrees of salt concentration in water and soil. They also tolerate varying periods of submergence by the tides. Salt grass and pickleweed live just above all but the highest tides; cordgrass grows where it is partly submerged at each tide. Pickleweed keeps salt in vacuoles, or cavities, in its stems, whereas cordgrass absorbs salt water and exudes little crystals of salt on its leaves.

Continue out the boardwalk to the viewing platform at the edge of the Bay. This vantage point offers a chance to see many species of shore birds, each feeding at the water level to which its legs and bill are adapted. Even the untrained observer can note the difference in bill lengths and in the motions the birds make in seeking their food. For example, the avocet uses its long, upward-curving bill to sweep the shallow waters and disturb small invertebrates for its meal. The short-legged and short-billed sandpipers find their food at the receding water's edge. The long-billed curlew is easy to spot by its downturned bill and its habit of feeding with its head down in the water as it probes for clams and worms.

Head back on the boardwalk until you reach the narrow catwalk going south over the marsh. This walk has no railing, and users are cautioned by the owner, the Pacific Gas and Electric Company, to proceed at their own risk. Although some feel timid about venturing out onto the catwalk, others are comfortable enough to jog its length. You are crossing the Harriet Mundy Marsh, named for one of the early advocates of Baylands preservation.

The marsh from a distance seems an unbroken stretch of cordgrass. At close hand from the walkway, however, you see it in its complexity—broken by little sloughs, muddy-banked at low tide or brimming with water at high tide. As you cross the sloughs, you can look down at the banks of mud 3–4' thick, composed of layers of silt

A catwalk leads over the marsh

washed down from the hills—and now rich enough to grow cordgrass, one of the world's most productive land plants as measured by yield per acre.

Pass under a great steel tower of the transmission lines, where the catwalk turns off to the right. Here you are back on land and are looking out at the wide channel where the waters of Charleston and Mayfield sloughs and Matadero Creek join and enter the Bay between Sand Point and Hooks Point.

You soon come to a parking lot and at water's edge are benches where you can sit with binoculars to watch birds and boats or just enjoy the vastness of the South Bay and the ring of mountains surrounding it. A pier will be built out into the channel for launching windsurfers' craft and for other small hand-carried boats.

From here it is just a step to the parking lot and your car across the road.

Trip 2. Walk to San Francisquito Creek

A bird-watching trip takes you along the lagoon and out to the mouth of San Francisquito Creek.

Distance 1.6 miles round trip.

Time 1 hour round trip.

Elevation Change Level. The first ¼ mile is suitable for wheelchairs.

TRAIL NOTES

For this trip take the levee path north of the Interpretive Center that leads beside the lagoon, with its population of fishermen, birds and birdwatchers. On the other side of the path, the Harriet Mundy Marsh extends to the Bay.

At any tide you will see in the lagoon some of the birds that reside in these Baylands. In fall and winter, especially in the early mornings and evenings when low tides expose mud flats in the lagoon, this levee walk is a birder's delight. Snowy egrets stalk the waters; flocks of willets alight and take off with a flash of black-and-white wings; muddy banks are alive with scampering least sandpipers; northern pintails, the commonest of California ducks, dot the waters or fly off in a haphazard **V**. You may catch a flight of white pelicans, their immense white wings catching the light as they turn in perfect formation. Mallards, which are Baylands residents, will usually be in sight. And always there are gulls of many species taking off, alighting and wheeling in the air on their way to and from the nearby garbage dump.

Even experienced birders may pick up a new find for their lists. The rank amateur will soon be able to identify a good many birds with the help of the illustrated leaflet from the Center. Shore and water birds, in general, are easier to identify than the modest little birds of the woodlands, which are so quick to dart out of sight into the trees. In contrast, birds of sloughs and marshes congregate in numbers, often stand still and have bold markings—and most are of good size.

A conducted bird walk with a Baylands naturalist will have you confidently checking off your list on your next visit. Ask at the Interpretive Center for the walk schedule. Even on your own, however, you are bound to enjoy the sights and sounds on this fringe of the Bay.

Our trail continues beyond the lagoon on a straight levee between Palo Alto's airport and marshlands. Take the second path to the right (bayward); the first follows the channel from the sewage-treatment plant, where effluent flows to the Bay after tertiary treatment. Another turnoff, left, is closed to the public because it is too near the airport's runway. Our trail parallels the runway at a safe distance, but the sight and sound of planes are constant.

In spring, watch the edge of the path for pygmy blue butterflies, pale blue and fingernail-sized, the smallest butterfly in North

Cordgrass in Bay marshes is washed by the tides

America. You will find them clustered on the foot-high Australian saltbush, which has been naturalized here. At any time of year you will see California ground squirrels scurrying from the weeds to their burrows.

Cattails and tules grow near the trail, attesting to the existence of a fresh-water marsh. In a little over ½ mile the trail ends at the San Francisquito Creek Channel. Gathering waters from the eastern flanks of the Santa Cruz Mountains, this creek is one of the largest on the Peninsula, forming the boundary between San Mateo and Santa Clara counties where it flows across the Bay plain.

The trail ends at the creek channel, but you can walk 50 yards farther, toward the Bay. A bar across the mouth of the creek is a favored spot for shore birds, which find food in debris washed down by floodwaters. The return trip gives you a better view of the extent of the Baylands marsh, almost a mile to Sand Point. This broad expanse, now a protected habitat, is important not only for egrets, whose white plumage you can see far out in the cordgrass, but also for a host of other birds and animals on down the food chain to the microcrustaceans essential for sustaining this web of life.

Trip 3.   Duck Pond

Give your children a few scraps of dry bread, and the waterfowl in the Duck Pond will provide an exciting adventure, which you can follow with a walk around the pond's perimeter to a picnic area by the slough.

Distance   0.4 mile.

Time   ½ hour.

Elevation Change   Level.

TRAIL NOTES

You need no guidebook to bring the ducks to you begging for food. The year-round residents wait for handouts and jostle one another fighting for scraps. As early as February young mallards are hatching, and soon they are paddling after their mothers on the pond. Your young charges may be more interested in the action of the birds than in identifying the species, but you might enjoy the leaflet on ducks from the Interpretive Center.

After the bread is gone and the children need a romp, take the short path that circles the east end of the Duck Pond. In less than ½ mile you will find a picnic table set among remnants of plantings from a former dwelling. In spring birds nest in the undergrowth here, so it is best to stay on the walkway.

The path circles back to the Duck Pond, from where you can continue east along the road to the Interpretive Center. If time and attention allow, many of the displays there, such as mounted birds and a harbor seal, are interesting to small children.

Trip 4.   A Loop around the Flood-Control Basin

A trip around Palo Alto's flood control basin takes you to the bracing breezes at the Bay's edge and birdwatching along Charleston Slough.

Distance 6-mile loop.

Time 3–4 hours.

Elevation Change Level.

Connecting Trails Other Baylands trails and Mountain View's Shoreline trails.

TRAIL NOTES

Find the marked trail entrance by a parking lot across from Palo Alto's recycling depot and next to the city's "refuse area." Continue past the dump, no longer active at this point. This seagull-intensive operation has moved farther inland, but can be visited on an occasional docent-led "garbology" tour.

The dump behind, we stride out toward the open waters and fresh breezes of the Bay. In 10 minutes we reach a tide gate that controls the flow of water in and out of the flood-control basin. We are out on the edge of the Bay, with salt wind in our faces. This is one of the few places in the South Bay where one can have the experience of hearing the slap of waves against the shore. Directly east across the open water rise salt pyramids at Newark. Bayward of Charleston Slough is a marshy island forming Hooks Point, which stands opposite Sand Point, on the far side of the wide mouth where Charleston and the other sloughs enter the Bay.

At this point you are across from the Baylands Interpretive Center and its parking area. Here Mayfield and Charleston sloughs join to reach the Bay. Broad Charleston Slough winds south; our trail is on a levee at its edge.

Across Charleston Slough the island, Hooks Point, laced with small channels, ponds and marshes, is alive with water birds. Flocks of gray-brown willets and tall avocets search for food in the shallows, and pintail and mallard ducks dabble busily for food.

On the levee bank pickleweed shows its fleshy new growth in early spring. Its seeds do not germinate unless the soil is less salty than that supporting the parent plants. In a typical April recent rains have diluted the salt enough to bring up a crop of seedlings.

Beyond the shelter of Hooks Point, we are once again on the open Bay, where winds drive waves against the levee, here buttressed with broken concrete slabs. From this point we turn shoreward. For another mile the levee winds in and out, following the main channel of Charleston Slough to the junction with Mountain View's Shoreline trails, which circle the Charleston Slough forebay. You can take the path around the forebay past its information panels.

A good access to this end of the Charleston Slough Trail is from a short path to a parking area on Terminal Boulevard, which turns off the east end of San Antonio Road.

But our trail continues to East Bayshore Road, where it meets the wide, paved bicycle trail heading back north to Palo Alto Baylands. In the middle of the 1-mile stretch by East Bayshore Road is a small parking lot, difficult to turn in or out of when traffic is heavy. A nature trail extends into the flood basin. This nature trail is one for your binoculars and your bird book. In the rainy season the basin floods with water, becoming a haven for myriad shore and migrant water-bird species resting on their way along the Pacific Flyway.

Many species, from the awkward, white-billed black coots to the elegant white-plumed egrets, are found here all winter. The basin in summer is a dry meadow, harboring birds of the uplands—marsh wrens, meadowlarks, sparrows, burrowing owls and redwing blackbirds. You may startle a jackrabbit into bounding away over the dry grass.

You can complete the journey on foot on the Bayfront Trail by East Bayshore Road for a mile, until the trail curves behind some commercial buildings to emerge at Faber Place. From there you turn left (northwest) to reach Embarcadero Road; then turn right and find your car at the parking area. Bicyclists find this an easy and rewarding loop trip.

Or at Embarcadero Road you can continue on the Bay Trail route north into San Mateo County on a pedestrian-bicycle bridge over San Francisquito Creek. From the end of the trail at Faber Place, a few steps west on Embarcadero Road take you to Geng Road and the bike path to the bridge. A path from the bridge will go as far as Cooley Landing in East Palo Alto.

Appendix I

Trails For Different Seasons And Reasons

FOR THE SEASONS

SPRING FLOWERS
  Ed R. Levin Park
    Los Coches Trails
  Joseph D. Grant Park
    San Felipe Trail
    Hall's Valley Trail
    Los Huecos Trail
  Henry W. Coe State Park
    Corral Trail to Arnold Field
    Frog Lake Trail to Coe Monument on Pine Ridge
    Northern Heights Route to Miller Field
  Calero Park
    Figueroa Trail
    Javelina Loop to Fish Camp
    Cherry Cove Trail to Cherry and Miner's coves

SUMMER STROLLS Cool canyons, shady streams, breezy Baylands
  Alum Rock Park
    Creek Trail—upstream
  Sanborn-Skyline Park
    Skyline Trail
  Calero Park
    Figueroa Trail
    Cherry Cove Trail to Cottle Rest Site
  Uvas Canyon Park
    Swanson Creek Trail—1st part
    Uvas Creek Trail
  Mt. Madonna Park
    Redwood Trail
    Blackhawk Trail
  Coyote Creek
    Trail through Coyote Hellyer Park
  Baylands Trails for Bay Breezes

FALL COLOR
  Alum Rock Park
    Creek Trail
  Henry W. Coe State Park
    Poverty Flat
    The Narrows
    Gill Route on Orestimba and Red creeks
  Almaden Quicksilver Park
    Guadalupe Trail
  Calero Park
    Figueroa Trail along Calero Creek
  Uvas Canyon Park
    Uvas Creek Trail
  Mt. Madonna Park
    Blackhawk Trail

WINTER WALKING ON SURFACED PATHS
  BETWEEN SHOWERS
  Alum Rock Park
    Creek Trail
  Coyote Creek Trails
    Coyote Hellyer Park to Emado Avenue
    Kelley Park
  Penitencia Creek Trail
  Palo Alto Baylands
    Boardwalks to observation platform
  Los Alamitos Creek
    Villagewood Drive to Harry Road
  Los Gatos Creek Trails
    Leigh Avenue to Vasona Lake Park
  Mountain View's Shoreline
  Coyote Hills Regional Park
    Bayview Trail and Boardwalks
  San Francisco Bay National Wildlife Refuge
    Tidelands Trail
    Fremont/Warm Springs Bay Trail
WINTER HIKES ON SUNNY SLOPES
  Mission Peak Regional Preserve
    Peak Trail
  Alum Rock Park
    North Rim Trail to Eagle Rock
  Joseph D. Grant Park
    Hotel Trail to Eagle Lake
  Henry W. Coe State Park
    Corral and Springs trails
    Pacheco Route to Manzanita Point
    Coit Route from China Hole to Mahoney Meadows
  Sierra Azul Open Space Preserve
    Hike to Priest Rock
    Loop on Priest Rock Trail to Kennedy Road junction and P.G. & E.
      service road
    Bald Mountain Ramble
  Almaden Quicksilver Park
    Mine Hill Trail to Bull Run
  Uvas Canyon Park
    Fire Trail Hike to Nibbs Knob and Summit Road
  Coyote Hills Regional Park
    Bayview Trail

FROM SHORT WALKS TO LONG HIKES

EASY LEVEL STROLLS Walk as far as you wish
  Alum Rock Park
    Creek Trail
  Joseph D. Grant Ranch
    Hotel Trail—1st part
  Sanborn-Skyline Park
    Skyline Trail/Bay Area Ridge Trail to Saratoga Gap
    Lake Ranch Reservoir Trail
  Calero Park
    Figueroa Trail along Calero Creek
  Mt. Madonna Park
    Loop Trail—1st mile from Old Mt. Madonna Road
  All Baylands and Creek Trails

SHORT TRIPS Less than 5 miles round trip
  Ed R. Levin Park
    Los Coches Trails
  Alum Rock Park
    South Rim Loop
    Circle Hike to Eagle Rock
  Joseph D. Grant Park
    Trails in Hall's Valley
    The Lake Loop
    Hike to Park's East Ridge
  Henry W. Coe State Park
    Corral Trail to Lion Springs
    Frog Lake to Coe Monument on Pine Ridge
  Sanborn-Skyline Park
    Circle Hike to Todd Redwoods
    Loop Trip to Summit Rock and Bonjetti Creek
  St. Joseph's Hill Open Space Preserve
    A Loop Trip to the Hilltop and back by the Creek
  Sierra Azul Open Space Preserve
    Bald Mountain Ramble
    On the Lower Slopes of El Sombroso
  Almaden Quicksilver Park
    Senator Mine and Guadalupe Trails Loop
  Santa Teresa Park
    All Trips in this park
  Calero Park
    Climb to the Ridge and Return along the Lake
    Figueroa Trail by Calero Creek to the Old Corral
  Uvas Canyon Park
    Loop Trip to Waterfalls
  Mt. Madonna Park
    Circle Trip through Banks and Blackhawk Canyons
    Ecological Sampler
  Los Gatos Creek
    Campbell Park to Vasona Lake Park—one way
    Forbes Mill to Lexington Dam

LONG TRIPS From 5 to 10 miles round trip
  Mission Peak Regional Preserve
    The Three Trips to the Peak
  Ed R. Levin Park
    Monument Peak Trail
  Joseph D. Grant Park
    Dutch Flat Trail to the West Ridge
    Canada de Pala Trail on the East Ridge
  Henry W. Coe State Park
    Loop Trip to Middle Ridge via Frog Lake
    Poverty Flat Circle Hike via Middle Ridge
  Sanborn-Skyline Park
    Skyline Trail/Bay Area Ridge Trail to Saratoga Gap—one way with
      shuttle
  Sierra Azul Open Space Preserve
    Kennedy Trail Ascent of the North Slopes
    Hike to Priest Rock and Loop on P. G. & E. service road
  Almaden Quicksilver Park
    Mine Hill Trail—one way with shuttle
    Randol Mine and Mine Hill Trails Loop

TRAILS SUITED TO DIFFERENT TRAVELERS

FOR EQUESTRIANS With horse staging area—H
  Mission Peak Regional Preserve
    Trails from Stanford Avenue—H
  Ed R. Levin Park—H
  Alum Rock Park
  Joseph D. Grant Park—H
  Henry W. Coe State Park—H
  Sanborn-Skyline Park
    Skyline Trail/Bay Area Ridge Trail from Peak to Castle Rock State
      Park
  Sierra Azul Open Space Preserve
    Kennedy Road Trail
  Almaden Quicksilver Park—H
  Calero Park—H
  Santa Teresa Park—H
  Mt. Madonna Park—H
  Coyote Hills Regional Park
    Alameda Creek Regional Trail to Niles (north side)

PAVED PATHS FOR BICYCLISTS
  Alum Rock Park
    Creek Trail
    Park entrance road and old park road from Alum Rock Avenue
      entrance
  Los Gatos Creek
    Leigh Avenue to Vasona Lake
    Forbes Mill to Lexington Dam
  Coyote Creek
    Coyote Hellyer Park to Emado Avenue
  Coyote Hills Regional Park
    Bayview Trail
    Alameda Creek Regional Trail to Niles (south side)
    Dumbarton Bridge Bike Lane
  Mountain View's Shoreline
  Palo Alto Baylands
    Bayfront Trail

PARKS PERMITTING MOUNTAIN BICYCLES ON CERTAIN
    DESIGNATED UNPAVED TRAILS
  Mission Peak Regional Preserve
  Ed R. Levin Park
  Joseph D. Grant Park
  Henry W. Coe State Park
  El Sereno Open Space Preserve
  St. Joseph's Hill Open Space Preserve
  Sierra Azul Open Space Preserve
  Santa Teresa Park

WHEELCHAIR RAMBLES
  Alum Rock Park
    Creek Trail
  Kelley Park
  Los Gatos Creek
    Leigh Avenue to Los Gatos Creek Park to Vasona Park
  Coyote Hills Regional Park
    Muskrat Trail
    Chochenyo Trail

San Francisco Bay National Wildlife Refuge
Phone for information on access
Mountain View's Shoreline
Palo Alto Baylands
Boardwalk to observation platform
Walk to San Francisquito Creek

RECOMMENDED FOR RUNNERS Training runs on hills and levees
and beside creeks
Alum Rock Park
Rim Trails
Almaden Quicksilver Park
Sierra Azul Open Space Preserve
Kennedy Road Trail
Santa Teresa Park
Coyote Peak Climb
Hidden Springs/Ohlone Trail Loop
Mt. Madonna Park
Merry-Go-Round Trail
Coyote Creek
Coyote Hellyer Park upstream
Penitencia Creek Trail
Guadalupe River Trail
Los Gatos Creek
Leigh Avenue to Vasona Lake Park
Coyote Hills Regional Preserve
Bayview Trail
Alameda Creek Regional Trail
San Francisco Bay National Wildlife Refuge
Newark Slough Trail
Alviso Slough Trail
Sunnyvale Baylands Trail
Mountain View's Shoreline
Palo Alto Baylands
Loop Trail around the Flood-Control Basin

SPECIAL DESTINATIONS

PEAK CLIMBS
Mission Peak Regional Preserve
The three trips to Mission Peak
Ed R. Levin Park
Monument Peak Trip
Henry W. Coe Park
Northern Heights Route to Mt. Sizer
Uvas Canyon Park
Fire Trail to Nibbs Knob and Summit Road
Santa Teresa Park
Coyote Peak Climb

LUNCH BY THE LAKE Short walks to picnic places
Ed R. Levin Park
Sandy Wool Lake
Joseph D. Grant Park
Grant Lake
The Lake Loop
Eagle Lake Loop
Calero Park
Climb to the Ridge and Return along the Lake

Los Gatos Creek
    Los Gatos Creek Park percolation ponds
    Vasona Lake Park
Mt. Madonna Park
    Sprig Lake

SECLUDED SITES Get away from it all
    Joseph D. Grant Park
        Deer Valley
        Eagle Lake
    Henry W. Coe State Park
        Madrone Soda Springs
        Skeel's Meadow
        Poverty Flat
        Orestimba Wilderness
    Sanborn-Skyline Park
        Bonjetti Creek
        Todd Redwoods
    Sierra Azul Open Space Preserve
        Bald Mountain
    Calero Park
        Cottle Rest Site
        Old Corral
        Hidden Reservoir at Fish Camp
    Santa Teresa Park
        Laurel Springs Rest Area
    Uvas Canyon Park
        Nibbs Knob
        Triple Falls and Old Logging Camp
    Mt. Madonna Park
        Banks Canyon
        Miller's Spring on Loop Trail

BAYLANDS TRIPS TO THE SPECIAL WORLD OF SALT
    MARSHES
    Coyote Hills Regional Park
        Shoreline Trail to Ideal Marsh
    San Francisco Bay National Wildlife Refuge
        Newark Slough Trail
        Alviso Slough Trail to Triangle Marsh
    Mountain View's Shoreline
        Walk South to the Marsh
        North Bayfront Trail to Forebay
    Stevens Creek Nature Study Area
        Crittenden Marsh
    Palo Alto Baylands
        Catwalk and Boardwalk

HIKES INTO HISTORY Early ranchos and historic sites
    Mission Peak Regional Preserve
    Ed R. Levin Park
    Alum Rock Park
    Joseph D. Grant Park
    Henry W. Coe State Park
    St. Joseph's Hill Open Space Preserve
    Almaden Quicksilver Park
    Calero Park
    Mt. Madonna Park

Coyote Creek
  Kelley Park San Jose Historical Museum
Los Gatos Creek
  Forbes Mill Museum

NATURAL HISTORY AND SCIENCE Interpreted at Visitor Centers
  Alum Rock Park
  Joseph D. Grant Park
  Sanborn-Skyline Park
  Almaden Quicksilver Park
    New Almaden Mercury Mining Museum
  Mt. Madonna Park
  Coyote Hellyer Park
  Children's Discovery Museum at Guadalupe River Park
  Vasona Lake Park
  Coyote Hills Regional Park
  San Francisco Bay National Wildlife Refuge
  Palo Alto Baylands

SPECIAL OCCASIONS

CHILDREN'S OUTINGS Short walks, playgrounds, zoos, picnic tables
  Alum Rock Park
  Ed R. Levin Park
  Mt. Madonna Park
  Coyote Creek
    Kelley Park
    Coyote Hellyer Park
  Los Gatos Creek
    Campbell, Los Gatos Creek and Vasona Lake parks
  Coyote Hills Regional Park
  San Francisco Bay National Wildlife Refuge
  Palo Alto Baylands

LET'S GO FISHING In lakes and streams
  Ed R. Levin Park
    Sandy Wool Lake
  Joseph D. Grant Park
    Grant, Bass and McCreery lakes
  Henry W. Coe State Park
    Middle Fork of Coyote Creek
    China Hole
  Sanborn-Skyline Park
    Lake Ranch Reservoir
  Mt. Madonna
    Sprig Lake For children 5-12 only
  Coyote Creek
    Cottonwood Lake at Coyote Hellyer Park
    Parkway Lakes at Metcalf Road
  Los Gatos Creek
    Los Gatos Creek Park percolation ponds
  Vasona Lake Park

CAMP IN THE PARK Out early on the trail
  Joseph D. Grant Park
  Henry W. Coe State Park
  Sanborn-Skyline Park
  Uvas Canyon Park
  Mt. Madonna Park

GROUP GATHERINGS With site reserved ahead, hike before lunch
  Ed R. Levin Park
  Alum Rock Park
  Joseph D. Grant Park
  Sanborn-Skyline Park
  Santa Teresa Park
  Uvas Canyon Park
  Mt. Madonna Park
  Coyote Creek
    Kelley Park
    Coyote Hellyer Park
  Los Gatos Creek
    Campbell, Los Gatos Creek and Vasona Lake parks

YOU CAN GET HERE BY BUS **your bicycle can go too
  Mission Peak Regional Preserve
  Alum Rock Park
  Almaden Quicksilver Park
  Santa Teresa Park **
  Coyote Creek
    Kelley Park **
  Penitencia Creek Park **
  Los Gatos Creek
    Campbell, Los Gatos Creek and Vasona Lake parks   all **
    Forbes Mill Museum
  Sunnyvale Baylands **

Appendix II

Information Sources on Parks, Preserves, Trails and Trail Activities

Public Agencies

City of San Jose Department of Parks, Recreation and Community Services	
333 W. Santa Clara St.	408-277-5134
San Jose, CA 95113	408-277-4661
City of Palo Alto	
Lucy Evans Baylands Nature and Interpretive Center	
2775 Embarcadero Road	
Palo Alto, CA 94301	415-329-2506
East Bay Regional Park District	
11500 Skyline Boulevard	
Oakland, CA 94619	415-531-9300
Midpeninsula Regional Open Space District	
201 San Antonio Circle, Suite C-135	
Mountain View, CA 94040	415-949-5500
San Francisco Bay National Wildlife Refuge	
P.O. Box 524	
Newark, CA 94560	415-792-0222
Santa Clara County Parks and Recreation Department	
298 Garden Hill Drive	
Los Gatos, CA 95030	408-358-3741
Henry W. Coe State Park	
P.O. Box 846	
Morgan Hill, CA 95038	408-779-2728

Organizations Supporting Parks, Sponsoring Hikes, Bicycle and Equestrian Trail Activities

Trail Center	
4898 El Camino Real, Office 205 A	
Los Altos, CA 94022	415-968-7065

The Trail Center acts as a clearinghouse of information on trails and trail activities; coordinates volunteer programs for trail maintenance and construction; promotes trail access and open space; and maintains lists of hiking, running, equestrian and bicycling events.

American Youth Hostels	
Golden Gate Council	415-863-1444
Santa Clara Valley Council	408-298-0670
Audubon Society of Santa Clara County—bird	415-329-1811
Bay Area Orienteering Club	
3152 Holyrood Drive	
Oakland, CA 94611	
Bay Area Ridge Trail Council	415-543-4291
Santa Clara County Committee	
Call the Trail Center	415-968-7065
California Native Plant Society	415-494-9301
Castle Rock Horsemen's Association	408-446-4584

Castle Rock State Park	408-867-2952
Docent-led hikes	408-335-7077
Companions of the Trail—	408-379-4809
Community Colleges	see local numbers
Some offer group hiking classes	
East Bay Trail Council	415-531-9300
Friends of the Grant Ranch Park	
1127 Sierra Avenue	
San Jose, CA 95126	
Hayward Shoreline Interpretive Center	415-881-6751
Hidden Villa—farm tours, group hikes,	
summer camp, hostel	415-948-4690
Los Altos Hills Horsemen's Association	
P.O. Box 425	
Los Altos, CA 94023-0425	
Midpeninsula Regional Open Space District	
Docent-led hikes	415-949-5500
New Almaden Quicksilver County Park Association	
P.O. Box 124	
New Almaden, CA 95042	
Peninsula Conservation Center	415-494-9301
Pine Ridge Association—Henry Coe State Park	408-779-2728
ROMP—bicycling events	415-941-7433
San Francisco Bay National Wildlife Refuge	415-792-0222
San Mateo Horsemen's Association	
P.O. Box 620092	
Woodside, CA 94062	
Santa Cruz Mountains Trail Association	
P.O. Box 1141	
Los Altos, CA 94023	
Dial-A-Hike Program—Portola State Park	415-948-9098
Sempervirens Fund	415-968-4509
Senior Centers—some sponsor group walks;	see local numbers
Sierra Club—Regional Groups, Sierra Singles,	
Family Outings	415-494-9901
Skyline Cycling Club	
P.O. Box 60176	
Sunnyvale, CA 94088	
Western Wheelers Bicycle Club	
P.O. Box 518	
Palo Alto, CA 94302	
Youth Groups	
Call local Boy Scouts, Girl Scouts and Campfire units	
Youth Science Institute	408-356-4945

For Information on Bus Service to Parks

Santa Clara County Transit	408-287-4210
East Bay—AC Transit	415-797-6811
BART	415-873-2278

Appendix III

Selected References

History

Brewer, William H., *Up and Down California in 1860–1864,* Berkeley: University of California Press, 1974.

Water in the Santa Clara Valley: A History, Cupertino, CA: California History Center, DeAnza College Local History Studies, Vol. 27, 1981.

Hoover, Mildred B., and Hero Eugene Rensch, *Historic Spots in California,* Stanford, CA: Stanford University Press, 3rd edition, 1966.

Johnson, Kenneth M., *The New Almaden Quicksilver Mine,* Georgetown, CA: Talisman Press, 1963.

Margolin, Malcolm, *The Ohlone Way, Indian Life in the San Francisco-Monterey Bay Area,* Berkeley: Heyday Books, 1978.

Payne, Stephen M., Santa Clara County, *Harvest of Change,* Northridge: Windsor Publications, 1987.

Pierce, Marjorie, *East of the Gabilans,* Fresno, CA: Valley Publishers, 1977.

Sanchez, Nellie Van de Grift, *Spanish and Indian Place Names of California,* San Francisco: A. M. Robertson, 2nd edition, 1922.

Sepeda, Dolores De Moro, *Hills West of El Toro,* Ann Arbor, MI: Braun-Brumfield, Inc., 1978.

Natural History

Bakker, Elna S., *An Island Called California,* Berkeley: University of California Press, 1971.

Conradson, Diane R., *Exploring Our Baylands,* Point Reyes, CA: Coastal Parks Association, 1982.

Birding at the Bottom of the Bay, Santa Clara Valley Audubon Society, Palo Alto, 2nd edition 1990.

Crittenden, Mabel, and Dorothy Telfer, *Wildflowers of the West,* Berkeley: Celestial Arts, 1975.

Lyons, Kathleen and Mary Beth Cuneo-Lazaneo, *Plants of the Coast Redwood Region,* Los Altos: Looking Press, 1988.

Murie, Olaf J., *A Field Guide to Animal Tracks,* Boston: Houghton Mifflin, 2nd Ed. 1974.

Peterson, Roger Tory, *A Field Guide to Western Birds,* Boston: Houghton Mifflin, 1975.

Scott, Shirley, *Field Guide to the Birds of North America,* Washington, D.C.: National Geographic Society, 2nd edition 1987.

Sharsmith, H. K., "The Flora of the Mt. Hamilton Range of California," American Midland Naturalist. Vol. 34, no. 2 (September 1945).

Thomas, John Hunter, *Flora of the Santa Cruz Mountains of California,* Stanford, CA: Stanford University Press, 1961.

Uvardy, Miklos D. F., *The Audubon Society Field Guide to North American Birds,* New York: Alfred A. Knopf, 1977.

California Natural History Guides, Berkeley: University of California Press.

Berry, William D. and Elizabeth, *Mammals of the San Francisco Bay Region,* 1959.

Cogswell, Howard L., *Waterbirds of California,* 1977.

Ferris, Roxana S., *Native Shrubs of the San Francisco Bay Region,* 1968.

Gilliam, Harold, *Weather of San Francisco Bay Region,* 1966.

Howard, Arthur D., *Evolution of the Landscape of the San Francisco Bay Region,* 1962.

Metcalf, Woodbridge, *Native Trees of the San Francisco Bay Region,* 1959.

Sharsmith, Helen K., *Spring Wildflowers of the San Francisco Bay Region,* 1965.

Smith, Arthur C., *Introduction to the Natural History of the San Francisco Bay Region,* 1959.

Stebbins, Robert C., *Reptiles and Amphibians of the San Francisco Bay Region,* 1960.

Trail Books

Doss, Margot Patterson, *Bay Area at Your Feet,* Lagunitas, CA: Lexikos Publishing, 1987.

Hosler, Ray, *Bay Area Bike Rides,* San Francisco: Chronicle Books, 1990.

Rusmore, Jean, and Frances Spangle, *Peninsula Trails,* Berkeley: Wilderness Press, 2nd edition 1989.

Taber, Tom, *The Santa Cruz Mountains Trail Book,* San Mateo: The Oak Valley Press, 5th edition 1988.

Whitnah, Dorothy L., *An Outdoor Guide to the San Francisco Bay Area,* Berkeley: Wilderness Press, 5th edition 1988.

Transit Service

Regional Transit Guide, Berkeley: Metropolitan Transportation Commission, 3rd edition 1989.

Index

South Bay Trails Update—1995

Acknowledgments

In addition to those who graciously helped us with the first and second printings of the second edition of *South Bay Trails* and who again provided updated information for this printing, we gratefully acknowledge the assistance of David Pierce, Julie Bondurant, Lisa Kilow, Elish Ryan, and Debbie Turpin, Santa Clara County Parks and Recreation Department; Craig Britton, General Manager, Randy Anderson and Sheryl Cochran, Midpeninsula Regional Open Space District.

We particularly thank our friend and hiking colleague, Betsy Crowder, who helped with the research for this 1995 Update.

Park Plans and Acquisitions

p. 12, 4th paragraph. In 1994 an advisory vote passed in Santa Clara County setting up the open space authority and electing a governing board. The phone number is 408-358-9443.

New Trails and Campgrounds

p. 12 and 13. The Trails and Pathways Committee has disbanded. A new Santa Clara County Master Plan for Trails is nearing completion.

Rules for Parks and Preserves

p. 18, last paragraph. Sharing the Trails

MROSD and Santa Clara County now require bicyclists on all their lands to wear helmets and to observe a 15-mile-per-hour speed limit, reduced to a 5-mile-per-hour speed limit when passing. In 1994 MROSD instituted a ranger bicycle patrol and also radar enforcement of speed limits, which will continue indefinitely. MROSD also began a volunteer patrol, made up of hikers, equestrians and bicyclists, to provide education and information on the District trails.

After three years of intensive study and public workshops MROSD adopted a set of Trail Use Policies. Studies to implement these policies are ongoing. Preserve trails slated for comprehensive review in 1995 are those in El Corte de Madera, Purisima Creek Redwoods, Fremont Older and Rancho San Antonio open space preserves. Notice of trail use-changes will be clearly marked at trailheads.

Cautions for Trail Users

p, 19. **Mountain Lions** Sightings of these shy, native residents of wild lands have become more frequent due to increased use of their habitat by the public.

A mountain lion is about the size of a small German shepherd with a furry tail as long as its body. It is recommended that trail users stand facing any mountain lion they encounter, make loud noises while waving their arms, and not run away.

Bobcats are not hazardous to humans. They are about twice the size of a house cat with six-inch-long tails.

Feral Pigs These have spread over many acres of wild lands since their introduction for hunting in the 19th century. While generally not dangerous to humans, they can be fierce when cornered.

Mission Peak Regional Preserve

p. 27, 2nd paragraph. A tall wooden post with directional signs identifying local landmarks marks the summit of Mission Peak.

p. 27, 2nd paragraph, last sentence. Mission Peak Preserve and Ed Levin Park in Santa Clara County are now joined by the 9.7-mile Bay Area Ridge Trail route using the Peak Trail, trails in the Monument Peak area, and the Agua Caliente and Calera Creek trails in Ed Levin Park.

p. 28, 6th paragraph. The 130-year-old house is used as a ranger residence. Nearby a backpack camp, available by reservation, is on the route of the Ohlone Wilderness Trail.

Ed R. Levin Park

p. 37, 1st paragraph. The last 2 sentences should read: "Continue on Calaveras Road to park headquarters and a series of picnic grounds. Then turning left off Calaveras Road onto Downing Road, you reach pretty little Sandy Wool Lake..."

p. 37, Facilities. Recently re-named park trails will appear on a new park map. A new, improved playground by Sandy Wool Lake opened in spring 1994.

The park no longer has horse rental stables. (See also p. 38, Trip 1, 4th paragraph.)

p. 42, Trip 3. The Calera Trail is now the Calera Creek Trail. and it forms one segment of the Bay Area Ridge Trail to Mission Peak Preserve.

Alum Rock Park

The new 0.9-mile loop trail, named for former ranger Todd M. Quick was built in 1994 by volunteers from the Trail Center and sponsored by REI. It zigzags uphill from the east end of the North Rim Trail to far-flung views of the Santa Clara Valley.

Joseph D. Grant Park

p. 58. This park now encompasses 9,522 acres. Stocking fish in Grant Lake and two smaller lakes is being re-evaluated in a new resource management plan underway.

p. 59, 1st paragraph. The nature-study program, conducted hikes and the Friends of Grant Ranch Park have been discontinued. However, the county is running a training program for volunteer patrol.

p. 60, 2nd paragraph. The new Joseph D. Grant park brochure contains an updated map with topographic lines and explanations of park history and activities.

p. 60. Facilities. There are 38 drive-in sites for families. Horse rental at nearby stables is no longer available.

Park Rules. The park is open from 8 A.M. to sunset. Fees are collected every Saturday, Sunday and holiday and on weekdays from the Saturday before Memorial Day to the Saturday after Labor Day. Camping fee is $8/night/site.

p. 61, Trip 1. Only the old corrals remain from former ranching days.

p. 68, Trip 6. The Dutch Flat Trail is on the proposed route for the Bay Area Ridge Trail.

p. 71, 2nd paragraph. The corrals and cattle chutes are no longer beside the Cañada de Pala Trail.

p. 71–73, Trip 8. The Digger Pine Trail is now called the Foothill Pine Trail.

Henry W. Coe State Park

p. 79, 5th paragraph. Plans are ready and a funding effort, spearheaded by the volunteer Pine Ridge Association, is underway to construct an expanded museum and visitor center.

p. 81, 1st paragraph. Two maps are available at the park visitor center for $1/ each. One is a detailed trail map without contour lines, the other a large format, three-color relief map covering the entire park. A new brochure explains regulations, fees, and amenities for hikers, bicyclists, backpackers, equestrians, dogs, and campers.

p. 85, Facilities. In addition to 19 backpack camps in the original park area near headquarters, backpack groups can stay in designated zones in the outlying regions. Permits are required.

p. 85, Park Fees. The fee for a horse campsite is $12/night; $2/night/horse; $5/ night/additional vehicle.

p. 87, after 1st paragraph add: Across the road to Manzanita Point, at the Fish Trail junction, a new foot trail, the Forest Trail, takes off to contour along the east side of Pine Ridge. Shaded by big oak trees and clumps of bay trees and resplendent with wildflowers in spring, this is a lovely trail to take to the picnic and camping areas at Manzanita Point.

p. 87, Trip 2. Loop Trip to Middle Ridge via Frog Lake

A new trail to Frog Lake, the Flat Frog Trail, is under construction at this writing. From the Fish Trail/Forest Trail junction this new, somewhat longer trail reaches Frog Lake on a much gentler grade and brings new views of Middle Ridge.

p. 98, Trip 6. A re-routed trail on a better grade leaves Manzanita Point, Camp 7, at the Madrone Springs Trail junction and contours around the west side of Pine Ridge to reach China Hole. This 1-mile-longer trail goes through a greater variety of habitats than that described on the Loop Hike to Mahoney Meadows.

As you leave China Hole enroute to Mahoney Meadows a new, 0.8-mile-longer trail on a much better grade ascends the hillside.

Sanborn-Skyline Park

p. 106, Facilities. A new ⅛-mile, paved loop trail provides access to redwood forest and pond environments for people of all abilities.

p. 106, Park Rules. Some fees have changed: Camping is now $6/walk-in site; $20/night/RV.

p. 109, Trip 2. Level Walk to Lake Ranch Reservoir

How to Get There. In addition to the access off of Black Road, there is limited parking in the valley at the end of Sanborn Road, which is now in public ownership. There is no vehicle access to the reservoir. There is now a trail over steep terrain from the Day Use Area on Skyline Boulevard to Lake Ranch Reservoir.

Trail Notes. This area is good for winter birding.

p. 113 and 114. The park's southern day-use trailhead parking area on Skyline

Boulevard is near an area marked on the USGS maps as "The Peak," but not marked as such on the county park map.

St. Joseph's Hill Open Space Preserve

p. 124, 2nd paragraph. The "Walking Zone" requires all users to walk in the 0.3-mile section of the Jones Trail. The nearby Historic Jones Trail, opened in late 1994, is a multi-use trail, and the former Jones Trail, with walking zone, may be named the Flume Trail, and be for hiking only.

Sierra Azul Open Space Preserve

p. 127. Bicyclists, too, are invited to use the Kennedy Road Trail.

p. 128. From the top of Kennedy Road you can see Jacques Ridge, south of Almaden Quicksilver Park, the new joint purchase of MROSD and Santa Clara County. Strategically connecting Sierra Azul OSP and Almaden Quicksilver Park, this new acreage could form the link to carry the Bay Area Ridge Trail into the Mt. Umunhum Area and then northwest along the ridges of Sierra Azul.

Almaden Quicksilver Park

p. 137, 1st paragraph, 2nd sentence, the architectural drawings are extant.

p. 137, photograph. "English Town" is now demolished.

p. 138. Facilities. There is now potable water also at The Hacienda, the main park entrance on Almaden Road.

p. 139, Trip 1. All the mines in the park are closed.

p. 141, 3rd paragraph. The old brick powderhouse has been restored.

Santa Teresa Park

p. 150, 2nd paragraph. The master plan for this park, completed in 1992, calls for two new trails. (1) The Fortini Trail will reach the park's southwest corner. (2). Another trail from the small parking area at the Mine Trail junction with the road to the IBM research facility parallels that road northeast and continues east on the south side of the park entrance road to the Pueblo Group Area. The Boundary Line Trail and the northwest Bicycle Loop Trail shown on the map, pp. 156–57, stay entirely within park lands.

p. 151, Park Rules. The park office phone is 408-225-0225.

p. 154, last paragraph. The Mine Trail and the Stile Ranch Trail connect with the Los Alamitos/Calero Creek Trail, forming a dedicated 6.25-mile segment of the Bay Area Ridge Trail.

Calero Park

p. 158, 5th paragraph. The historic Murphy house, which serves as headquarters for the Calero Stables, is not open to the public.

p. 159, Facilities. The horse rental stables, horse staging area, and ranger's office are near the park entrance at McKean Road. A new trail crosses the ridge between the Pena and Figueroa trails.

Park Rules. A $3/car entrance fee is now charged for boat launch entry.

p. 162, Trip 3. At the Hidden Reservoir, known as Fish Camp Pond, there are now an observation deck and a picnic table.

p. 163, photo. Under the big oak tree above the stock pond near the Juan Crespi Trail there are a new observation deck and a picnic table.

Uvas Canyon Park

p. 172, 2nd paragraph. Most of the Swanson Creek log jam resulting from the severe storms of 1986 has been cleared and the trail up the creek is quite navigable. The effects of 1995 winter storms have not been assessed at this writing.

p. 173, Trip 2, last paragraph. A picnic table on a small flat on the west side of Alec Creek makes a fine, shady place for lunch. Sounds of the creek tumbling over boulders and bird-song in the trees add to the pleasure of a stop in this remote part of the park. Signs on the far side of the creek forbid access beyond this point.

Mt. Madonna Park

p. 179. A new brochure explains the park's natural and cultural history and provides a map of the park.

p. 180, Facilities. There are now 17 RV sites at Valley View Camp #1. Sprig Lake, a fishing pond exclusively for children 5–12 years, is open from the last weekend in April until approximately mid-July.

Park Rules. Vehicle entry fees are collected year-round on weekends and holidays, and are also collected on weekdays from one week before Memorial Day until one week after Labor Day. Park office phone: 408-842-2341.

Creekside Park Chains

Coyote Creek

p. 192, paragraph before Trip 1. Fourteen miles of trail extend southeast from Coyote Hellyer County Park to the Anderson Lake Ranger Office on Burnett Avenue in Morgan Hill. Plans to extend the paved trail south to the face of Anderson Dam are under consideration. Currently 7 miles of equestrian/hiking trail parallel the paved bicycle trail on opposite sides of the creek from Metcalf Road to Burnett Avenue.

p. 194, Trip 2. Title should read: Coyote Hellyer County Park Trails South to Burnett Avenue.

This is now a 14-mile trail extending all the way to Burnett Avenue. At the visitor center in Coyote Hellyer County Park there is a small natural-history exhibit.

A new park brochure shows the Coyote Creek Parkway and the Coyote Creek Trail in detail. From Coyote Hellyer County Park to Metcalf Road this trail is the route of the Bay Area Ridge Trail.

How To Get There. Bernal Road changes to Silicon Valley Boulevard on the east side of Highway 101. Going south, take Bernal Road exit, cross over the highway and follow Silicon Valley Boulevard to trail parking on the south side of the road. Going north, take Silicon Valley Boulevard and follow directions in previous sentence.

Metcalf Road access: From Highway 101 take Bernal Road exit, go south to Monterey Highway (82), go left (southeast) for 1 mile, make a U-turn at Metcalf Road and go north ¼ mile to staging area on right.

p. 195. Bernal Road on the east side of Highway 101 has been re-named Silicon Valley Boulevard. The Coyote Creek Trail now extends to Burnett Avenue, 7 miles from Metcalf Road.

p. 196, 1st paragraph, last sentence. Stream banks are fragile and easily eroded. Users are encouraged to remain on the trails.

p. 197. Add after 4th paragraph. Just south of Silicon Valley Boulevard on your right is a 24-acre mitigation site. Here Caltrans created and planted a riparian habitat to mitigate for all wetlands destroyed in the course of completing Highway 85 in this area.

p. 197, (3). Bernal Road on the east side of Highway 101 has been re-named Silicon Valley Boulevard. The distance from Silicon Valley Boulevard to Metcalf Road is 3 miles.

p. 200, Trip 3. Metcalf Road to Burnett Avenue (This text appears in the 2nd edition, 2nd printing, but for those who have the 1st printing, it is repeated here.)

A new, 7-mile paved hiking and bicycling path and parallel equestrian trail continue upstream from Metcalf Road to Burnett Avenue. The trail is accessible from Monterey Road (Highway 82) in south San Jose at Metcalf Road and at Burnett Avenue, its southern terminus. Officially dedicated in May 1992, this southern leg of the Coyote Creek Parkway meanders through public lands where the lush creekside environment of evergreen oaks, rangy sycamores, graceful willows and an understory of berries and shrubs is preserved. This is some of the most beautiful and intact floodplain in the county. At three rest areas you can enjoy this quiet scene while eating your lunch at one of the picnic tables. A pause to watch the model airplanes take off and land at their own airport will add variety to the day's outing.

At the Anderson/Burnett Ranger Office on the east side of the creek the paved trail ends. Across the creek is a staging area for hikers, bicyclists and equestrians at the end of Burnett Avenue.

Penitencia Creek

Facilities. There are new facilities at Penitencia Creek County Park at Jackson Avenue and Mabury Road, including a 2-acre pond, drought-tolerant shrub gardens and meadows of native grasses and wildflowers. Parking is still on-street at this park. At the Piedmont Road/Penitencia Creek Road junction a large park developed jointly by San Jose City and Santa Clara County, managed by San Jose, includes large playgrounds, restrooms, community center, and parking.

p. 203, 2nd paragraph. The formal trail ends at the west end of Penitencia Creek County Park at Mabury Road.

Guadalupe River

p. 205, 5th paragraph. The Guadalupe River Parkway Plan is a joint project between Santa Clara County and the City of San Jose.

p. 206, 2nd paragraph. A segment of the riverwalk exists from Woz Way by the Children's Discovery Museum to Santa Clara Street. It is hoped that the parkway project from Santa Clara Street to West Mission Street will be completed in the mid-1990s. In and around the Guadalupe River area are many points of interest, including the Technical Museum of Innovation, the San Jose Museum of Art, San Pedro Square, the Peralta Adobe, and the Fallon House.

Los Alamitos and Calero Creeks

p. 209, Trail Notes. The path south of Almaden Lake now continues on a trail paralleling Graystone Lane to the vicinity of the confluence of Los Alamitos and Calero creeks. The Calero Creek Trail from its intersection with the Stile Ranch Trail to the confluence of Los Alamitos Creek is a dedicated segment of the Bay Area Ridge Trail. The Ridge Trail then follows Los Alamitos Creek paths to the Harry Road/McKean Road intersection.

Los Gatos Creek

A new Santa Clara County brochure for Vasona and Los Gatos Creek parks has a splendid map of both parks and the Los Gatos Creek Trail. Distances of each segment of the trail are marked, as are the location of telephones, restrooms and park amenities.

Facilities. Los Gatos Creek Park added new casting ponds and Vasona Lake Park now has paddle boat rentals and a new playground.

p. 214, Trip 1. Construction completed in 1994 and '95 closed the gap between Vasona Lake Park and the beginning of the trail to Lexington Dam at Forbes Mill. The trail passes under the huge Highway 85 complex and beside a native plant revegetation area. When dedicated in April 1995, the Los Gatos Creek Trail, completed from Willow Street at the Blackford School in San Jose to Lexington Dam in Los Gatos, stretched 14 miles through the cities of Los Gatos, Campbell and San Jose, as well as through the two county parks and Campbell Park.

p. 215, Trip 2. The trail downstream from Campbell Park now passes under Leigh Avenue and extends to Willow Street.

San Francisco Bay National Wild-life Refuge

p. 237. Caption on photo is incorrect. Change to "Tidelands Trail crosses bridge over Newark Slough."

Alviso.

p. 245, last paragraph. A Santa Clara County master plan for the Alviso Marina is underway at this writing. The marina is currently unusable except for boat launching at high tides. The marina offers parking, restrooms and access to the trail into the New Chicago Marsh.

Sunnyvale/Santa Clara County Baylands Park

p. 249, 1st paragraph. The 220-acre Baylands Park when completed will feature a protected seasonal wetlands preserve with interpretive displays, nature trails, picnic areas, and recreation areas, in addition to the existing softball complex.

Jurisdiction. Santa Clara County and the City of Sunnyvale.

Facilities. Recreation areas, commercial softball diamonds and clubhouse, group and family picnic areas, nature areas, restrooms, children's play area, ranger station and parking.

Trail Notes. The existing commercial Twin Creeks Softball Complex in the northwest corner of the park includes a clubhouse and 10 baseball diamonds available for club games.

The rest of the park emphasizes the natural setting, featuring seasonal wetlands and interpretive displays. Along nature trails interpretive signs explain the unique dynamics of wetlands. A state-of-the-art creative play area gives children a hands-on experience in this Baylands world.

In upland areas native grasses and shrubs provide habitat for such creatures as burrowing owls and the rare harvest mouse. An open water bird preserve will attract local and migrant species.

Major picnic areas for large groups and families are sheltered by plantings. Nearby are play areas and large meadows. Parking is ample.

This park will serve as an important trailhead for the Bay Trail, which already circles much of the South Bay. A connecting trail south to Alviso is underway, and a short connector is planned north to adjacent Sunnyvale Baylands.

Changes in Appendix II

Audubon Society of Santa Clara County—bird walks
   Sequoia Chapter 415-345-3724
   Santa Clara Valley Chapter 408-252-3747
Bay Area Ridge Trail Council 415-391-0697
   311 California Street, Suite 510
   San Francisco, CA 94104
Bay Trail, ABAG 510-464-7935
Committee for Green Foothills 415-968-7243
Companions of the Trail 415-968-7065
East Bay Regional Park District 510-635-0135
East Bay Trail Council 510-635-0135
Hayward Shoreline Interpretive Center 510-881-6751
Midpeninsula Regional Open Space District
   330 Distel Circle
   Los Altos, CA 94022 415-691-1200
   docent-led hikes 415-691-1200
Peninsula Conservation Center 415-962-9876
ROMP (Responsible Outdoor Mountain Pedalers) 408-534-1130
San Francisco Bay National Wildlife Refuge 510-792-0222
SF Bay Bird Observatory 408-946-6548
Environmental Education Center, Alviso 408-262-5513
Santa Cruz Mountains Natural History Assoc. 408-335-3174
Santa Cruz Mountains Trail Association 415-968-2412
Sierra Club, Loma Prieta Chapter 415-390-8411
The Trail Center 415-968-7065
   3921 E. Bayshore Road
   Palo Alto, CA 94303
Women's Outdoor Network 415-494-8583
For Info on Bus Service
   Santa Clara County Transit 800-894-9905
   East Bay—AC Transit 510-797-6811